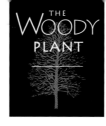

Trees and Shrubs for Fragrance

Glyn Church

Photographs Pat Greenfield

FIREFLY BOOKS

A FIREFLY BOOK

Published by Firefly Books Ltd. 2002

Originated in 2002 by David Bateman Ltd.,
30 Tarndale Grove, Albany, Auckland, New Zealand

First Printing

National Library of Canada Cataloguing in Publication Data

Church, Glyn
Trees and shrubs for fragrance
(Woody plant series)
Includes bibliographical references and index.
ISBN 1-55297-633-5 (bound)
ISBN 1-55297-632-7 (pbk.)
1. Ornamental trees. 2. Ornamental shrubs. 3. Fragrant gardens.
I. Greenfield, Pat II. Title. III. Title: Fragrance. IV. Series: Church, Glyn.
Woody plant series.
SB454.3.F7C48 2002   635.9'771   C2001-903296-X

Publisher Cataloging-in-Publication Data (U.S.)

Church, Glyn.
   Trees and shrubs for fragrance / Glyn Church ; photographs by Pat Greenfield. – 1st ed.
[160] p. : col. photos., maps ; cm. (Woody Plants)
Includes bibliographic references and index.
Summary: An illustrated gardening guide to over 100 trees and shrubs selected for their fragrance.
ISBN 1-55297-633-5
ISBN 1-55297-632-7 (pbk.)
1. Gardens, Fragrant. 2. Ornamental shrubs. 3. Ornamental trees.
4. Aromatic plants. I. Greenfield, Pat. Title. II. Series.
635.968   21   CIP   SB454.3.C58   2002

Published in Canada in 2002 by
Firefly Books Ltd.
3680 Victoria Park Avenue
Willowdale, Ontario
M2H 3K1

Published in the United States in 2002 by
Firefly Books (U.S.) Inc.
P.O. Box 1338, Ellicott Station
Buffalo, New York
14205

Design by Errol McLeary
Typesetting by Jazz Graphics, Auckland, New Zealand
Photographs by Pat Greenfield
Printed in Hong Kong through Colorcraft Ltd

Above: *Hydrangea paniculata* 'Kyushu'

Opposite top: *Perovskia atriplicifolia* 'Blue Spire'

Opposite below: *Genista* 'Yellow Imp' with *Dimorphotheca* flowers.

Page 1: *Salvia involucrata* 'Bethellii'

Pages 2 and 3: *Philadelphus coronarius* and *Rhododendron* 'Razzle Dazzle'.

Contents

Introduction   6

How to use this book   8

Hardiness zone map   9

A to Z of trees and shrubs for fragrance   12

Ready-reference table   148

Mail-order sources for trees and shrubs   154

Glossary   156

Bibliography   157

Index   158

Acknowledgements   160

Picture credits   160

Introduction

Our sense of smell is an amazing thing. It keeps us safe by alerting us to dangerous or unpleasant things but it also brings us pleasure. Most of our sense of taste comes from what we smell, and we enjoy the pleasant scents of cosmetics, soaps and perfumes. I believe that fragrance is at its best when it is natural, and from earliest times we have been using the scent of plants to mask unpleasant odors, flavor our foods and simply for enjoyment. The joy of smelling a rose or a jasmine gives us a lift and one that we can keep returning to. Scents are also fantastic memory triggers. We inhale a scent and are transported back in time; perhaps back to your grandmother's garden, or a long-forgotten holiday or your first date. You can't put a price on fragrance when it works in this way. It is an instant and wonderful experience as the memories come flooding back.

Often these trigger scents are from flowers and somehow we expect that flowers will always have a smell. Offer someone a bloom and they invariably sniff it. We are disappointed when roses don't have a fragrance, and we blame the breeding of many of the modern roses for denying us this pleasure. Most often we think of fragrance being associated with flowers, though some plants in this book have scented leaves or stems. The flowers aren't releasing the fragrance for our benefit, they are trying to attract pollinating insects, like bees, often with a honey or sweet nectar scent. Some plants have a strong smell to their leaves to ward off insect pests, and we have used these properties throughout history to protect our homes and ourselves.

Fragrance adds another dimension to our gardens, making them a truly sensual experience. Once you are aware of the vast array of fragrant plants, you will regard any non-scented specimen as less worthy. This is especially so if you have a small garden, where you need your plants to perform a variety of functions. I always regard a scented plant as giving double the pleasure.

When choosing a tree or shrub for fragrance, take extra care when deciding where to plant it. We usually place scented plants near the house so we can enjoy the perfume. However, while some scents are initially attractive, they can become heavy and

Left: Spartium junceum
Opposite: Mandevilla laxa
Below left: Kalmia latifolia 'Raspberry Glow'

cloying on longer acquaintance, so it is best to plant these species further away. Plants with scented leaves often need the leaves to be touched to emit the fragrance, so plant them next to a path so you brush past them or so you can clutch a leaf as you walk by.

This book focuses on woody plants and, because space is restricted, I have had to select only some of my favorites for fragrance. "One man's meat is another man's poison," so some of your favorites may have been omitted, but I hope the selection presented here has something new and interesting for you to try.

A woody plant is one with a permanent woody structure. Some woody plants die back to some extent in the winter but there is always some woody part visible throughout the year. My own garden has well over 2,000 different woody plants, and many of the photographs in the book were taken there. I have used this garden and also my experience of growing plants in windy, dry or cold climates to explain the likes and dislikes of the plants. Zones are given to show how cold a climate a plant will cope with, but they are only a guide. When a plant does not like warm or hot regions, I have included an upper as well as a lower limit.

It is very hard to generalize about the climate a plant needs in order to thrive. Within any region and even within a garden there are microclimates—places that are warmer or colder than the surrounding area. Even planting a shrub next to a wall where it gets the reflected heat can make the difference between success and failure. Similarly with soil, we can improve it and irrigate if necessary. The type of soil is critical to the well-being of some plants and irrelevant to others. Over the years I have gardened on heavy clay soils with a pH of 7.0, on rocky soil with a pH of 6.0, and currently a free-draining acidic loam of pH 5.5, so I have used my experience regarding soil types when writing the plant descriptions.

I have also included plants that may have naturalized in your region. The more I travel the more I find that what is regarded in one region as a weed is a treasure somewhere else. Sometimes this is based on the plant actually self-perpetuating in that region and sometimes it is just plain bias against a certain plant or group of plants.

I want to take you on a journey of scented woody plants. Not all of them are "pleasantly" scented, some might say a few are downright noisome, but all of them give off a fragrance that is pleasing to someone. Describing fragrance is a difficult task, as it is very subjective, rather like taste. I have tried to indicate the main groupings of scent—whether savory, fruit, honey or nectar, citrus or pepper. I only wish there was a way to convey the fragrance of the following plants through these pages, but I hope my efforts give you some guidance as to what will be best for your garden.

How to use this book

The plants presented in this book are organised alphabetically by genus. If you know the common name only, you can find the botanical name entry through the index, where both botanical and common names are listed.

Each entry has a variety of information laid out in the format illustrated below, so you can quickly find what you need to know about a particular plant. The text includes not only notes on cultivation, but anecdotes and historical information, making this a fascinating book to browse through.

The table at the back of the book will help you to find plants by hardiness zone and size whether they are evergreen or deciduous, or native to North America. An extensive glossary covers the botanical terms used throughout the book.

Genus

Common name

Family
Taxonomic grouping of genera to which this genus belongs.

Species name

Common name
These names vary from place to place. To be sure of what you are buying, always check the species name.

Cultivar or form
Cultivated variety, usually bred but can be a natural variety, then often called a "sport." Can only be propagated true from cuttings.

Elaeagnus

THORNY ELAEAGNUS
Elaeagnaceae

*E*laeagnus is a large genus of plants with a widespread distribution from southern Europe through to Asia and over to North America. Some are deciduous while others are super-hardy evergreens, though few of them have enough merit to be brought into our gardens.

The most useful aspect of these plants is the wind-hardiness of *E. pungens* and *E. macrophylla* and the dazzling variegated leaf forms of *E. pungens* and *E.* x *ebbingei*.

Elaeagnus = wild olive (from Greek *elaeagnos*, in reference to the fruits).

Elaeagnus angustifolia
OLEASTER OR RUSSIAN OLIVE
Oleaster makes a large deciduous shrub or small tree with a billowy habit, reddish stems and hidden spines. The tiny, fragrant, creamy yellow flowers appear in summertime. However, the prime reason for growing this is the silvery willow-like leaves, and it is often confused with a *Pyrus salicifolia*. It is found native in southern Europe to central Asia. Height x width 20 ft (6 m). ZONE 3.

'Quicksilver' is an excellent silvery leaf form grown for its consistency. Height x width 12 ft (4 m).

Angustifolia = narrow leaf.

Description of genus

Meaning of botanical name

Species description and cultivation notes

Hardiness zone
These zones are guides only (see page 9). The zone range is given at the end of each species entry. If no upper limit is given, the plants will grow to zone 10, though possibly with some change to habit, e.g., some deciduous trees can become semi-evergreen. Unless otherwise stated, cultivars grow in the same zone range as the species.

Approximation of size
Height and width can be an approximation only as it varies enormously depending on your climate. If you are concerned about something growing too big, check with a local garden center to find out how they grow in your area.

Right: *Salvia involucrata* 'Bethelli'
Far right: *Luculia grandifolia*

Hardiness zone map

This map has been prepared to agree with a system of plant hardiness zones that has been accepted as an international standard and range from 1 to 11. It shows the minimum winter temperatures that can be expected on average in different regions. Where a zone number has been given, the number corresponds with a zone shown here. That number indicates the coldest areas in which the particular plant is likely to survive through an average winter. Note that these are not necessarily the areas in which it will grow best. Because the zone number refers to the minimum temperatures, a plant given zone 7, for example, will obviously grow perfectly well in zone 8, but not in zone 6. Plants grown in a zone considerably higher than the zone with the minimum winter temperature in which they will survive might well grow but they are likely to behave differently. Note also that some readers may find the numbers a little conservative; we felt it best to err on the side of caution.

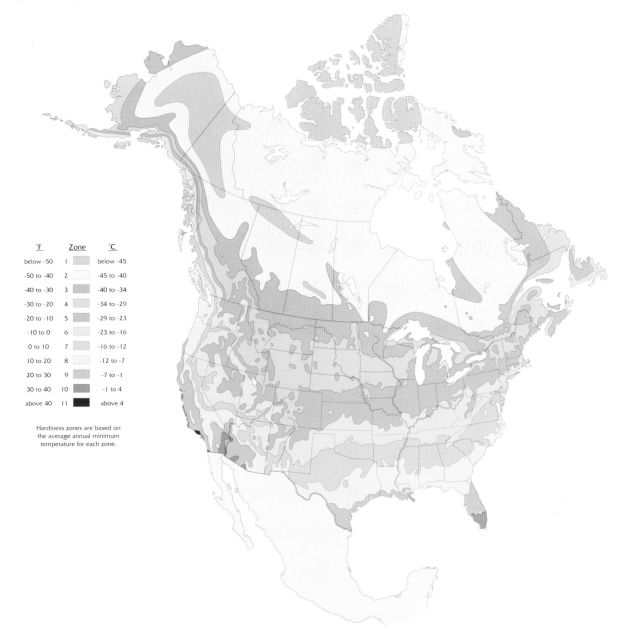

°F	Zone	°C
below -50	1	below -45
-50 to -40	2	-45 to -40
-40 to -30	3	-40 to -34
-30 to -20	4	-34 to -29
-20 to -10	5	-29 to -23
-10 to 0	6	-23 to -16
0 to 10	7	-16 to -12
10 to 20	8	-12 to -7
20 to 30	9	-7 to -1
30 to 40	10	-1 to 4
above 40	11	above 4

Hardiness zones are based on the average annual minimum temperature for each zone.

Left: *Laburnum anagyroide*
Far left: *Hydrangea macrophylla* 'Rotschwanz'
Following pages: Deciduous hybrid azaleas.

Abelia

Caprifoliaceae

*A*belia are a group of unsung garden heroes that work away quietly, growing in difficult sites or being put to work as hedges, and yet they are rarely noticed. Many garden species are summer flowering and the blooms have a sweet, honey fragrance. Abelias will grow in full sun or in the shade of deciduous plants, and will take any soil they are given, from acidic to alkaline, clay to sand. Most are easy to grow and can be transplanted with ease, pruned at will and clipped to form hedges or any shape you wish. Abelias grow in wet or dry climates and put up with quite a lot of wind. They are not bothered by any pests or diseases. Generally they are arching shrubs. For all their ease of growth and similar appearance, however, the species of this genus come from diverse homelands, including the Himalayas, China, Japan and Mexico. Some are evergreen, some are deciduous and some are deciduous only in cold regions.

Abelia = after Dr. Clarke Abel (1780–1826), who was part of a British delegation to the emperor of China in 1816. As the delegation traveled back to the coast, Abel surreptitiously collected nearly 300 types of seeds, including Abelia chinensis.

Abelia chinensis
CHINESE ABELIA

Some shrubs are instantly desirable, while others need time to grow on you. *Abelia chinensis* is one that grows on you. It has become my favorite *Abelia* because it is reliable, constant and easy to grow and because it flowers in late summer when few shrubs are out. The real highlight of the soft pink flowers is the delicious sweet, sugary scent. The blooms appear in clusters near the tips of the stems and last a good few weeks.

This *Abelia* grows in full, hot sun or in the difficult shade underneath birch trees. It is happy in wet or dry climates, tolerates some cold and is fine in any soil. Native to China. Height x width 5–6 ft (1.5–2 m). ZONE 8.

Chinensis = from China.

Abelia x grandiflora (A. chinensis x A. uniflora)
GLOSSY ABELIA

To call this plant *grandiflora* is a bit of an exaggeration unless it refers to the sheer quantity of pale pink, sweetly scented blooms. This is a hybrid *Abelia* with dark, glossy leaves and masses of pale pink, almost white, flowers all through late summer. It is evergreen in a mild climate and semi-evergreen elsewhere; the leaves take on a reddish tinge at times. It makes an excellent small hedge for suburban gardens. There is a variegated form called **'Frances Mason'**, as well as several gold versions. A hybrid between *A. x grandiflora* and *A. schumannii* called **'Edward Goucher'** has beautiful gold and bronze new leaves, later turning bright green, and is evergreen in warm places. The pinky lilac flowers in late summer are a bonus. All have the same sweet scent. Height x width 6 ft (2 m). ZONE 5.

Grandiflora = having big flowers.

Abelia schumannii

An ungainly shrub that sends shoots in all directions. It makes up for this by producing masses of soft purple-lilac flowers, with a

Left: *Abelia chinensis*

Right: *Abelia* x *grandiflora* 'Edward Goucher'

Below: *Abelia schumannii*

sweet tea scent, all through summer. Even the red calyxes protecting the flowers are pretty, and new stems are red, too. A plant deserving of more attention and an ideal shrub for those difficult spots at the back of a border or between buildings. From China, evergreen in warm climates. Height x width 6 ft (2 m). ZONE 7.

Schumanni = named for Karl Schumann (1851–1904), a German botanist.

Abelia triflora

The summer flowers are not much to look at, being small and an extremely pale pink. But it's worth planting one in a corner somewhere just for the wondrous honeysuckle scent. Originates from the Himalayas. Height x width 6 ft (2 m). ZONE 6.

Triflora = appearing in threes.

Abelia uniflora

This *Abelia* is better looking than *Abelia triflora*, with showier, prettier flowers, though the scent is not as strong as some other species. It is not a common garden plant and often hard to find in garden centers. Native to China. Height 6 ft (2 m) x width 6 ft (2 m). ZONE 7.

Uniflora = appearing singly.

Abeliophyllum

Abeliophyllum distichum
KOREAN ABELIALEAF, WHITE FORSYTHIA
Oleaceae

I first came across this plant at the Chelsea Physic Garden on the banks of the Thames in London. It was a month after midwinter, there was a crisp frost on the ground, and the only woody plant brave enough to open was a little bush with dainty white flowers that smelled like almonds. The plant was brought into cultivation in the West in 1924 when Mr. Ishidoya from Korea sent seeds to Ernest Wilson, keeper of the Arnold

Above: *Abeliophyllum distichum*

Arboretum in Boston. Wilson was one of the few plant hunters to include Korea on his itinerary and *Abeliophyllum* is found naturally only in that country. I'm told by Korean plantspeople that this shrub is quite rare and is close to extinction. *Abeliophyllum* is monotypic, which means that there is only one plant in its genus.

Abeliophyllum is usually seen with pure white flowers and yellow anthers. The four outstretched petals remind me of a forsythia, which is not surprising really because the plants are in the same olive family. In its native Korea there are forms with pink flowers, or cream with orange centers. In the wild the plant tends to have an upright, bushy habit not unlike forsythia, but it is not as tall. However, most of those in cultivation seem to be more rounded, with an almost horizontal habit that is probably caused by propagating them from cuttings. (Conifers are a classic instance of this, producing horizontal plants from horizontal cuttings. Cultivation techniques change the natural shape of the plant.)

Being a Korean native means it can handle bitterly cold winters and equally hot summers. It seems to need extremes to thrive and is lackluster in a mild climate. In Korea spring comes slowly and consistently with no false starts, and so in milder climates this plant is inclined to flower at the first hint of warmer weather. These early flowers may be frost-damaged, but the plant will not suffer. It is therefore hard to predict when it will bloom because it depends on when spring comes in your zone. I can say it will be one of the earliest of the spring shrubs in your garden and is worthy of a place for its flowers and scent. I always imagine they would be good cut-flowers but have to confess I never have enough to practice with.

If you decide to plant *A. distichum*, choose a warm sunny site with good drainage. Like its relative forsythia, it will grow equally well in alkaline and acidic soil. Provided it has enough winter cold and summer heat and some shelter from strong winds, it will grow easily and is unhindered by pests or diseases.

The small, simple, *Abelia*-like leaves are opposite along thin, rather brittle, twigs. These stems are usually a creamy pale brown and occasionally take on a purplish tinge where they catch the sun. The plant is deciduous but there is no fall color worthy of mention. Find a spot in your garden where you will notice it during those late winter days and it will lift your spirits to know spring is on its way. Native to Korea. Height 2–3 ft (60 cm–1 m) x width 3 ft (1 m). ZONE 4.

Abeliophyllum = leaf (*phyllum*) like an *Abelia*; *distichum* = two rows.

Acacia

WATTLE, MIMOSA
Mimosaceae, part of Fabaceae

Most Australian acacias have fragrant blooms in early spring, and are popular for cut-flowers and as "instant" trees in new city suburbs. The fragrance is like sweet honey.

When is a leaf not a leaf? When it's an acacia leaf. Let me explain: acacias have two types of leaves. The first are fine and feathery juvenile leaves, found on seedlings and young plants. Some acacias such as *Acacia baileyana* keep these true leaves throughout their lives. However many acacias change from these feathery leaves to much thicker, almost fleshy, leaves. The catch is, these are not true leaves at all, but are flattened leaf stalks or petioles. They are known as phyllodes and act like ordinary leaves. Because they have chlorophyll and photosynthesize, to all

intents and purposes they are leaves. These tough phyllodes have adapted to cope with heat, drought and strong winds, which is why acacias can survive and thrive in hot and dry or windy climates. In some of the African species these phyllodes have adapted even more to become spines.

Acacias are found in many sub-tropical regions, especially Africa and Australia. Ornamental acacias are evergreen, prefer an acidic soil and are generally easy to grow if the drainage is good. For the most part, acacias are very fast-growing and many are not long-lived. This is what I call a "grow fast–die fast" syndrome. Some species only live for around 10–15 years. Sometimes they fall over as young plants, breaking off at ground level, and they can be uprooted in a storm. Many have brittle branches, easily broken in strong winds, while others such as *A. longifolia* are tough and wind-hardy.

Typical legume trees, acacias have very hard seed coats. To speed up germination, put the seeds in very hot, almost boiling, water and leave them to soak overnight before sowing. The hot water softens the coat and allows the seed to absorb water. They then germinate easily and can be grown in pots for a while. Take care that they don't become root-bound, as the fast-growing roots twirl round and round the bottom of the pot. Tease out the roots and spread them in a star fashion at planting time or else the plant will not live long—the roots will twist around each other until they strangle the plant. Most acacias need an acidic, free-draining soil, although they will grow in poor sites. Some are grown specifically for the cut-flower trade, either for foliage or flowers, and are often referred to as "mimosa."

Acacia = from Greek "akazo," meaning sharp point, referring to the spiny species.

Above: *Acacia baileyana*

Below: *Acacia longifolia*

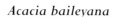

Acacia baileyana
COOTAMUNDRA WATTLE

In spring, *Acacia baileyana* is covered in a brilliant mass of honey-scented, yellow puffball flowers.

This is one of the few acacias that displays true leaves. They are soft and fern-like in a lovely shade of blue. Delicate appearances can be deceptive, however, as acacias are surprisingly tough plants. Each leaf consists of four pairs of bipinnate leaflets and each of these has dozens of mini-leaflets. They are a blue-gray color, a rare hue in the plant world. The plant forms a small, round-headed tree with a billowy habit that is slightly pendulous. It grows so fast it becomes an "instant" tree and is therefore popular in new suburbs. Acidic or neutral soil and free drainage are essential. In windy climates it needs some shelter, as it is prone to blow over at ground level, especially in its early years. Also, the branches can be brittle and occasionally break during a storm. The form **'Purpurea'** has purple-bronze new growth, contrasting with the blue. Native to New South Wales, Australia. Height x width 15 ft (5 m). ZONE 8.

Baileyana = after Frederick Bailey (1827–1915), Australian botanist and author; *bipinnate* = doubly pinnate, having leaflets on leaflets.

Acacia dealbata
SILVER WATTLE

It has silver fern-like leaves and is surprisingly tough, sometimes being grown as a windbreak. A froth of yellow flowers with a delicious honey fragrance appear in spring. Often used for cut-flowers, florists sell sprays of bloom as "mimosa." It is also one of the hardier species, along with *Acacia longifolia* and *A. melanoxylon*. From New South Wales and Tasmania, Australia. Height 20–30 ft (6–10 m) x width 30 ft (10 m). ZONE 8.

Dealbata = whitened, referring to the silvery white leaves.

Acacia longifolia
GOLDEN WATTLE

This is one of the tougher acacias and a hardy, rugged tree that grows speedily to create an immediate impact. The tough, leathery leaves or phyllodes are like long, thin strips of plastic. In spring the bush is covered in slender cones of bright yellow, fluffy flowers contrasting with the grass-green leaves. The scent is a typical acacia smell of strong honey. It is one of the few acacias to tolerate pruning, which is best done immediately after flowering. It is more lime-tolerant than most species. Popular in Europe, being quite hardy. Native to Australia. Height x width 15 ft (5 m). ZONE 8.

Longifolia = with long leaves.

Acacia melanoxylon
BLACKWOOD

The creamy-colored little puffballs of flowers are honey scented and appear in spring. The fine, ferny, blue-green juvenile foliage is another reason to grow this tree. When you plant a blackwood it is a bit of a lottery. It may keep its juvenile foliage for years, but the tougher, waxy phyllodes most often take over. Surprisingly, although one of the fastest-growing trees on the planet, it still manages to produce excellent timber. Usually fast-growing trees only yield poor-quality timber. When used for fine furniture, it is on a par with walnut and mahogany. It is also an ideal tree for a firewood lot, with good burning qualities and speedy growth. Typically the trunks are about 2 ft (60 cm) around after 6 or 7 years. The growth habit can be ungainly, with multi-trunks prone to splitting, so regular pruning for shape is necessary. From Australia. Height 50–80 ft (15–25 m) x width 30 ft (10 m). ZONE 8.

Melan = black; *xylon* = wood.

Acacia pravissima
OVEN'S WATTLE

One of the hardier, more resilient species, with a fabulous froth of sugary-scented flowers in the spring. The chains of golden yellow flowers cascade in pendulous fashion like a firework just past its zenith. It seems to grow in any soil and is hardier to cold than most. The bluish triangular leaves are really phyllodes and not leaves at all. Originates from southern Australia. Height 20 ft (6 m) x width 15 ft (4.5 m). ZONE 8.

There is also a prostrate form called **'Golden Carpet'**. Height 3–6 ft (1–2 m) x width 6–10 ft (2–3 m).

Pravissima = crooked or deformed.

Acacia verticillata
PRICKLY MOSES

A large shrub or small tree with whorls of spiny, dark green leaves and lemon-yellow spikes of sweetly scented flowers like mini-bottlebrushes in spring. *Acacia verticillata* grows naturally in damp areas, but in cultivation it is best grown in free-draining soil. A good plant for seaside gardens. It is sometimes attacked by acacia gall, which disfigures the bush. From southern Australia. Height 10–12 ft (3–4 m) x width 6 ft (2 m).

There is a compact fragrant form called **'Rewa'**, growing only 6 ft (2 m) high and wide, with softer foliage and a more weeping habit. ZONE 8.

Verticillata = having whorls of leaves.

Acradenia

Acradenia frankliniae
WHITEY WOOD

Rutaceae

The first thing you will notice about this plant is that it is almost black—certainly the darkest foliage I have seen in the woody plant world. Then you will see that the leaves are slightly puckered with prominent glands, and if you crush a leaf you will discover a strong citrus-like scent, which is typical of all the plants in the lemon family. Tiny, lemon-scented white flowers appear in early summer. "Once seen, never forgotten" is how I describe this shrub, as the tiny, trifoliate leaves are unique. Each trio of leaflets is opposite another set and it looks like a single leaf enveloping the stem. *Acradenia frankliniae* forms a neat, columnar shrub if grown in full sun and remains leaf-covered to the ground, which is unusual, as most shrubs eventually lose their lower branches. The bush looks so neat and formal, you may think someone has diligently clipped it to create such a perfect shape.

The flowers are quite cute, but they won't set the gardening world on fire. Sometimes I think we gardeners want only highlight shrubs, but if they were all "stars" then none of them would shine. I feel it is much better to have some hard-working "bit players." You won't regret planting one, as they add shape and form to a garden and are ideal to screen an entrance, a role usually given to a conifer. The bush prefers full sun and good drainage but otherwise is not too fussy as to site. It is only marginally hardy to cold, needing a moist, mild climate to thrive. It grows best on river banks and in other moist places. It is easy enough to transplant, with a good root system, but it does tend to be very slow-growing in the early years. It pays to plant a quick-growing bush like broom beside it so that by the time it has died the *Acradenia* is established. This temporary bush is called a "nurse plant," as it protects the slow-growing one and gives color while we wait for the longer-term plant. Native to Tasmania. Height 10–15 ft (3–5 m) x width 3–6 ft (1–2 m). ZONE 8.

Acradenia = referring to the glands on the fruits; *frankliniae* = after Lady Franklin, wife of Governor Sir John Franklin of Tasmania. The Franklins were traveling in the party that discovered this plant in 1842.

Agonis

Myrtaceae

If you live in a warm, dry climate but you have a fancy for a weeping willow, then this genus could provide the tree for you. Willows need a lot of moisture, while *Agonis* can cope with hot and dry conditions. The leaves of these evergreen trees have a tangy, minty fragrance. They are quite happy in a warm, wet climate, too, thriving in high rainfall areas. Any soil including clay or limestone will suffice and they are also very wind-hardy.

These plants are ideal for new suburbs because they grow fast and mature quickly to become "instant" trees. Eventually they become large trees, but in a gardener's lifetime they are quite a manageable size. If your climate is warm enough, then they will be easy to grow and seemingly free of pests and diseases. Being native to western Australia, they are able to withstand heat and drought.

Agonis = from "agon," meaning a gathering, referring to the mass of seeds in the capsules.

Agonis flexuosa
PEPPERMINT TREE, WILLOW MYRTLE

The leaves are long, thin and willow-like, but made of much thicker, harder material that helps them withstand wind and drought. They release a tangy, peppermint scent when they are

Left: *Acradenia frankliniae*

matures, the stems hang down gracefully, creating a curtain of feathery foliage. Trim the tree occasionally in the early years to keep a good, dense shape as it can reach skyward and become very open. If you want a light, open, airy tree then you will have the added attraction of the fibrous, furrowed bark. Tiny white flowers appear in winter or early spring, and it is sometimes grown for the cut-flower and foliage trade (as evident in the named form, **'Florist Star'**). Originates from western Australia. Height 15–25 ft (5–8 m) x width 10 ft (3 m). ZONE 8 OR 9.

Juniperina = like a juniper.

Above: *Akebia quinata*

Akebia

Akebia quinata
CHOCOLATE VINE
Lardizabalaceae

Chocoholics, have I got a treat for you! Chocolate-scented flowers. They even look like chocolate. These intriguing, purplish-brown flowers are held out like little lanterns in springtime, but it is often the scent that leads you to them rather than their color or showiness. Once you have seen them in flower you wonder how you ever missed them before. The fruits look something like purple sausages, although the plant is not inclined to set fruit in cooler areas.

This semi-evergreen climber tends to keep some or most of its leaves in a mild climate. A fabulous contrast is created between the older, dark green leaves and the newly emerging spring leaves. Smooth-edged leaflets sit neatly in a hand fashion

Above: *Agonis flexuosa*

touched or bruised. Among these leaves are tiny, white, rose-like flowers tucked in close to the stems all along the new growths. These spring flowers may be small but they are produced in abundance and are sweetly scented. There is a beautiful variegated form, **'Variegata'**, that unfortunately is very difficult to propagate and therefore very scarce. It is not often that I rave about variegated plants but I make an exception here. The combination of pink, cream and green on a small weeping shrub is phenomenal. A new dwarf variegated form called **'Grace'** will soon become popular. Native to western Australia. Height 15–25 ft (5–8 m) x width 10 ft (3 m). ZONE 9.

Flexuosa = crooked or zigzag, because of the twisty branches.

Agonis juniperina
JUNIPER MYRTLE
This is aptly named, as the foliage looks just like a juniper—dark green, crusty and spiky to touch. Like a juniper, the leaves are scented; only these smell of peppermint when touched or brushed past. Initially the bush has a strong, vertical growth habit but as it

Below: *Agonis juniperina*

and always manage to look elegant. Many plants appear jaded or ragged by fall but *Akebia*, being healthy and pest-free, looks as fresh in the fall as it did in the spring. It is worthy of a place in your garden even just as a foliage plant and in many ways it is the perfect vine for a patio or entranceway because of its delicious scent and amazing leaf patterns. I hear occasional complaints "that it is too vigorous," but its growth is never on the scale of a jasmine, and nothing that can't be solved with secateurs. Like most climbers it seeks to cover any prop it is given, so the answer is to give it a small trellis, say 6 ft (2 m) high. Sometimes it is a good idea to cut it back hard about every 6 or 7 years. Cut back to ground level or to a few long whips in springtime and let it start again.

Akebia quinata is perfectly hardy, but it pays to protect young plants for the first winter. I can vouch for its hardiness, having seen it growing as a stunted little vine on the freezing, desolate peaks of Mount Hallasan on Cheju Island, off the south coast of Korea. Yet it is equally happy in a warm zone 9 or 10 climate. Strong winds will not bother it too much, and it is certainly happy in both sunny and shady spots and virtually any soil.

It was introduced to Western gardens in 1845 by Robert Fortune (1812–1880), the man responsible for smuggling tea plants out of China. There are other species, including a three-leaf version logically called **Akebia trifoliata**. It is a native of Korea, China and Japan. Height 10–30 ft (3–10 m). ZONE 5 for both species.

Akebia = from the Japanese name for this plant;
quinata = refers to the five leaves.

Aloysia

Aloysia triphylla, syn Lippia citriodora
LEMON SCENTED VERBENA
Verbenaceae

Some plants have only one purpose, and *Aloysia* is just such a plant. Were it not for the overpowering, citrus-scented leaves, we would never give it a space in our gardens.

The plant is a stalked, untidy bush with arching branches, some of which are strong and vigorous while many are weak and fragile. The stronger growths have leaves in threes at every node, while on the weaker stems the leaves are opposite. The thin, pale green, willow-like leaves have nothing special to commend them and the overall bush is rather sparse. Often semi-evergreen in mild regions, it is deciduous in cooler climates. It will be much improved if you prune the bush drastically in the spring before the new growth comes away, as you will have a denser, tidier plant. From midsummer onward pale blue flowers appear at the tips of the stems and they are suitable cut-flowers for a vase.

It is an easy plant to please in terms of soil, growing anywhere except poorly drained places. Drought poses no threat, but wet climates are fine, too, if the drainage is good. Plant it in a sheltered place, as strong winds will damage it (and it looks bedraggled enough already). Perhaps grow it as a wall shrub in colder regions, allowing it full sun and as much heat as possible. Ideally, place it near a path so you can pluck a leaf as you pass by or brush against the bush to release the glorious scent. The strong citrus smell keeps all pests at bay. It transplants easily from pots and could possibly be moved if you cut it back

very hard. It is so easy to root that it is probably easier to grow your own cuttings than to buy new plants. The plant comes from Chile. Height x width 6 ft (2 m). ZONE 8.

Aloysia = Queen Maria Louisa of Spain; *triphylla* = having leaves in threes.

Above: *Aloysia triphylla*

Amelanchier

JUNEBERRY, SHADBUSH, SNOWY MESPILUS
Rosaceae

Amelanchiers are a confused group of plants. They have at times been cataloged as *Mespilus*, *Aronia*, *Pyrus* or *Crataegus* and with the species it seems that only botanists can tell one from another. From the viewpoint of ordinary gardeners they are simply beautiful plants and we should select named forms so that we get the bush we need. Most have flowers with an apple blossom scent to attract the pollinating insects.

Although the individual flowers are small, when they are massed together the overall effect is stunning. Amelanchiers grow all across the cooler regions of the Northern Hemisphere and the flowers must be very tough to survive frost, snow and biting cold winds. They are all hardy, deciduous shrubs or small trees with clean, oval leaves and simple, white, apple blossom-like flowers followed by small black or purple fruits. It is not for the outright showiness of the flowers but for their abundance and bravery at flowering in adverse conditions that they are so attractive. Then, at the end of summer, they oblige us with stupendous fall colors in shades of orange and red.

Amelanchiers are easy to grow in any soil that is not too dry or too poor. Most of them need an acidic or neutral soil. As you will have gathered, they are supremely cold- and wind-hardy,

growing on mountaintops. Full sun is ideal as they become thin and unloved in the shade. With an upright, brush habit they are an ideal plant for the back of a perennial or shrub border. Some form small trees and can be used as lawn specimens. I have

moved very big specimens quite successfully, and they can be transplanted at any time during the dormant winter period. They don't mind being pruned, either for outline shape or more drastically, if your plant gets too big for its allotted space.

Amelanchiers are prone to cankers and fireblight.

Amelanchier = an adaptation of "amelancier," an old name for *Amelanchier ovalis* in Europe.

Amelanchier arborea
DOWNY SERVICEBERRY

This species is bigger than the above and becomes a tree, thus the name *arborea* (tree). It may need pruning in a garden situation to make it into a tidy, rounded, small tree. The oval leaves are slightly hairy or downy and have colorful fall tints. The arching racemes of white flowers are a sweet apple blossom scent and are followed by red berries. This plant comes from northeast U.S.A. Height 20 ft (6 m) x width 15 ft (5 m). ZONES 4 TO 9.

Arborea = tree-like.

Amelanchier asiatica
ASIAN SERVICEBERRY

In the spring the Asian serviceberry has racemes of white, apple blossom scented flowers. It is a large, upright shrub with bronzy new growth and nice smooth stems. Copes with limy soil. It hails from China, Korea and Japan. Height 6–10 ft (2–3 m) x width 5 ft (1.5 m). ZONES 5 TO 9.

Asiatica = from Asia.

Amelanchier canadensis
SHADBUSH

A handsome, upright shrub with a tendency to sucker. Typical white flowers with an apple blossom scent on erect racemes in the spring followed by black berries. The smooth leaves are green

through summer and turn to fiery reds and orange in the fall. This plant is from northeast U.S.A. Height 10 ft (3 m) x width 6 ft (2 m). ZONES 3 TO 9.

Canadensis = from Canada.

Amelanchier laevis
ALLEGHENY SERVICEBERRY

A large shrub or small tree covered in fragrant, white flowers in spring. The new leaves are often bronzy red, changing to green for the summer and to rich colors in the fall. One of the best Amelanchiers for flowers and leaf color. The cultivar **'Cumulus'** is bigger and more disease-resistant. Another species that originates in North America. Height 10–12 ft (3–4 m) x width 6–10 ft (2–3 m). ZONES 5 TO 9.

Laevis = smooth.

Amelanchier lamarckii

This is a fabulous plant with neat foliage, great fall color and pollen-scented flowers. The new growth in spring is bronzy-colored, quickly followed by a mass of dainty white flowers. During the summer the leaves always look fresh and presentable and they turn fiery oranges and reds in the fall. It is a bush with a very tidy habit and it can be trained into a small tree or standard shape. This lovely plant has confused gardeners and botanists alike for many years. It was first called *Crataegus racemosa* by Lamarck as long ago as 1783. At times people have thought it a European species, then a hybrid, and then perhaps an obscure American species. At times it has been lumped in with *A. canadensis* and *A. laevis*. Now it is thought to be a minor North American species. Height 10–12 ft (3–4 m) x width 6–10 ft (2–3 m). ZONES 5 TO 9.

Lamarckii = after Jean Baptiste de Lamarck (1744–1829).

Amorpha

Fabaceae

Sometimes known as "false indigo" or "bastard indigo," because the early American settlers used it as a substitute for the true indigo blue dye, *Indigofera tinctori*. There are lots of similar species of amorpha and most have sweetly fragrant flowers. They are all American shrubs or sub-shrubs with pinnate leaves typical of legumes.

Amorphas love hot, sunny places and can cope with any soil, providing the drainage is good. They also tolerate wind, cold and drought, so you can see that they are easy-care plants. They are technically part of the legume or pea family, although you would need better eyesight than mine to see this, as the individual flowers are very small. They are so small, in fact, they only have room for one petal instead of the usual five in a legume, with wings and keel. At least the seed pods are easily recognizable as typical legumes.

A = not; *morph* = form, referring to the irregular shape of the flowers.

Amorpha canescens
LEAD PLANT

So called as it was thought to grow where the mineral lead was in the soil. A low, deciduous bush, growing from a woody base and sending up new shoots to form a thicket, usually only knee to waist high. Intriguing purple-blue flowers with a heavy, cloying candy-like scent appear at the tips of the erect growths in late summer. The leaves are covered in gray down, helping it survive heat and drought, but it will also grow in wetter climates. In extremely cold climates the plant dies down to the rootstock each

Left: *Amelanchier lamarckii*

Above: *Amorpha fruticosa*

Below: *Argyrocytisus battandieri*

the tips of the stamens. Each tiny flower is not much bigger than a grain of rice. The flowers open in succession from the base to the tip, meaning the display lasts for well over a month, from late spring on through summer. Each flower has a central spike and three smaller finger-length spikes to the side.

Although it naturally frequents riverbanks and flood plains of eastern North America, it's equally happy in hot, dry conditions and will survive drought-prone regions. In fact, if you saw this plant and had to guess its natural habitat, I'm sure you would choose hot and dry rather than wet. It will also handle some shade, giving us several possible sites in the garden.

It looks good in a mixed border or at the back of a herbaceous bed. Native to eastern North America. Height x width 6 ft (2 m). ZONE 5.

Fruticosa = shrubby.

Argyrocytisus

Argyrocytisus battandieri, syn Cytisus battandieri
SILVER BROOM, MOUNT ATLAS BROOM
Fabaceae

This was, until recently, just another broom—or at least was listed as such—but when you see it you will have to agree it looks different enough to be in a genus of its own. Grow one near a path so that you can enjoy the lovely texture of the leaves and the strong, fruity scent of the flowers. The cones of golden-yellow flowers appear in summer on the tips of the arching stems and smell like ripe pineapples or strawberries. Actually, men are far more enamored of the smell than women. I'm convinced the sexes differ in the way they interpret fragrances. All the flowers open at the same time, creating a good display.

Silver broom is very appropriately named, given the silky-haired, silver leaves divided into three leaflets, a bit like a bird's foot imprint. These soft, gray hairs protect the plant from drought and hot sun. It is certainly used to hot, dry conditions, coming from the Atlas Mountains in North Africa. It was only discovered in 1915 and introduced into cultivation about 1922. The same region is home to the *Cedrus atlantica* or Atlas cedar.

Argyrocytisus battandieri forms an open, rangy sort of plant and so it is not a good choice for tidy gardeners. It grows between 6–12 ft (2–4 m) high and wide, depending on your climate and the soil conditions, and is semi-evergreen in warmer climates. When grown in the open garden it often has a loose, wayward appearance but thankfully it responds well to a "haircut" and can even be pruned back hard, which is most unusual for a broom.

Gardeners in cooler climates are happy just to keep it alive and resort to growing it as a wall shrub to give it heat and protection. It suits being grown this way because it is tidier, and keeps the root zone drier. It is not happy in cold, wet or humid climates, but give it good drainage and lots of sun and hope for the best. It can be easily raised from seeds or cuttings, so try and keep a younger plant in reserve because they're not long-lived in cool, moist regions. Native to North Africa. Height x width 6–12 ft (2–4 m). ZONE 8 OR 9.

Argyr (from argent) = silver; *cytisus* = broom; *battandieri* = Jules Aimé Battandier (1848–1922) who studied the flora of the Atlas Mountains.

winter, but it will survive to zone 2. A great plant for the front of a sunny border. *Amorpha nana* is similar, with purplish, fragrant flowers but is not downy in the leaf. Native to North America. Height 1–3 ft (30 cm–1 m) x width 3 ft (1 m). ZONE 2.

Canescens = gray or hoary.

Amorpha fruticosa
FALSE INDIGO
See this plant in flower for the first time and you will be taken by its unusual purple, almost black, flowers. They have a pleasant, wholesome, honey scent, and so are popular with bees. The long, thin, rat-tail spikes of flowers have tiny specks of orange pollen on

Left: *Artemisia arborescens*

Artemisia

MUGWORT, SAGEBRUSH, WORMWOOD
Asteraceae

The scent of these plants is sharp, almost curry-like, but very pleasant. They are grown solely for their foliage and scent because the small daisy flowers are quite unexciting. *Artemisia* are wonderful landscape plants with silver, feathery foliage. They are perfect contrast plants and can be used as a foil for roses or summer-flowering perennials, or maybe to brighten up dense, dark evergreens such as rhododendrons. They are a mix of herbaceous and woody plants and most of the garden-worthy ones come from the Mediterranean region. The woody ones can be tidy, upright plants, while others are more rambling, scrambling, lax ground covers. All of them are heat- and sun-lovers, although they cope with a little light shade. They grow almost as well in wet climates, providing they get lots of sun and the drainage is good. Otherwise they are not at all fussy about soil and grow easily in alkaline and acidic conditions. In wet climates or if the soil is too rich, the plants may sometimes be sparse, prone to mildews and short-lived. Typical of gray-leafed plants, they cope with windy places, as the leaves are covered in soft hair or down.

Some gardeners trim them at flowering time to remove the dull daisies. If you need to shape them you can prune at any time and some of the bushier sorts need an occasional clip to improve their shape. You can even prune them drastically back to short stumps and they will regenerate.

Artemis = from the twin sister of the Greek god Apollo. Artemis was a virgin
goddess noted for her prowess in hunting and her abhorrence of men.

Artemisia absinthium

ABSINTH, WORMWOOD
A silky-haired bush with soft, feathery foliage. The leaves of some forms are a dull gray color, so choose **'Lambrook Silver'** for its fine, silvery appearance and sharp, curry-like fragrance. Grows to

around waist-high, but can be trimmed to keep it dense and bushy. Absinthe was a popular aperitif at the end of the 19th century and was distilled from the leaves of this plant. Originates in Europe and Asia. Height x width 3–4 ft (1–1.2 m). ZONE 4.

Absinthium = old Latin name for wormwood.

Artemisia arborescens

A bold, upright shrub, it has a sharp, curry-like fragrance. Initially a dense, rounded mound, it may need pruning to keep it tidy and trim. The soft, silver-gray foliage is a highlight in any garden as a contrast to green shrubs, roses or perennials. From the Mediterranean. Height x width 3–5 ft (1–1.5 m). ZONE 5.

Arborescens = woody or tree-like.

Artemisia 'Powis Castle'

Sometimes thought of as a clone of *Artemisia arborescens* or perhaps a hybrid form. Either way this magnificent plant is worth seeking out. It has a sage-like fragrance. With very fine, feathery foliage in silver-gray, it is a brilliant contrast shrub. Tends to stay low and compact, making it an ideal ground cover plant. Height 3 ft (1 m) x width 5 ft (1.5 m). ZONE 5.

Azara

Flacourtiaceae

This is an unusual and neglected group of plants, which is a shame, because wind-hardy evergreen shrubs with scented flowers are a scarce commodity. They are usually seen as thin, upright shrubs in sheltered gardens and are grown for the dainty leaves. They have superbly scented, acacia-like flowers. Some say they smell like vanilla, others, chocolate. Either way, it's pleasant. I've had great success growing them in windy and even coastal sites—they love it.

I am a bit of a fan for clipping or nipping them back when young to keep them bushy. This stops them getting too thin and leggy because if they get top-heavy they are likely to be flattened in stormy weather. I don't usually recommend staking young plants, but I'll make an exception here.

Surprisingly, they grow well in acidic or alkaline soil as long as it is well drained. Grow them on a slope among other shrubs or use them instead of conifers for shape and height in a mixed border. Transplanting from open ground or pots is easy, as they have a good ball of roots. They do not like droughts or very hot climates and neither do they tolerate extreme cold. Azaras can look fantastic grown against a high wall and, being narrow, can be placed between two windows.

Most leaves seem to be in pairs but one is much smaller. The flowers are a little strange, too, as they have no petals and look like balls of fluff—a bit like acacias. All of them hail from Chile and Argentina.

Azara = after J.N. Azara (1731–1804), an early Spanish botanist.

Azara integrifolia
GOLDSPIRE

A small, upright tree with pompom flowers in late winter to early spring. This *Azara* smells like vanilla to some and chocolate to others. The oval leaves have no teeth or serrations, a good clue to its identity. Probably better as a foliage plant, as the flowers are small. More cold-hardy than most azaras. A variegated form with

Below: *Azara lanceolata*

Above: *Azara microphylla*

pink, cream and green leaves is quite pretty. Native to Chile and Argentina. Height 15–20 ft (5–6 m) x width 6 ft (2 m). ZONE 8.

Integrifolia = having whole or entire leaves.

Azara lanceolata
LANCELEAF AZARA

This is an upright, evergreen bush with green, arrowhead-shaped leaves with saw-toothed edges. The foliage tends to tumble down in a graceful fashion and the golden yellow, pompom flowers appear at every node on last summer's stems. Not only are the flowers nicely scented but this is possibly the best of the genus for flower display.

The plant has the distinction of being discovered by Charles Darwin in 1834 on the voyage of the ship *Beagle*. It was not introduced as a garden plant until 1926 when Harold Comber found it growing in southern Chile. It needs a cool, moist climate and is not as hardy as some. Native to Chile and Argentina. Height 15 ft (5 m) x width 6 ft (2 m). ZONE 8.

Lanceolata = lance-shaped.

Azara microphylla
BOXLEAF AZARA

You will smell the delicious vanilla scent long before you notice the plant. The hardiest species and possibly the most handsome. Initially it is a thin, upright shrub, but as it gets older it forms a small, upright tree with arching branches like a series of open umbrellas or fern fronds. It can be trained to shape for Japanese or Asian-style gardens. The overall appearance is unique. The leaves are blackish green, each one like a tiny boxwood leaf. The tiny, yellow, brush-like flowers are on the underside of the stem, so the scent and foliage are outstanding but the flowers are visually disappointing. A creamy variegated form is sometimes available.

In its native Chile and Argentina, *Azara microphylla* grows in drier districts but it is equally at home in a moist climate, providing the drainage is good. Introduced for the Veitch nursery around 1860 by Richard Pearce. Veitch's nursery in England was famous in the 1800s for sending plant hunters around the world. Height 15–20 ft (5–6 m) x width 6 ft (2 m). ZONE 8.

Microphylla = having small leaves.

Azara petiolaris

The small, creamy yellow flowers of this species are nicely vanilla scented and quite showy against the shiny, deep green foliage. The small, tooth-edged leaves resemble those of holly. Originates from Chile. Height 15 ft (5 ft) x width 6 ft (2 m). ZONE 8.

Petiolaris = with stalks or prominent petioles holding the leaf to the stem.

Azara serrata

Bright yellow balls of honey-scented flowers appear above the leaves in summertime and visually the flowers are only bettered by *Azara lanceolata*. Lovely, glossy green, serrated leaves are a picture of health and this plant from Chile is cold- and wind-hardy. *A. dentata* is similar. Height 15 ft (5 m) x width 6 ft (2 m). ZONE 8.

Serrata = serrated around the edges.

Backhousia

Backhousia citriodora
LEMON IRONWOOD, LEMON-SCENTED MYRTLE
Myrtaceae

Plant this fabulous fragrant shrub where you can readily enjoy its scent. The citrus odor (hence, *citriodora*) is evident when you crush or even just brush past the leaves: the scent is overpowering, even compulsive, because you will be drawn back to it again and again. We used to live in a house with a large *Backhousia* bush next to the garage entrance, and each time the car brushed past it, it released its scent. Parking the car was never more pleasant. *Backhousia* should be in everyone's top-five scented plants. I would like to say the scent is unique, but that is not true. *Aloysia triphylla* has an identical smell, although the bush is nowhere near as exciting as this Australian treasure.

It is an evergreen shrub, or more often a small tree 6–10 ft (2–3 m) high, with an upright, fairly dense habit and pointed, finger-length leaves. The leaves are light green, smooth above and rather leathery. Large viburnum-like flower heads composed of masses of tiny, greenish-yellow flowers usually appear en masse in late summer but sometimes *B. citriodora* flowers in fits and starts. The blooms have a pleasant, spicy scent and seem highly attractive to bees.

Backhousia needs a hot position and is fine in full sun. It will grow in the shade of high trees and buildings, although it will be spindlier and not inclined to flower as well. If your bush becomes open and sparse you can prune it back quite hard as long as you leave some foliage lower down the trunk to maintain the plant. They bush up surprisingly well. It seems most plants in the Myrtaceae family can be cut back to bare stems and still regenerate (*Callistemon* and *Metrosideros*, for example). If in doubt, prune lightly every year.

Backhousia citriodora will take a fair amount of wind but bear in mind that it needs heat and also protection from heavy frosts. I have seen this plant growing in heavy clay soils as well as free-draining loam, and acidic or neutral soil is certainly fine, but I doubt it would like very limy ground. It accepts moist, humid climates and can cope with modest droughts. An occasional caterpillar has a chew of the new leaves but otherwise it is

Above and left:
Backhousia citriodora

problem-free. Transplants easily from pots and big specimens can be shifted, too, if you reduce the leaf cover.

Use it as a wall shrub in cooler areas and if you're lucky enough to grow it as a full shrub, you can use it as an isolated specimen next to a building, where you can pluck a leaf to enjoy the scent and share it with your friends. I can assure you they will be impressed.

It is named after Yorkshireman James Backhouse (1794–1869), who was a Quaker missionary and temperance crusader in Australia in the 1830s, but also spent time collecting plants and writing about his travels. His family had a nursery in York, England. Native to Queensland, Australia. Height 6–10 ft (2–3 m) x width 3–5 ft (1–1.5 m). ZONE 9.

There is another species, **Backhousia anisata**, with pleasantly anise-scented leaves that are narrow, glossy and wavy. It is an endangered plant in the wild and worth growing to help preserve it from extinction. Height 10–15 ft (3–5 m) x width 10 ft (3 m). ZONE 9.

Backhousia = after James Backhouse, plant collector;

citriodora = with a citrus odor.

Boronia

Rutaceae

Boronias are very hard to grow, but it is certainly worth a try because of all the plants in this book, they have the most heavenly scent of all. How to describe the perfume? It is heavy and heady, almost like a sweet liqueur. Even the foliage is deliciously spicy when you brush past it.

These Australian natives grow naturally in swamps and on heaths, which makes them all the more frustrating because any hint of poor drainage in your garden and they die. So although they need a moist climate, in a garden situation the drainage must be near-perfect. Perhaps a sandy soil in a moist, warm climate is the ideal but whatever you do, expect your boronias to be short-lived. I know of some gardeners who manage to grow them in pots for a while. A light prune with the shears after flowering theoretically extends the life of these plants and keeps them bushy.

Boronia = after Francesco Boroni, an 18th-century Italian plant collector.

Below: *Boronia heterophylla*

Above: *Boronia megastigma*

Boronia heterophylla
RED BORONIA

The thin, spiky leaves of this boronia are soft to the touch and delightfully scented, almost like pine. Spring clusters of cerise, shocking-pink flowers are slightly perfumed and make good cut-flowers. Thankfully an easier plant to cultivate than *Boronia megastigma*, but still not classed as easy. Has the same rigid requirements about soil conditions but is likely to live longer, so the plants seen are often taller, even up to head high, and with a very narrow, column habit. Australian native. Height 3–6 ft (1–2 m) x width 2 ft (60 cm). ZONE 9.

Heterophylla = with different leaf shapes.

Boronia megastigma
BROWN BORONIA, SCENTED BORONIA

The bush is very upright, growing just over waist high, although it would be higher if it survived long enough. The feathery, dark, evergreen foliage is made up of soft, needle-like leaves. It is quite brittle, so shelter from wind is essential. Plant in full sun in an acidic or neutral soil and mulch the ground as the fibrous roots do not like to be disturbed. Whatever you do, don't ever try to shift it to another spot in the garden or it will be doomed. When the flowers open in the spring, the scent will alert you before you notice the small, bell-like, chocolate-colored flowers, with a yellowish center hanging down beneath the stems. The flowers are very pretty up close and very cute when seen from below.

There are several good named forms, including **'Heaven Scent'** and a yellow version called **'Lutea'**. The species is native to Australia. For all, height 2–3 ft (60 cm–1 m) x width 1–2 ft (30–60 cm). ZONE 9.

Megastigma = with a large stigma.

Brugmansia

ANGELS' TRUMPETS
Solanaceae

A s the common name suggests, the long, tubular flowers of this genus look just like the trumpets the angels blow in bible-story pictures. These plants are almost constantly in flower, especially the common *Brugmansia suaveolens*—they seem to be perpetually in bloom in mild climates. Actually this plant has it all: it is handsome, has huge, showy flowers all year in frost-free climates, and is fragrant to boot. And oh, what a fragrance! It can bowl you over. It is sweet, heady and seems to go straight to the center of your brain. Perhaps this effect explains why the plant has been used for hallucinogens. Although *Brugmansia* are related to tomatoes and potatoes, the whole genus is poisonous. Some gardeners are reluctant to plant them for this reason, but in fact many of our garden plants are poisonous.

All *Brugmansia* are evergreen, often with huge, felted leaves, and are usually multi-trunked. Although the tops are frost-tender, if you can build up enough strength in the plant in the first summer, the rootstock will regenerate the next spring. The large, heavy stems are laden with water and are thus more frost-prone, and they are thirsty plants in summer. To keep these stems and big, lush leaves in tip-top condition give them plenty of water in hot periods; they will grow in swampy ground or places occasionally inundated with water. They are not fussy about soil or acidity, being just as happy on chalk as anywhere. Full sun in a hot location is best, although they cope with some shade in warm regions. Strong winds can break and blast the

Above left:
*Brugmansia
chlorantha*

Left: *Brugmansia
sanguinea*

Above: *Brugmansia* 'Noel's Blush'

leaves. They have a strong odor, which is enough to keep most pests at bay, but they can be attacked by spidermite and whitefly in very warm regions.

Transplant in the spring after the danger of frosts is past. Older specimens can be cut back and moved but it is far easier to make a new plant from a cutting. Cut off two thick branches, remove the leaves and push them into the ground where you want a new plant. One of them is sure to grow, and if both grow then give one to a friend. You can prune them drastically if you ever need to, and you will be staggered at the weight of the branches.

Try one in a planter indoors if your climate is really too cold for outdoor growth. Alternatively you can over-winter a rootstock in a shed as you might a dahlia, keeping it on the dry side to prevent fungus attack. You can then replant outdoors in the spring. *Brugmansia* are natives of Mexico and the South American Andes. There are many hybrids with large, showy flowers in peach, pinks and creams. In some of these hybrids, the flowers are held at an angle of 45° rather than in the usual vertical direction. Examples are **'Grand Marnier'**, **'Noel's Blush'** and **'California Peach'**. For all, height x width 15 ft (5 m). All ZONE 9 or warmer.

Brugmansia = after Sebald Justin Brugmans (1763–1819), a professor of natural history from Leiden in Holland.

Brugmansia chlorantha, syn B. lutea

A bush around 6 ft (2 m) high, although I have seen it as a small tree. Long, narrow trumpets hang vertically under the tips of the stems and the five long, curly petal tips reflex to touch the outer tube. The flowers release a sweet smell after dark. The pointed green leaves are around 6 in (15 cm) long.

It is a slightly ungainly bush with branches going this way and that, but the beautiful yellow trumpets deserve a place in the garden. This plant needs shelter but copes with shade. Height x width 6 ft (2 m). ZONE 9.

Chlorantha = having green or yellow flowers.

Brugmansia sanguinea, syn B. rosei

RED ANGEL'S TRUMPETS

The unusual red flowers of this novel species are streaked with yellow and have a sweet scent at night. It has small, dark green leaves. The leaves of *Brugmansia chlorantha* and this species seem very alike; they may be color variants of the same thing. Like its yellow cousin, it copes with more shade than the larger species. Native to Central and South America. Height 6–10 ft (2–3 m) x width 3–6 ft (1–2 m). ZONE 9.

Sanguinea = from *sanguine*, blood.

Brugmansia suaveolens, syn B. x candida, B. knightii

The huge flowers of this plant have a widening trumpet, flared at the bottom, and a sweet perfume that lives up to their name. The perpendicular flowers hang beneath the tips of the stems and seem to be on show nearly all year, although in cold climates it only flowers in summer. This species has big, bold leaves in a dull gray-green with a felted surface. They would be nice to touch except that they produce a putrid smell. They are very pointed and have a lush, tropical look. A double-flowered form is available, but you need to examine it to realize that it is double, so it is not a great improvement. It seems B. x *candida* and B. *knightii* are very similar to B. *suaveolens* or possibly the same thing. Some suggest that B. *candida* has wider-mouthed petals with an accentuated tip and that B. *suaveolens* has a narrower, more bell-like flower, but I have seen both types of flower on the same bush. Native to southeast Brazil. Height x width 10–15 ft (3–5 m). ZONE 9.

Suaveolens = sweet-smelling.

Above: *Brugmansia suaveolens*

Brunfelsia

YESTERDAY, TODAY AND TOMORROW
Solanaceae

The heady gardenia scent of this plant is almost cloying and can be overpowering if it is grown in a tub in a confined space, such as a greenhouse. Outdoors the scent is described as "blissful," in a sweet, talcum-powder way. *Brunfelsia* is called yesterday, today and tomorrow, as the flowers open as rich violet ("yesterday") and fade to soft lilac the second day ("today") and then to white on the third day ("tomorrow"). The bush will have all three colors as it will have flowers of different ages. Sometimes they have those of day four, burnt and brown, hanging on, but we won't dwell on that. Like most of the shrubby *Solanum* family they hail from South America and, as you would imagine, they need plenty of heat. Part-shade is fine in a hot climate but they generally need all the sun they can get for the extra warmth. Cold and frost are their main threat, although whitefly and mealy bugs can also cause them problems.

The leaves emerge a bright green and fade to a duller gray-green. In cool winters the leaves often take on a purplish tinge or they may look pale and anemic. This is typical of hot climate plants when grown in a region cooler than they would like. It seems the cold weather prevents the sap flowing well enough, and the leaves are lacking in certain nutrients. As the warm weather returns they soon green up and look healthy again. The warmth encourages flowering, and clusters appear at the tips of the new growths. They grow well in containers, and in cold regions the plant can be over-wintered under cover and placed out on a deck or patio again after all risk of frost is past. With their strong scent and long-lasting flowering season they are the ideal patio plant.

Above: *Brunfelsia calycina*

Surprisingly, they will grow near the ocean, as long as the winds are not too extreme or cold. They require free-draining soil and, like many in the tomato family, have a high water requirement in summer. Acidic or neutral soil is ideal but most Solanaceae plants cope with lime, too. Transplant young plants from small tubs. It would be risky to move established plants.

Brunfelsia = from Otto Brunfels, a German monk who was a physician and a botanist. He published an early work on herbs in 1530.

Brunfelsia calycina, syn B. pauciflora

A neat little shrub, ideal for small borders next to the house. It is evergreen but tends to lose some leaves in the cold. Its mass of talcum powder-scented spring flowers more than earn its keep. The form **'Eximea'** is the best one to buy. Native to Brazil. Height x width 3 ft (1 m). ZONE 9.

Calycina = cup-shaped or in the form of a calyx.

Brunfelsia latifolia

A big, upright shrub with wavy-edged leaves. The sweet, cloying fragrance is delicious in small doses. This species is more impressive than *Brunfelsia calycina* when in bloom but, as is always the case, it is not as hardy as the less showy variety. There seems to be some inverse proportion whereby the more spectacular the plant, the harder it is to grow or to propagate. Native to Brazil. Height 3–10 ft (1–3 m) x width 3–5 ft (1–1.5 m). ZONE 9.

Latifolia = having broad leaves.

Buddleja

BUTTERFLY BUSH
Loganiaceae

Prior to cultivation, buddlejas managed to colonize large parts of the globe including large parts of Asia, Africa and South America and now, with our help, they are colonizing even more land, especially as *Buddleja davidii* is naturalized in many countries. They are a mix of evergreen and deciduous shrubs, usually with long, lance-like leaves often covered in hair or down and panicles of small, fragrant flowers.

They are almost too easy to grow and handle virtually any soil. Heavy clays, sand, chalk—all are fine. I have even seen them growing out of brick walls and gutters, so there is no place this plant considers out of bounds. They are best in full sun but they will grow in the shade of buildings and most are wind-hardy, some extremely so. They do vary in their cold-tolerance, some being supremely cold-hardy while others are tender. Left to their own devices they spread and sprawl, taking up more ground every year, and can even root down where stems touch the ground. To keep the more robust ones tidy, select one stem to be the main structure and cut all the branches back to this trunk every winter. This works especially well for *B. davidii*.

Buddleja = after the Reverend Adam Buddle (1660–1715), an English vicar and botanist who wrote a volume on plants using Dr. Houston's new system of botanical classification. Dr. Houston repaid the compliment, naming *Buddleja* after him.

Buddleja alternifolia

A big, arching shrub with an open, airy appearance. The small clusters of soft lilac flowers appear in early summer on last year's growth, so wait until after flowering to do any pruning. Winter

Right: *Buddleja alternifolia*

Far right: *Buddleja asiatica*

Below: *Buddleja madagascariensis*

pruning will remove all the flowers. These sweetly scented clusters appear at every node like chains of bloom.

The tiny leaves fail to create a full canopy but this allows us to use the plant where we need something light and ethereal. Train it high as a standard and let the stems flow down, creating a naturally weeping bush. The plant is from China. Height x width 6–10 ft (2–3 m). ZONE 6.

Alternifolia = having alternate leaves.

Buddleja asiatica

This is usually the first of all the buddlejas to flower in early spring and therefore is likely to be frosted. The flowers are frequently a muddy off-white and don't always have a pleasant smell—in fact it can be too strong to be called pleasant. I suggest you look for the selected cultivar **'Spring Promise'**, as it has crystal-clear, white flowers with a heavenly scent like highly refined sugar. As you might imagine, *Buddleja asiatica* grows throughout Asia, from the Himalayas through China to the Philippines. Like most *Buddlejas* it grows rapidly to 6–10 ft (2–3 m) and more, and may need ruthless pruning after flowering to keep the bush tidy. The leaves are long and thin and similar *to B. davidii*, green above and silvery gray and hairy beneath.

The long, thin spikes of flower appear in the axils of the upper leaves and can be as much as 8 in (20 cm) long. Each tiny flower is white with a pale yellow center; only the mass of blooms and especially the scent make the plant worth having in your garden. In cooler districts it would be worth finding a warm wall to train this shrub against and protecting it from the winter chills. Believe me, you won't regret it. Height 6–10 ft (2–3 m) x width 6 ft (2 m). ZONE 8 OR 9.

The tender **B. madagascariensis** is similar, except the flowers appear in winter and are in smaller racemes in a pale orange yellow. The scent is fabulous. For most gardeners this plant is too delicate to cultivate. On the other hand, when it does do well, it quickly outgrows its welcome by becoming huge in no time. ZONES 9 TO 10, but try it against a wall in a warm ZONE 8.

Asiatica = from Asia; *madagascariensis* = from Madagascar.

Buddleja davidii
BUTTERFLY BUSH, SUMMER LILAC

Aptly named the butterfly bush as its sweet, heady, honey scent has a hypnotic effect on butterflies and gardeners alike. A big, sometimes sprawling bush that we can keep tidy by drastic pruning in winter. The long racemes of flowers are produced on the tips of forming the typical brush shape. New flowers have yellow pollen at the tip of each stamen, which gives them a golden sheen. If you have the right climate, grow them in mixed borders, shrubberies or even as isolated specimens in a lawn. I don't usually like lawn shrubs but these are so spectacular they will look good. Try not to crowd them, as they look their best where they have room to show off.

Callistemons have a surprising box of talents. Although we think of them as drought- and wind-hardy shrubs, they naturally grow in water courses in their native Australia—although bear in mind that these water courses can be dry for years. It does mean that they have the ability to grow in wet places, so they are equally happy in a mild, moist climate and in a dry, arid site. All winds are a breeze for them and even the flowers are unscathed by heavy storms. The tough, waxy leaves are almost like plastic in texture. Some cultivars, like 'Little John', have hairy new leaves to protect them from the elements, before they harden to reduce water loss from sun and wind. The wood is extremely tough and hard, and the trunks are covered in long strips of peeling bark. This joint strength of leaf and wood makes them ideal plants for windy, coastal regions. Even if the trees get damaged in heavy weather, they quickly regenerate. This means you can prune them drastically to stumps without leaving a leaf on, or even cut to ground level, and they will sprout up again.

The flower clusters are peculiar in that they appear part way along the stem, so the new season's growth consists of a portion

Above: *Buddleja davidii*

the new summer's growth so it doesn't matter how ruthless you are when winter pruning. Left to its own devices it becomes a very large shrub with a thin veneer of grayish, lance-like leaves. It has purple or lavender flowers and if you look closely you will see that they have an orange throat. There are many superb clones with rich red, purple, blue, pink or white flowers. Grow it for the flowers, for the sweet, heady perfume or as a wind- or coast-hardy plant. The wild species was collected in western China. Height x width 6–10 ft (2–3 m). ZONE 6.

Davidii = after Père David (1826–1900), a French missionary to China.

Callistemon

BOTTLEBRUSH
Myrtaceae

The flowers of *Callistemon* are made up of thousands of stamens, explaining its common name of "bottlebrush." This mass of stamens looks just like those laboratory brushes used to clean test tubes and bottles. It is hard to imagine that a flower so striking and beautiful has no petals. Take the petals away from most flowers and you have nothing worth shouting about, but not in this case. *Callistemon* is one of those dazzling shrubs every gardener ought to grow. Bottlebrushes flower in spring with honey-scented blooms full of nectar. A large bush will seem to have the entire hive busily working away. Nectar-feeding birds are not slow to appreciate callistemons either. At the base of each flower is a cup full of liquid nectar, with a shuttlecock of bright red stamens shooting up from it. Each flower head is composed of dozens of these cup flowers,

Below: *Callistemon citrinus*

Right: *Callistemon*
'Little John'

of leaves followed by a cone of flowers and then more radiating leaves at the end. Another fascinating thing is the seed heads, which consist of nugget-like, rounded woody balls tightly clustered around the stem. They stay on the bush unopened for years, so on an old tree you can see several years' worth of seeds all wrapped up in their cones waiting for something to happen. The "something" is fire: in the natural bush fires of Australia, the heat makes the cones open and release their bounty of hundreds of thin, pin-like seeds.

Thrips can twist and distort the leaves and the plants do get a few leaf spots, but they are generally easy-care. Hard, heavy frosts are their biggest threat, so in colder regions planting them against a wall may be the answer. Callistemons will tolerate any soil, as tough as you like, even heavy clay, although I would choose as light and well-drained a soil as I could find in a cold climate to help them survive the winters. Tender plants are far more likely to survive cold winters if grown in light and sandy soils, while growing in wet, heavy soils tends to make the plant growth lush and thereby prone to frost. Transplants easily but make sure the roots are radiating out from the trunk as they can spiral into a ball.

Callistemon = beautiful flowers, or beautiful stamens.

Callistemon citrinus
CRIMSON BOTTLEBRUSH

The new leaves are pink and their tangy, lemon scent accounts for the name. This callistemon was one of the first Australian plants in cultivation after it was taken to England by Joseph Banks, the botanist on Captain Cook's first voyage to the antipodes. A tough, somewhat straggly bush that is prone to frost damage. Look for the form **'Splendens'**, with its bright, crimson flowers. Native to southern Australia. Height x width 10 ft (3 m). ZONE 8 OR 9.

Citrinus = lemon-scented.

Callistemon 'Little John'

An unusual hybrid in that it only grows between 3–6 ft (1–2 m) high and with pruning can be kept very low and bushy. The leaves and stems have a pleasant, camphor-like fragrance. The scent is stronger in dead or dried stems. The leaves are soft and silky initially and harden to a waxy, blue-gray color. Possibly the best of the genus for foliage, and the flowers are pretty, too. Rich, dark red flowers topped off with a sheen of yellow from the pollen glisten in the sunlight. Height 3–6 ft (1–2 m) x width 3–5 ft (1–1.5 m). ZONE 8 OR 9.

Callistemon salignus
WHITE BOTTLEBRUSH, WILLOW BOTTLEBRUSH

Most of these plants in the wild grow in swampy country and have yellow flowers, although red forms are cultivated. The leaves and stems have a pleasant, camphor-like fragrance. The scent is stronger in dead or dried stems. This species is hardier and more resilient than most and a good starter if you haven't grown bottlebrush before. Also has pinky-red new growth. Originates from southern Australia. Height x width 15 ft (5 m). ZONE 8.

Salignus = willow-like, referring to the leaves.

Callistemon viminalis
WEEPING BOTTLEBRUSH

The best bottlebrush for shape, with a lovely, weeping habit. The sugary-scented scarlet blossoms appear in spring and are often followed by another burst of flowers in fall. An excellent small tree with spikier, smaller leaves. Tolerant of any soils, including damp places, but not as cold-hardy as some. Native to Queensland and New South Wales, Australia. Height x width 15 ft (5 m). ZONE 9.

Viminalis = bearing osiers, stems of a willow.

Calocedrus

INCENSE CEDAR
Cupressaceae

The dense, dark green foliage comes in flattened sprays in much the same way as some *Thuja*. And like the related *Thuja* they have a pleasant, tangy smell that hangs in the air in hot weather and becomes even more marked when we crush some leaves. We are mostly familiar with just one of the three species and even then we tend to grow just one form of it, so we have a limited idea of these trees. We picture the incense cedar as a narrow, columnar tree, but in the wild there are more horizontal forms with widespread branches. They seem to handle hot and dry weather better than most conifers except junipers and pines. Poor soils are acceptable, too, as long as the drainage is reasonable.

Calocedrus = beautiful cedar.

Calocedrus decurrens, syn Heyderia decurrens, Libocedrus decurrens
INCENSE CEDAR

This tree grows from Oregon to Mexico, usually in cool mountain regions, and yet it is far more resilient than this distribution suggests. It thrives in hot and dry climates, making it a valuable conifer, and the leaves are generous with their spicy scent in hot weather in much the same way as herbal plants are. Although the tree has a neat, conical habit, the branches seem to twist and turn within this shape and the trunks have attractive, peeling, reddish bark. In gardens we usually see the narrow, columnar form grown to give a tree height and stature. This form is sometimes known as **'Columnaris'** or **'Fastigiata'**. Height 60–80 ft (18–25 m) x width 30–40 ft (10–12 m). ZONE 5.

'Aureovariegata' is a gaudy, gold-splashed variety and **'Berrima Gold'** is an Australian cultivar with yellowish foliage tipped with gold in wintertime. Both height 40 ft (12 m) x width 20 ft (6 m). ZONE 5. If your garden is small, perhaps you could try **'Intricata'**, a miniature variety ideal for rock gardens. Height 3–6 ft (1–2 m) x width 3 ft (1 m). ZONE 5.

Calocedrus macrolepis is a rather tender tree with a handsome, open habit, showing off the flattened stems that are deep green above and silvery beneath. Introduced by E.H. Wilson (1876–1930) from southwest China in 1900. Height 100 ft (30 m) x width 25 ft (8 m). ZONE 8 or 9. *C. formosana* is a tender species from Taiwan. Height 80 ft (25 m) x width 30 ft (10 m). ZONE 9.

Decurrens = extending or running down the stem.

Calycanthus

Calycanthaceae

Calycanthus is one of my favorite shrubs, and yet I am hard-pressed to explain why. I wouldn't be without one, even if I lived in a small suburban garden. *Calycanthus* flowers have a strong aroma that can be too strong for some tastes. Some would also disagree with the term "scent," and describe it as closer to a stench. Some say they smell of cloves and the fragrance seems sweet until you get too close. Then it hits you and is vaguely reminiscent of vinegar. It is astringent and tends to catch you in the throat. This strong fragrance does not appeal to everyone, but I like it. The leaves and stems, however, have a pleasant, camphor-like fragrance that appeals to most people. This scent is even stronger in dead or dried stems and has been used as a substitute for cinnamon, as allspice.

Calycanthus have the richest red-maroon flowers in the plant world, apart from some velvet maroon roses. To me there is something magical about that color. The flowers vary quite dramatically from plant to plant, which is why I have many seedlings in the garden in the hope that I can select good forms. Usually the flowers are in opposite pairs, sitting just up above the new leaves. The floral display is quite sparse and it would be easy to walk past a flowering plant and not notice the blooms if it were not for their scent. These dark flowers are very primitive, as the petals we see are not really petals at all but sepals or a calyx. This is usually the part that protects the petals. For example, the calyx on a rose is the green bract that forms the bud and protects the petals until the flower opens. Each

Left: *Calocedrus decurrens*

flower has a central cone of these sepals and they gradually reflex backwards to create a starry base. The flower is pollinated by beetles that come to feed on the oil-bearing, sterile stamens within.

The oval leaves can be rounded or pointed at the ends and are usually about thumb-length, but they can be as long as a hand. They are always opposite and emerge before the flowers, providing a backdrop for them. Sometimes the leaves are delightfully textured, feeling smooth if you run your finger down the leaf and rough if pushing up it. It resists your touch, almost like the pile on velvet. This feature seems to be a characteristic of this plant family, as *Chimonanthus praecox* has the same feel.

The plants are deciduous and sometimes have a clear yellow fall color, but don't rely on it. Stems are often long and whippy, and it is generally not a tidy plant. Although I love them I cannot heartily recommend them for town or suburban gardens. They are more a plant for woodland spaces although they do need sun and summer heat to shine.

Calycanthus like deep, moist soil. My plants get flooded periodically but bear no grudge. Really, any soil will do, but the plants become anemic on limestone. Easy to transplant, easy to prune if necessary, and no pest problems.

Calycanthus = calyx flower.

Above: *Calycanthus floridus*

Calycanthus floridus
CAROLINA ALLSPICE, COMMON SWEETSHRUB, STRAWBERRY SHRUB

The strongly fragrant flowers appear in late spring and, as the blooms appear intermittently, there is never a great show as such. However, each flower is a wonderful deep rich red color. I have seen stupendous cherry-red forms in Williamsburg, Virginia, but the only named cultivars seem to be yellow, such as **'Athens'**. A drawback with the maroon flowers is that they tend to get scorched and often have unsightly burns from the tips to the sepals. This species grows naturally near waterways from North Carolina down to Florida. Height x width 6 ft (2 m). ZONE 5.

Floridus = having rich or plentiful flowers, and not "from Florida," as you might imagine. Plants from Florida are called *floridana*, as in *Leitneria floridana*.

Calycanthus occidentalis
CALIFORNIA ALLSPICE

A vigorous, lax shrub with horizontal, flexible stems. Similar to *C. floridus* in its scent, but the leaves are never downy and the flowers are redder on longer stalks. Grows naturally on stream banks in California. Height x width 6 ft (2 m). ZONE 6 OR 7.

Occidentalis = western.

Left: *Calycanthus occidentalis*

Camellia

CAMELLIA
Theaceae

Camellias are not only beautiful and versatile, they are also the ultimate easy-care shrub. If ever I need an upright evergreen to make a garden more secluded, or to shield the eyes before emerging into a new garden area, then a camellia is always the first plant to come to mind. Then there are the wonderful flowers, in different shapes and colors, early flowering and late, with many having a lovely fragrance. As with other popular flowering shrubs, such as rhododendrons and roses, it is impossible to generalise about flowers or fragrance across species. However, the needs of the different camellias are quite similar.

Camellias take either full sun or quite dense shade. Some insist they must be grown in shade, perhaps to protect them from heavy frosts or to prevent the soil from drying out. But camellias tolerate very strong light intensities and are perfectly happy out in the full blaze of the sun, as long as they have a mulch of leaves or bark chips to keep the soil cool and moist. With this protection for the roots, I have even seen them planted on bulldozed clay hillsides. They seem oblivious to soil conditions, other than needing it to be acidic or neutral and well drained soil. Sometimes you see them looking anemic and yellowing in the leaf, but this is easily fixed with a dose of Epsom salts (magnesium sulfate), containing the wonderful greening magnesium fertilizer. They like regular rainfall, although this is not essential, and prefer constant humidity, but will cope with hot, dry summers.

Camellias are easy to transplant from pots and even large, aged specimens can be moved. I find that it pays to move them in the fall, as the success rate of transplanting declines if they are transplanted in the spring. It is also a good idea to reduce the amount of foliage on the bush when moving large specimens.

Camellias have a good natural shape and rarely need pruning, but should you need to do this they can be trimmed lightly with

Above: *Camellia yunnanensis*

shears, or you can make them into interesting shapes by removing branches and opening them up. You can even prune them drastically to bare stumps if you wish and they will quickly regenerate.

Strong winds are no problem to most of them, although the flowers may be battered by storms and white flowers are particularly susceptible in this regard. The plants even tolerate coastal winds with no lasting damage. Camellias seem affected by cold in some mild climates, while in other colder regions they seem to thrive. Perhaps hot summers ripen the wood to cope with the winter frosts. They act as host to the occasional caterpillar or cluster of aphids, but never in such numbers that you need to venture out with a remedy.

All the known species come from Asia, notably China and Japan.

Camellia = after George Joseph Kamel (1661–1706), a Jesuit missionary who traveled widely in Asia and wrote an account of the plants he found in the Philippines. He Latinized his name as Camellus, and then Carl Linnaeus (1707–1778) chose to name this group of Asian shrubs after him. Linnaeus simplified the Latin naming of plants and animals and also Latinized his own name from Carl von Linné.

Camellia japonica
COMMON CAMELLIA

Camellia japonica is the ultimate easy-care, free-flowering shrub. The flowers of the scented varieties of this species have a very pleasant tea fragrance. Hundreds of big, bold, equidistant pink, red or white flowers appear from winter through early spring. Different cultivars flower at different times, so through careful selection you can have your camellias flowering over much of the year.

Above: *Camellia japonica* 'Kramer's Surprise'

They are very popular as flowering plants and the big, dense, upright bush can be clipped or shaped. If ever you need a dense, evergreen shrub to block out a view, flower superbly and provide fragance in your garden, then this species and its cultivars are very hard to beat. As the name suggests, its home is Japan, but it is also found in Korea and China. Height 6–12 ft (2–4 m) x width 3–6 ft (1–2 m). ZONE 8.

Look out for the following scented varieties: **'Kramer's Gold'**, **'Kramer's Supreme'**, **'Scented Gem'**, **'Scented Sun'**, **'Scentsation'** and **'Superscent'**. For all height 6–12 ft (2–4 m) x width 3–6 ft (1–2 m).

Camellia lutchuensis

A small-leafed species with tiny white flowers flushed with pink appearing in midwinter. The flowers have a sweet, spicy smell and are worthy of a spot near a path so that you can enjoy the perfume as you walk by. New leaves are a reddish color as they emerge. It makes an ideal column shrub for narrow borders by the house. Native to Japan and Taiwan. Height 6–10 ft (2–3 m) x width 3–6 ft (1–2 m). ZONE 8.

> *Lu-tchu* or *liu-kiu* = old European names for the southern Japanese island now called Ryuku, home to this beautiful but tender species.

Camellia oleifera

OIL SEED CAMELLIA

The single white flowers of this camellia appear in early winter

and smell like smoky tea. This seems to be the hardiest of the camellias and so is cherished by gardeners in the cooler parts of North America. This ability to cope with cold is rather odd as it is thought to have a similar lineage to the more tender *Camellia sasanqua*. Originates from China. Height 20 ft (6 m) x width 10 ft (3 m). ZONE 6.

> *Oleifera* = oil-bearing. The fruits were squeezed for camellia oil, and used for cooking and cosmetics.

Camellia sasanqua

SASANQUA CAMELLIA

One of the joys of fall for me is the flowering of the sasanqua camellias, coinciding as it does with the fall leaves. Strangely enough, even though the camellias tend to be in pink and cerise (and white), they seem to blend with the reds and golds of fall, which is not what you would expect.

If they are close to a path, you can enjoy the wonderful sweet tea fragrance of the flowers. Another reason I like the sasanquas is their smaller blooms and the more informal shape of the shrub. It is a breath of fresh air compared with the more overblown flowers and more formal shape of *C. japonica*.

Sasanquas initially have a fairly tidy, upright habit and then take on a wider, arching shape with age. It is at this stage you can trim the basal trunks and turn them into a more interesting open shrub, showing off their smooth, gray trunks to advantage.

The flowers are usually small, varying from a single row of petals to semi- and fully-double blooms. Most have a central clus-

Right: *Camellia lutchuensis* hybrid, C. 'Fairy Bush'.

Above: *Camellia sasanqua* 'Plantation Pink'

ter of stamens above a source of nectar highly prized by bees and nectar-feeding birds. Leaves are generally smaller than most other camellias, being slightly longer than a finger-joint, with a toothed or serrated edge. They have the typical glossy surface of camellias and, being evergreen, look good year-round.

Sasanquas are more tender than most camellias and don't thrive in colder climates, but if your conditions suit them, then you should find room for at least one of these excellent plants. In cooler regions they can be trained espalier-style against a wall to give them extra heat and protection. From Japan. Height 6–10 ft (2–3 m) x width 6 ft (2 m). ZONE 8 OR 9 (they will grow in ZONE 6 or 7 if they get hot summers and a slow spring).

The following varieties are all scented, and around the same height and width as the species. **'Hiryu'** has an unusual, rather loud, cerise-colored flower and looks good against a building and the reddish color of brick walls.

'Mini-no-yuki' (also known as **'Moonlight'**) is my personal favorite; see the double white blooms covered in dew or raindrops in the fall sun and you will be hooked too.

'Plantation Pink' is a lovely single pink and a great favorite with bees and nectar-feeding birds.

Sasanqua = from the Japanese name for these plants.

Camellia tsaii

Camellia tsaii has an almond scent that is not too strong either outdoors or indoors. If you visualize camellias as big, bold shrubs with large, glossy leaves and even larger, showy flowers, then you are in for a surprise when you see *C. tsaii*.

The 3½ in (9 cm) long, grass-green leaves look more like a willow than a typical camellia. Each leaf is slightly upturned to form a valley, with the added twist of wavy, undulating edges. These long, pointed leaves indicate that it is a wet climate plant as the thin tip, or "drip-tip" as it is known, sheds water much faster

than ordinary leaves. The new spring growth is a reddish bronze color.

A mass of tiny, white, cup-shaped flowers the size of a fingernail appear in pairs at the base of each leaf, with a group of four or five at the tip of the stem. Hanging down among the leaves, they are hidden to some extent by the foliage, although from a distance the overall froth of flowers is quite delightful. It is almost like a dusting of snow against the green background. Only last season's growth produces flowers, and any long stems can be cut for floral decoration. Because the flowers appear in early spring there is a risk of frost damage.

The bush has a natural, upright habit, lending itself to mass planting as a hedge or screen. It comes from Yunnan (southwest China), Burma and Vietnam and does not like cold or dry climates. It was collected by George Forrest (1873–1932) in 1924. Height 6–10 ft (2–3 m) x width 3–6 ft (1–2 m). ZONE 8 OR 9.

Tsaii = a native name.

Camellia yunnanensis

This camellia's flowers have a lovely spicy smell, so plant one near a path where you can enjoy the scent. It is unusual in that it has leaves with a rough surface. Most camellias have shiny, dark green foliage, but in this case the contoured leaf is a duller, paler green. It forms a slightly open, upright bush to around head-high and it is a good idea to prune it to enhance this open effect and show off

Below: *Camellia tsaii*

Above: *Camellia sasanqua* 'Hiryu'

Above: *Carpenteria californica*

the fine orange-brown bark. Even the flowers are different from the typical camellia in that they are more open and fragile-looking; the widely-spaced white petals have a slightly haphazard look. Height 6 ft (2 m) x width 3 ft (1 m). ZONE 8.

Yunnanensis = from Yunnan Province in southwest China.

Carpenteria

Carpenteria californica
TREE ANEMONE
Philadelphaceae

*C*arpenteria is a one-off; there is only one species and, as you might guess from its name, it hails from California. It loves long, hot, sunny days and tends to sulk if it's too wet or cloudy. It is a bushy evergreen with bold, sticky leaves in a deep, almost blackish green, but it is the flowers we are interested in. The plant produces masses of beautiful white flowers with a central boss of golden stamens and a tangy scent of fresh oranges. It is reminiscent of a Japanese anemone in both size and shape, and is sometimes known as tree or bush anemone. Flowers appear in clusters at the tips of the stems in high summer and present themselves nicely for us by facing out from the bush. At first glance it could easily be mistaken for a *Cistus* or *Philadelphus* with its white saucer-shaped flowers.

Give *Carpenteria californica* the right environment and it will thrive. However, you often see straggly specimens that are not getting all their needs met. As well as needing maximum heat and sun it also needs good drainage; and yet strangely enough it doesn't like to dry out. Sometimes you see plants with burnt edges to the leaves caused by wind or drought. If you are in a cooler climate, planting against a wall is an option to increase the

heat, and it does look good as a wall shrub. Like *Ceanothus*, it seems designed to be grown in this way and with minimal training it can be a highlight plant in your garden. You can also grow one in a shrubbery, but it should be a prime site and somewhere you can enjoy the subtle fragrance. **'Ladham's Variety'** is a selected cultivar with larger flowers (3 in/8cm across) and the same scent of oranges. Native to California. Height 6–10 ft (2–3 m) x width 6 ft (2 m). ZONE 8.

Carpenteria = after Professor William Carpenter of Louisiana; *californica* = from California.

Caryopteris

BLUE SPIRAEA
Verbenaceae

*C*aryopteris are easy to overlook when planning a garden. But do take a closer look, because otherwise you will miss one of the best blue flowers in the business. Smothered in a delightful soft blue haze of flowers from midsummer onward, these deciduous shrubs will grow in any sunny border. The small, arrowhead, opposite leaves are a dull gray-green and frankly not the best to highlight blue flowers. However, these small-toothed leaves are aromatic, adding to the lavender-like comparison that some gardeners make. If you crush a leaf it is really quite pungent, but it is pleasant on the air. You will want to plant more than one of these, and they have more impact in threes and fives. You should always plant in odd numbers and avoid the straight lines made when planting in twos or fours. *Caryopteris* are small enough to grow at the front of a border, and blend well with

Left: *Caryopteris* x
clandonensis
'Heavenly Blue'

annuals, perennials and other shrubs. The hybrid forms are easy-care shrubs, given a sunny, well-drained site. They are very hardy, coping with winter cold, wind and drought. Any well-drained soil will suffice—a bonus for those gardening on limestone. They are easily transplanted from pots when young, but they resent being moved at a later date. They are not hurt by pests. The flowers are on new growth near the tips of the stems, so a winter trim keeps them tidier and bushier, encouraging new growth and therefore more flowers. The wild species are temperamental and rather tricky to grow.

Carya = nut or fruit; *pteron* = wing, thus *caryopteris* = winged seeds.

Caryopteris x *clandonensis* (*C. mongolica* x *C. incana*)

Easily the best and most easy-care of the genus, this plant grows just over waist-high and with regular pruning will stay neat and compact. It combines the brighter color of the *Caryopteris mongolica* flowers and the vitality of *C. incana*—in other words the best of both. The clusters of violet-blue flowers appear from midsummer onward and have a slight lavender scent; the foliage is sage scented. Save for the efforts of one man and a smidgen of luck we would never have seen this plant in our gardens. Arthur Simmonds (1892–1968), secretary of the Royal Horticultural Society in England, grew both *C. incana* and *C. mongolica* together and the two plants naturally hybridized. Various named cultivars are available. **'Arthur Simmonds'** was named after the grower of the original clone. It has bright blue flowers on a low, knee-high bush. Height

2 ft (60 cm) x width 2 ft (60 cm). **'Blue Mist'** has soft, powder-blue flowers. **'Heavenly Blue'** has deep blue flowers and **'Ferndown'** has dark, violet-blue flowers. All have the same lavender and sage scent. For all, height x width 3 ft (1 m). ZONE 6.

Clandonensis = plant was discovered as a natural hybrid in Clandon near London, England.

Caryopteris incana

A variable shrub when grown from seed, usually with soft gray, felted leaves and flowers from dull blue to a fabulous haze of purple-blue generally appearing in late summer to early fall. Looks great in a perennial border as it is slightly taller than the hybrid forms. The whole plant has a sage essence. This Chinese native was originally introduced to the West in the 1840s by Robert Fortune (1812–1880). In those days every exotic plant was considered tender and grown in greenhouses. But as is often the case, gray-leafed plants hate humidity and so this plant died in the humid hothouse atmosphere.

It was later reintroduced by Charles Maries (1831–1902) in 1880 and again in 1915 by Reginald Farrer (1880–1920). So it took several attempts to establish it in western gardens. Height x width 5 ft (1.5 m). ZONE 6.

Incana = woolly and gray, referring to the leaves.

Caryopteris mongolica

This plant, too, had a bumpy ride to make it into cultivation. It was first discovered by Dr. Alexander von Bunge (1803–1890) in

1830 and introduced to France, where it died out. Père David (1826–1900) sent it again in 1866. A smaller plant than *C. incana*, it has rich blue flowers in summer and a herby scent. Height x width 3 ft (1 m). ZONE 6.

Mongolica = from Mongolia.

Catalpa

Bignoniaceae

Catalpas have big, bold leaves and yet somehow we manage to overlook or ignore them. True, they do have some serious drawbacks, yet when they are good they can rival the best *Paulownia*. If you want to add drama to your garden then look no further. They have it all—big, bold, heart-shaped leaves and generous heads of delightfully pollen-scented, white flowers, all on stately, spreading trees. When we think of fragrant plants, we usually imagine roses or magnolias, or maybe the intense, sweet scent of lilac, rather than a mammoth plant such as *Catalpa*. But next time you see one in flower, take a moment to pull a head down and inhale the sweet pollen-like perfume. The big leaves are usually in opposite pairs but sometimes in threes at a node. They are often rather pale and almost anemic-looking. In cool climates the fall color is bright yellow, but in milder climates the trees just gradually lose their leaves without any farewell. The seed pods are like long, thin beans; hence the common name Indian bean tree.

These big, rounded trees are ideal lawn specimens providing you have enough room to accommodate them. Young trees need to be trained in the early years to make a strong single leader. They have two buds at the tip of each stem, causing them to grow every which way, so some early training is necessary. Like the paulownias they will regenerate easily, so if your tree is messy you can cut it to ground level and you will be rewarded with a very strong new shoot to shape into a new tree. They will grow in virtually any soil, including moist, heavy soils or light sands. While they have the ability to grow in cities and don't mind being the only tree in a sea of concrete, this hardiness is often denigrated.

Catalpa are strange trees. Find the right climate and they are fabulous, but in many situations they are a dismal failure. For a start they don't like wet conditions, and they don't like too mild a climate, but give them a dose of drought and cold and suddenly we're getting close to what they desire. They seem to need hot summers and preferably a period of dry or cold.

Shelter is essential for the soft, luxuriant leaves. The young stems are stalky and quite brittle with a hollow, pithy center. The combination of weak young stems and huge leaves makes them a

Right: *Catalpa speciosa*

poor choice for windy sites. Occasional attacks of mildew on the leaves are not life-threatening, while stem borer can devastate them, and they are prone to dieback. In some regions they spread naturally by seed and can be a minor nuisance but they are easily disposed of.

Catalpa = Native American word.

Catalpa bignonioides
INDIAN BEAN TREE, SOUTHERN CATALPA

This tree has handsome, gray trunks and an informal, open habit topped with huge, heart-shaped leaves. The overall impression is of an open, airy tree with no fussy twigs or superfluous growth. Open panicles of white, hooded flowers decorate the tree in mid-summer and have a delightful sugary sweet perfume. Look inside and you'll see that each one has a yellow throat dotted with purple spots. We expect to find such intricate flowers on tiny perennials rather than on immense trees. Sometimes when grown as a lawn specimen the flowers are low enough to enjoy. Unfortunately the leaves have an unpleasant smell. The clone **'Aurea'** has yellowish new leaves turning to light green for summer and is good as a con-trast tree. Grows naturally in southeast U.S.A. Height x width 25–50 ft (8–15 m). ZONES 5 TO 9.

Bignonioides = like a *Bignonia* flower.

Catalpa ovata
CHINESE CATALPA

A more modest size than *C. bignonioides*, but still an imposing tree. The leaves can be even bigger than the latter and are a richer color. They are ovate or sometimes have three lobes. Flowers are a creamy or yellowish white, with purple or red spots and a sweet perfume. From China. Height x width 30 ft (10 m). ZONES 5 TO 9.

Ovata = ovate, after the shape of the leaves.

Catalpa speciosa
NORTHERN CATALPA, WESTERN CATALPA

This species from the American midwest is the tallest of the catal-pas. The leaves are not scented but the flowers have a pleasant honey perfume. Big, open panicles of white flowers with yellow stripes and purple spots appear in midsummer. The plant seems to be encouraged by a somewhat cold climate. In the early days the timber was used for fence posts and railroad timbers because it does not rot. Height x width 50–70 ft (15–20 m). ZONES 4 TO 9.

Speciosa = splendid.

Ceanothus

CALIFORNIAN LILAC
Rhamnaceae

How can anyone resist the scrumptious, rich blue flowers of a Californian lilac? Not only is blue an irresistible color but the evergreen plants all radiate an overpowering scent of honey, as evidenced by the hum of bees around every bush. Not all *Ceanothus* are blue, however, and not all are evergreen. There are white-flowered species, garden cultivars and several deciduous species, too, but I personally find their pink or off-white flowers and nondescript leaves less attractive than the evergreens.

Most species are Californian and evergreen with neat, dark leaves. They are always rough or corrugated and look as if the

Above: *Ceanothus papillosus*

leaf has been compressed sideways and needs ironing. The two essentials for a happy *Ceanothus* are good drainage and plenty of sunshine, just as you would expect from a Californian native. Choose your site very carefully because once you have planted it, it is too late to change your mind. Trying to shift a *Ceanothus* bush to another spot is almost certain doom for the plant. *Ceanothus* need to be grown in pots and transplanted carefully. Occasionally they turn up their toes when planted out, so take extra care.

Ceanothus grow in acidic or alkaline soil and almost prefer the poor soils that keep them neat and compact. While they are happiest in full sun, they will grow in the shade of a wall or building; they just don't like overhead tree shade. One of the things I like about them is that they flower dependably every year and don't need to be tidied up or have the spent flowers removed. Certainly you can prune them after flowering, but they will forgive you if you forget.

Ceanothus can play many roles in a garden. You can use them as a ground cover or a border shrub, and they look so sublime when trained against a wall that it seems as if they were bred for that purpose. Some of them are terrific foliage plants with rich, dark green, corrugated leaves. They are drought-hardy, and will grow in full, hot, baking sun, in windy places and by the sea. They are generally very tough and, being evergreen, they look good all year. They tolerate a certain amount of cold and frosts but are not super-hardy. Thankfully they seem free of pests.

Ceanothus = from the Greek for spiny.

Ceanothus arboreus
CATALINA CEANOTHUS

As the species name suggests this is a tree-sized version of the genus. The fantastic honey-scented flowers appear in spring and early summer and vary from rich blue to anemic blue when grown from seed, so choose cultivars such as **'Trewithen Blue'**. An excellent wall shrub, but it can become rangy and leggy. Native to the U.S.A. Height 12 ft (4 m) x width 10 ft (3 m). ZONE 8.

Arboreus = tree.

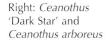

Above: *Ceanothus* 'Dark Star'

Right: *Ceanothus* 'Dark Star' and *Ceanothus arboreus*

Ceanothus 'Burkwoodii'

A complex hybrid, mixing spring-flowering evergreens and the late-flowering deciduous types. Valued for the lovely blue flowers with their heady honey fragrance in late summer, its hardiness and being evergreen. Height x width 6 ft (2 m). ZONE 7.

Ceanothus 'Concha'

Purple buds open to rich blue, sweetly honey-scented flowers on a big, handsome bush with very pleasing shiny foliage. It has a lovely arching habit and looks great planted *en masse* on a slope. Height x width 6 ft (2 m). ZONE 8.

Ceanothus 'Dark Star'

A tall bush with tiny leaves and possibly the darkest blue flower of any *Ceanothus*. The flowers appear in late spring and are delightfully honey-scented. Height x width 6 ft (2 m). ZONE 8.

Ceanothus impressus

SANTA BARBARA CEANOTHUS

A wonderful garden shrub, forming a low, dense bush smothered in deep blue, honey-scented flowers in the spring. The small, dark green leaves have deeply impressed veins. Hardier than most to both cold and wind. **'Puget Blue'** is a good selection. Native to California. Height x width 6–10 ft (2–3 m). ZONE 7 OR 8.

Impressus = referring to the deep veining on the leaves.

Ceanothus papillosus

A big, dense, evergreen shrub, in spring it has beautiful cobalt-blue flowers in little tight heads with a delicious honey fragrance. Discovered in 1833 by David Douglas (1799–1834) and introduced to the Veitch nursery in England by William Lobb (1809–1863) in 1850. Originates from California. Height x width 12 ft (4 m). ZONE 8.

Ceanothus papillosus **var roweanus** is a more compact, spreading version, and is ideal as a dense, high ground cover. Height 3–5 ft (1–1.5 m) x width 5–10 ft (1.5–3 m). ZONE 8.

Papillosus = having pimpled, rough leaves.

Cephalotaxus

PLUM YEW
Cephalotaxaceae

This is a genus not seen often enough in the garden. The plum yew has two styles of growth; short, curved leaves spiraled around the erect stems, and flatter, opposite leaves on the horizontal stems. Underneath they have two silver-gray stripes, distinguishing them from yew or *Taxus*. (*Torreya* is similar, with silver stripes, but it has a sharply pointed leaf.) If touched, the leaves of *Cephalotaxus* release a spicy, almost camphor-like perfume. The plum-like fruits are produced on female trees, the males being a separate bush.

As well as being dense evergreens, *Cephalotaxus* also have the ability to grow in alkaline soils and in heavy shade. These two factors alone should make them indispensable, because most other conifers seem to need maximum light and can cope with shade from buildings but not from overhead trees. *Cephalotaxus* also have the ability to grow in wet soils and in moist and humid climates, but they will be equally at home in hot, dry areas. They are fairly easy to transplant if you prepare them by cutting the roots, one quarter or one side at a time, over a period of two months before lifting. Some have been used for long-lived hedges and, surprisingly for a conifer, they tolerate heavy pruning as well as a light trim. All of the species are spread across Asia.

Kephale = Greek for "head," and *taxus* = yew, referring to the broad crown and yew-like appearance.

Cephalotaxus fortunei
FORTUNE PLUM YEW
This wide, spreading bush is great as an understory plant if you need a dense plant to block a view or enclose a garden. Touch the leaves to release the camphor-like scent. Older specimens show the peeling, red bark allowing you to open the bush Asian-style to show off the trunks. Native to China. Height x width 6–20 ft (2–6 m). ZONE 6.

Choose the **'Prostrate Spreader'** cultivar for a magnificent ground cover for shady places. Height 3–6 ft (1–2 m) x width 6–10 ft (2–3 m).

Fortunei = after Robert Fortune (1812–1880), who collected the plant in eastern China.

Cephalotaxus harringtonia
COWTAIL PINE, PLUM YEW
A wide, spreading bush to small tree with slightly paler leaves than the above. The leaves give off a spicy smell when brushed. Native to China, Japan and Korea. Height x width 6–10 ft (2–3 m). ZONE 6. The form we usually see in gardens is **C. harringtonia var drupacea** with shorter leaves in a "v"-shaped valley along the horizontal stems. This has a billowy habit and is ideal for training and clipping. Height x width 6–10 ft (2–3 m). The form **'Prostrata'** is a good ground cover. Height x width 2–5 ft (60 cm–1.5 m). If you want something different, try **'Fastigiata'**, a more narrow, upright form growing just over head-high. Height 6–10 ft (2–3 m) x width 1½–3 ft (0.5–1 m).

Harringtonia = named for English Utopian thinker James Harrington.

Cercidiphyllum

Cercidiphyllum japonicum
KATSURA TREE
Cercidiphyllaceae

When we think of fragrant plants we usually think of flowers, but many plants have pleasantly scented leaves, especially when we brush past them. This peculiar plant has a scent at just one time of the year and no one knows where the scent comes from—it is one of those garden mysteries. You may walk out into the garden on a fall day and discover that a smell of toffee being cooked is on the air. It is getting stronger and stronger, but where on earth is it coming from? You check the *Cercidiphyllum*, as the smell seems to be in that region. You smell the bush—no; take a leaf and crush it—no smell. Canny old gardeners will tell you it *is* the katsura tree,

Left: *Cephalotaxus harringtonia* 'Fastigiata'

Right: *Cercidiphyllum japonicum*

because they know from experience that is where the smell emanates from. But no matter how hard you try, you will not get the plant to release its scent on demand.

As a young plant it is multi-stemmed and very erect and yet strangely, as it matures, it becomes one of the most widespreading of trees. Site it on an open stretch of lawn where it can mature to become a real feature tree. You will not regret the choice when you see the combination of handsome leaves, excellent fall color and, in time, a fine character tree. The rounded, coin-like leaves have serrated edges and attractive reddish petioles or leaf stalks. Young stems are smooth and almost black, yet the older trunks have flaking, brown bark. All *Cercidiphyllum* have tiny red flowers at the time the new leaves emerge. Male and female flowers are on separate trees; that is, the species is "dioecious."

The tree is rather tricky to establish, which is possibly why we don't see it more often. Ideally, it needs a good, deep, rich soil, or even clay that is moist in summer, and not too hot a site. It does not like droughts. Shelter from cold or fierce winds is essential, but it is very cold-hardy. The new spring growth can be hit by frost in a fluctuating climate. It has no pests but does seem prone to root rots. Native to Japan and China. Height x width 50 ft (15 m). ZONES 4 TO 9.

There are several forms, including **Cercidiphyllum japonicum var sinense**, which usually has a single trunk and in the wilds of China is the largest of all deciduous trees. If, like me, you have only seen modestly-sized katsura trees in cultivation, it is hard to imagine them growing so big. The fall colors are usually shades of red, orange and salmon and the tree gives off a spicy odor of cotton candy at leaf fall. Height x width 50 ft (15 m). ZONES 4 TO 9.

The weeping form, **'Pendulum'**, is a magnificent sight but unfortunately very rare. Washington Arboretum has a splendid specimen in the Asian garden. Height 20 ft (6 m) x width 25 ft (8 m). ZONES 4 TO 9.

Cercidiphyllum magnificum from Japan is considered by some to be a separate species and by others to be a form of *C. japonicum*. The gardener in me says they are definitely different, but botanists generally go on flowers only, so it may be technically correct to say they are the same. The leaves are larger, paler and more wavy at the edges. *C. magnificum* is appropriately named as it is magnificent with these crinkle-cut leaf edges, like a cookie. Usually a single-trunk tree with smooth, light brown stems. Seemingly happy with very cold winters and hot, hot summers. Lovely yellow fall tints. Height 30 ft (10 m) x width 25 ft (8 m). ZONE 6.

Cercidiphyllum = having a leaf like a *Cercis*; *japonicum* = from Japan.

Cestrum

Solanaceae

Cestrums are a group of multi-trunked, shrubby relatives of the tomato from South America and Mexico. They are rangy, rambling shrubs with multiple stems capable of forming a thicket. Why would you want to plant a *Cestrum*? For the intense scent that varies from species to species and the colorful summer flowers of some.

Cestrums are evergreen in warm climates but often look scruffy and sparse in winter. Frosts will defoliate them, blackening the leaves and the soft, fleshy stems and even cutting them back to ground level. When this happens, it is a natural form of pruning: the bush regenerates in the spring with renewed vigor and is much bushier and tidier for this cutback. If frosts don't do the job for you, it is a good idea to give the plants a drastic prune in late winter. You can grow them under trees in an attempt to prevent frost damage, as they will grow quite happily in shade or full sun. In cold regions plant as big a specimen as you can find as soon as the threat of frost is past. Then feed and water it to get it as big as possible by fall. The larger the plant's rootstock, the more chance it has of surviving the impending frosts.

Apart from frosts, the biggest threat is strong winds that tear the soft foliage and break the sappy stems. It is not troubled by

Left: *Cestrum aurantiacum*

pests or diseases. I think the very strong smell of the leaves would deter even the hungriest bug.

Cestrums are not fussy about soil but do best in a dry piece of ground if you are in a frosty zone. (Plants are more likely to survive cold winters if they are in dry soil rather than wet, because the plant will be tougher and less sappy.) I have grown cestrums in swampy ground without any problems, but it was in a frost-free location. They do like plenty of water in the summer to keep them lush and attractive, so in dry regions either give them a mulch around the roots or water them regularly. Being indifferent to the acidity of the soil, cestrums may be a good choice for gardeners on limestone, where few shrubs grow well. They are easy to transplant at any stage; simply cut back hard if you are moving a large specimen. If you want a new plant in another location it is easier to take a section of the rootstock (almost like dividing a herbaceous plant), or grow a new plant from a cutting. They are easy to grow from cuttings, so it is not worth the effort of digging up an established plant.

They are not prime position plants but are a useful "fillers," especially if you want a quick-growing "instant" shrub to fill a gap or block a neighbor's view into your property. Typically they are 6–10 ft (2–3 m) high and wide. Grow them against a wall in cold areas, as they need a warm ZONE 8 or else ZONE 9 or 10.

Cestrum = from the Greek "kestron," meaning hammer.

Cestrum aurantiacum
ORANGE CESTRUM

Clusters of flowers at the tips of the stems appear in summer on the ends of the new growth. Unlike other *Cestrum*, this one usually has just one burst of flowers in mid- to late summer. They all come out in bloom at one time and last perhaps three weeks, with the bonus of being night-scented, almost like jasmine. Individually the tiny, tubular flowers have no impact, but the sheer number of soft apricot trumpets is superb. It is not a color to appeal to all gardeners and does not blend easily with other flowering shrubs. It is a typical *Cestrum* in that it has a loose, open habit and needs a spring prune to keep it tidy. It has long, thin, willow-like, green leaves. Native to Central America. Height x width 6–10 ft (2–3 m). ZONE 9.

Aurantiacum = orange.

Cestrum 'Newellii'
RED CESTRUM

This bright red version is thought to be a hybrid and is certainly the most attractive of the genus. It has a faint scent of talcum powder and the soft, felted, velvety leaves are oval and a rich, dark green. They are much healthier-looking than the anemic, pale leaves of *Cestrum aurantiacum* or *C. nocturnum*. The bright crimson flowers are shaped like an urn and appear in clusters at the tops of the stems in summer. Some flowers first appear in spring and it can flower intermittently all summer. **C. 'Hugh Redgrove'** is a similar hybrid with the same scent. For both, height x width 6–10 ft (2–3 m). ZONE 9 OR 10.

Cestrum nocturnum
NIGHT-SCENTED JESSAMINE

Just one amazing quality saves this shrub from obscurity—the perfume of its night-scented flowers. And it is not just a light perfume, it's a "knock your socks off," pungent smell. The initial waft is delicious, but it is followed by a stench like cheap perfume that really packs a punch. Most people rave about the smell but others find it too powerful. Greenish-yellow, thin, tubular flowers in clusters at the tops of the stems are the source of the perfume;

Above: *Cestrum*
'Newellii'

Below: *Cestrum*
nocturnum

they are followed by white berries. The flowering season is long, lasting from early spring through summer.

The shrub is uninteresting to look at, with plain, oval leaves in soft green. It forms an upright thicket of stems from waist- to head-high, depending on the lushness of your climate and soil conditions. It does tend to look scruffy and rangy at times and is not a plant for tidy gardeners. Give it a severe pruning every spring to try and keep it under control. Like all cestrums, it is evergreen and will grow in sun or shade. I have seen it buried deep in the back of a shrubbery under trees, and some would say that is the

best place for it, "out of sight out of mind"—until you get a whiff of it in the evening. Height x width 3–6 ft (1–2 m). ZONE 8 OR 9.

Nocturnum = at night, referring to when the scent of the flowers is released.

Cestrum parqui
WILLOW-LEAFED JESSAMINE, GREEN CESTRUM

This is probably the hardiest species and is quite similar to *Cestrum nocturnum*, being night-scented, but it is not as strong. It has pale, yellowish green flowers and slender, willow-like leaves. It hails from Chile, which explains why it is hardier than other species. Height x width 6–10 ft (2–3 m). ZONE 8.

Parqui = a Chilean name.

Chimonanthus

Chimonanthus praecox
WINTERSWEET
Calycanthaceae

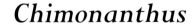

If ever there was a plant specifically designed to lift your spirits on a gray winter's day, then this is it. Imagine walking through your garden in the middle of winter, everything drab and closed down for the cooler months, and suddenly you spot these lemon-scented yellow flowers. You know the year has turned and spring is on its way. Even though wintersweet is willing to flower for us at such a cold and inhospitable time, it is not a super-hardy plant. However, it will cope with cold winters, providing it has had enough summer heat to ripen the wood. This early-flowering species is probably the hardiest shrub to flower in midwinter in its zone.

Above: *Chimonanthus praecox*

to transplant in winter. Even established bushes can be moved before the flowering season. These plants originate in China. Height x width 6 ft (2 m). ZONE 7.

Chimonanthus = winter flower; *praecox* = appearing early.

Choisya

Choisya ternata
MEXICAN ORANGE BLOSSOM
Rutaceae

Typical of the citrus family, *Choisya ternata* is strongly scented with a powerful orange aroma. I love the scent of the crushed leaves, but I know that a small percentage of people find it distasteful. The bird's-foot leaves have three or sometimes four leaflets and come in opposite pairs. You will be impressed with the lush, dark green leaves that appear regardless of the season or site. Clusters of starry white flowers appear in the spring or early summer. They smell better than they look, with a delicious orange blossom scent.

One of the great standby foliage plants, *Choisya* is capable of growing just about anywhere. A tough customer, it is the kind of shrub that you can be sure is going to thrive. It will cope with all that poor soil and leftover brick and concrete that builders bury around a new house, and is happy in alkaline or acidic soil. Further, it grows in sun or shade and is generally indestructible. It is evergreen and an excellent bold shrub for borders, especially near buildings in those difficult, drafty sites. It can be clipped to retain any shape, and it generally withstands poor treatment or neglect.

In a warm climate they are sometimes attacked by thrip or leaf hoppers, but otherwise they are invincible. As with most citrus, the leaves occasionally become pale and anemic due to a lack of magnesium, but a good dose of Epsom salts (magnesium sulfate) will soon put that right. Easy to transplant from a

Below: *Choisya ternata*

This gorgeous deciduous shrub deserves far greater recognition. It is a sign that you are in a real plantperson's garden if you see one of these, and while they look fairly drab throughout the summer, they repay you handsomely at flowering time. Flowers appear on the previous year's twigs and so any necessary pruning should be done immediately after flowering so as to allow the plant time to make new growth for next year's flowers. It is generally a twiggy bush and, while not the tidiest of shrubs, it should not really need more than occasional pruning for overall shape or outline.

It is most common to see the straight species, with yellowish to opaque flowers and an inner circle of dark red. The flowers are pleasing enough, but it is possible to pass by the plant and not know it is in flower except for the spicy lemon scent. Seek out grafted forms like **'Luteus'**, with pure yellow, showy flowers. Each flower glistens as if painted with gold, and a bush laden with blooms is breathtaking. The flowers last for two to three weeks and can be cut for a vase to cheer your winter days. Planting against a wall or a dark conifer highlights the pointed, arrowhead leaves and greatly improves their appearance. A dark background also throws the flowers on the bare stems into relief.

What conditions do you need to grow *Chimonanthus*? Any reasonable, free-draining soil will suffice, and they are one of the few shrubs to grow well on limestone soils. They seem equally happy in high and low rainfall areas. They love hot summers and cold winters, although neither are essential to success. Do give them all the summer heat and sun you can manage; in shade they sulk and don't flower as well. Plant away from cold or constant winds. These plants are generally easy-care, free of pests and easy

Right: *Choisya* 'Aztec Pearl'

container and certain to grow, but once you have chosen a site, it is best not to risk shifting it again. It will grow in cool or hot climates, in sun, shade or wind, and even in coastal gardens.

This plant is part of a small group of evergreen shrubs from southwestern U.S.A. and Mexico. *Choisya ternata* is usually around 3 ft (1 m) high and perhaps a little wider, but I have seen it grown as a wall shrub to over 10 ft (3 m) high. ZONE 8.

Choisya = after Jacques Choisy, a Swiss clergyman and botanist (1799–1859); *ternata* = having three leaflets.

'Sundance' is a super, yellow-gold leaf form that rarely flowers, but, as with the species, the leaves are aromatic. It is not so successful in warm climates or in hot sun, preferring a cool climate. Height x width 8 ft (2.5 m).

'Aztec Pearl' is a hybrid between the rarely seen *Choisya arizonica* and the common *C. ternata*. It has a real crow's-foot leaf with narrow, shiny, green leaflets, and the bigger, dazzling white flowers are much showier than the straight species. Height x width 8 ft (2.5 m). ZONE 9.

Cladrastis

YELLOWWOOD
Fabaceae

A small group of trees, and one of the many plants showing a historical plant link between China, Japan and eastern America. When you see the chains of pea-like flowers with the long, pointed panicles you will instantly think "wisteria," and,

what's more, they are sweetly scented. They may not be well known, but these deciduous trees have some winning ways. In a garden setting they do not grow too big and they have a neat, upright habit with the tops arching out like an umbrella. Handsome, pinnate, ash-like leaves have a lovely clean, almost glaucous, look about them. They are one of those plants that look almost as good at the end of summer as they did with the new leaves in spring. So many deciduous trees look rather scruffy by fall. *Cladrastis* also have excellent fall color in bright yellows. These plants are related to *Maackia* but differ in having next year's buds enclosed within the base of the leaf. Pull a leaf off and you will see what I mean. Plane trees also cover the new buds with the leaf petiole, protecting it from the elements.

Cladrastis thrives in a continental climate and prefers to be in full sun for healthy growth and maximum flowers. Any soil will suffice as long as there is good drainage. No major pests or diseases, but the branches are brittle and often break in storms. The young plant may need protection from frost for a few years.

Cladrastis = from the Greek, perhaps referring to the brittleness of the branches.

Cladrastis lutea, syn *C. kentukea*
YELLOWWOOD

What a splendid small tree—and yet it is often overlooked. In late spring to early summer the pretty clusters of white flowers tend to give the impression they are tumbling out of the bush and about to fall on you. They are worth a closer look: inhale the sweet scent and notice the smooth, gray trunks that tempt one to run a hand across them. Golden yellow fall color is a bonus. Brilliant green, smooth leaves form a dense canopy of foliage with a slight weeping habit. Each leaf is made up of 5 to 9 leaflets, somewhat remi-

Above: *Cladrastis lutea*

Above: *Cladrastis sinensis*

niscent of walnut. In the wild this tree can reach 30–50 ft (10–15 m) high and will eventually grow tall for you, but it has many years as a small tree to beautify your garden. It has a luxuriant look about it all summer. Called yellowwood because of its yellow timber. Native to southeastern U.S.A. Height 30–50 ft (10–15 m) x width 30 ft (10 m). ZONE 3.

'Rosea' is a light pink-flowered form that is very cute but somehow lacks the purity of the "true" plant.

Lutea = yellow.

Cladrastis sinensis

There are several Chinese species but this is the most well known. The panicles of erect flowers are white with a hint of red or pink and are sweetly scented, appearing in high summer. The alternate blue-green leaves are compound and held horizontally in a lovely attitude. Pale gray, upright trunks form a neat, small tree, giving a pleasing aspect in winter or summer. Nice clear yellow fall color. Native to China. Height x width 30 ft (10 m). ZONE 6.

Cladrastis platycarpa is a similar Japanese species with erect, white, scented flowers with a touch of yellow. Height x width 15–30 ft (5–10 m). ZONE 7.

Cladrastis wilsonii is a Chinese species with slightly hairy, bluish leaves and panicles of fragrant white flowers. Height x width 15–30 ft (5–10 m). ZONE 6.

Sinensis = from China.

Clerodendrum

Verbenaceae

Much as I love the hardy clerodendrums, they do tend to take over a garden with their suckering habits. They are a mix of evergreen and deciduous shrubs and a few climbers, with sugar-scented flowers, growing from China and Japan down to the tropics and across to Africa. Most are only suitable for large gardens. They grow easily in almost any kind of soil (sometimes heavy soils are the best as it restricts their suckering habit). Clerodendrums grow equally well in alkaline and very acidic ground and are at home in wet or dry climates, withstanding considerable drought at the base of old trees. Sun or shade makes no difference to their growth, although shelter from wind is advisable. If they are damaged by wind, prune them hard and watch them quickly regenerate. The combination of shade- and drought-tolerance makes them almost essential in large woodland gardens. Pests and disease seem to leave them alone, possibly because of their strong-smelling leaves.

Clero = from Greek "kleros," meaning chance. This name apparently refers to the uncertainty of the plant's medicinal qualities; *dendrum* = tree.

Clerodendrum bungei
GLORY BOWER
Having mentioned the bad suckering habits of *Clerodendrum*, let's concentrate on the good aspects of this plant, starting with the stunning pink flowers in fall. Imagine a small, inverted saucer the size of your palm in fluorescent shocking-pink sitting right on top of bold stems above large, heart-shaped leaves. The flowers produce a pleasant sugary scent, although it is a bit strong and better on the air than it is at close range. The leaves, too, are scented or stinky, depending on your point of view or your sense of smell. I find the smell of the crushed leaves to be quite interesting and pleasant. These leaves are a rich, dark, blackish color. Even the stems are the same color, and smooth except for the prominent lenticels. Each stem comes from below ground level, grows to around 6 ft (2 m) high and hardly ever branches, and so each one is like a single cane. The base of the plant is invariably leafless, showing a thicket of stems reminiscent of bamboo, with single canes suckering through the ground. To me the greatest value of *C. bungei* is that it flowers almost alone in the fall. It looks best in isolation, as its impact is lost among other shrubs and you will curse the way new suckers come up in adjoining bushes. From China. Height 6 ft (2 m) x 10 ft (3 m). ZONE 7.

Bungei = after Russian botanist Alexander von Bunge (1803–1890), who collected plants in northern Asia and China.

Clerodendrum trichotomum
HARLEQUIN GLORY BOWER
This slightly taller version is stalk-like, but the stems do branch out at around shoulder height, so it forms a bushier plant than *Clerodendrum bungei*. Like its sister plant it will sucker, especially on lighter ground, although it is less of a problem in that regard than *C. bungei*. The leaves are grayish and slightly hairy or felted.

Right: *Clerodendrum bungei*

Strange, sugary-smelling flowers appear in late summer on top of the bush. The little, white, starry flowers are normal enough but they sit on top of a fleshy calyx. Initially this calyx is green, later changing to bright, waxy red when it holds up the brilliant aquamarine-blue berries. As it is a tall plant, most of us miss this display so, if you can, plant one near the bottom of a slope where it can be viewed from above. Ideally you should plant it as a lone specimen to appreciate the tropical-looking foliage—and because it suckers.

There is another form of this plant, **Clerodendrum trichotomum var *fargesii***, with white flowers and a green calyx, and its leaves are less hairy. Introduced by Père Farges (1844–1912), this version is thought to be hardier than others, although not as pretty. Actually both types can be frosted and sometimes cut to the ground by cold, but they quickly regenerate in the spring. China and Japan. Height x width 6–10 ft (2–3 m). ZONE 6.

Tricho = hairy; *tomus* = cut or cleft.

Clerodendrum ugandense

BLUE BUTTERFLY BUSH, BLUE GLORY BOWER

If you are lucky enough to have a hot, sunny garden with no frosts, consider planting one of these climbers. All gardeners are fascinated by blue flowers, and this is one of the best. The upright panicles of flowers are loosely arranged to show off the beautiful, blue, winged flowers. Four of the petals are pale blue and shaped like the four wings of a butterfly, with a long tail or extra petal of purple-blue at the base of the flower. The sweetly scented blooms open in succession, providing a floral display for two months

Left: *Clerodendrum trichotomum*

Above: *Clerodendrum ugandense*

or more in late summer and fall. The leaves are quite small and nothing special. In fact, the whole bush is rather nondescript apart from the flowers. Give the plant a good, hard prune in late spring to tidy it, and to promote more new growth and lots more flowers. Originates from East Africa. Height 4–6 ft (1.2–2 m). ZONE 9.

Ugandense = from Uganda.

Clethra

SUMMERSWEET, SWEET PEPPERBUSH, WHITE ALDER
Clethraceae

*C*lethra is a wonderful genus and it has long been a favorite of mine. All species have white, fragrant flowers and nearly every one is pretty. Most *Clethra* are deciduous shrubs from China and Japan, with a few relatives in eastern U.S.A. This geographical link is common in the plant world. Clethras somehow managed to drop off a couple of strange siblings along their way. There is an upright, evergreen tree version growing in Madeira, off the coast of Spain, and another spreading, evergreen type with bronze leaves growing in Mexico. They like acidic, free-draining soil and need to be in sun or nearly full sun. A sheltered site is the next priority, as the leaves are usually delicate and the plants are prone to tip over at ground level in severe storms. In the wild some American species grow in swamps, but these conditions are not advisable in a garden setting as they would probably be fatal. They thrive in a moist climate, such as would suit rhododendrons and yet I have seen them doing well in drought-prone country. They need sun for most of the day to ripen the wood for flowering; plants in shade tend to be poor flower-bearers. The roots are fibrous and near the surface, like a rhododendron, so they are easy to transplant and will repay your kindness if you give them a mulch to keep the roots cool. Most are very cold-hardy and their only problem

Left: *Clethra barbinervis*

Above: *Clethra delavayi*

seems to be root rot. The fall color can be good but varies according to species and your climate—cool regions have the best color. Clethras are best sited in a woodland garden, although some would look fine in a suburban plot.

Clethra = from Greek, meaning alder.

Clethra alnifolia
SWEET PEPPERBUSH

Appropriately named, the sweet, sugary smell of the late summer flowers wafts around your garden, leading you to the source—the long, white, raceme-like fingers of flowers on the tips of the stems. Some gardeners complain because this plant suckers and spreads, while others have little or no problem; perhaps it depends on your soil type. Mine does sucker, but more like a clumping bamboo than like a runner, and it is only now just over 3 ft (1 m) high after 10 or more years: it is more like an erect thicket of smooth stems. The leaves are adequate as a foil for the flowers and in fall consistently turn a rich yellow. Native to eastern U.S.A., where it grows in moist places. Height x width 8 ft (2.5 m). ZONE 3.

A cultivar called **'Rosea'** has very pretty pink flowers. Height x width 8 ft (2.5 m). **'Hummingbird'** is a more compact white form at a height up to 36 in (90 cm) x width 8 ft (2.5 m).

Alnifolia = leaf like an alder or *Alnus*.

Clethra arborea
LILY OF THE VALLEY TREE

Fragrant flowers with a lily scent appear in late summer and show up well against the glossy foliage. The panicles of white, fringed, bell-shaped flowers are reward for growing this plant as, being evergreen, there is no fall color. Worth growing just for the rich, dark, evergreen leaves on an upright, columnar shrub. These shiny-topped leaves are the best of any hardy *Clethra*. Grow one where you might otherwise use a conifer for a column of dense, evergreen foliage. Native of Madeira. Height 10–15 ft (3–5 m) x 3–6 ft (1–2 m). ZONE 8 OR 9.

Arborea = tree-like.

Clethra barbinervis
JAPANESE CLETHRA

The flowers open from the base toward the tip, thus flowering in succession for several weeks. The scent is reminiscent of fresh green apples or apple cider, as it is slightly "ripe." This open, rather sparse shrub has nice smooth stems, so the interior of the bush looks quite tidy. The very old trunks have peeling bark that adds even more appeal. Each year new growths are topped with a whorl of leaves that are slightly furry and rough to touch. At the base of each of these new growths a multiple raceme of flowers appears in summer. Good fall color in orange tones. Native to Japan. Height 6–10 ft (2–3 m) x width 6 ft (2 m). ZONE 6.

Barbi = bearded; *nervis* = nerves or veins; thus hairy veins.

Clethra delavayi
The racemes of white flowers appear in late summer in almost horizontal fashion from the tips of the stems. Each bell-flower encloses the hidden stamens and the scent is sweet. A neat-looking, deciduous shrub with red-tinged, wrinkled leaves. Height x width 6 ft (2 m). ZONE 7.

Clethra monostachya is very similar.

Delavayi = after Abbé Delavay (1838–1895), a French missionary in China who collected thousands of new plants. He discovered this one in 1884 and it was later introduced by George Forrest (1873–1932) in 1913.

Clethra fargesii
A hardy, deciduous shrub, its dull grayish leaves are a weak point because in summer the pure white, apple-scented flowers are delightful. Each raceme has a main stem and secondary flower stems. Found in Szechwan Province in western China and introduced by Ernest Wilson (1876–1930) in 1900 for the Veitch nursery, England. Height x width 10 ft (3 m). ZONE 6.

Fargesii = after Abbé Farges (1844–1912), one of the French missionaries in China in the late 19th century.

Above: *Clethra arborea*

Colletia

ANCHOR PLANT OR CROWN OF THORNS
Rhamnaceae

The tiny, white, cup flowers of this plant can be singles or in dense clusters and have an exquisite scent of ice-cream and honey—just take care how you approach the blooms to enjoy the perfume. Anchor plant forms a gangling sort of bush best kept away from paths because of its ever-present sharp spines. This is a strange genus from South America, found mostly in Argentina but also in neighboring countries. The branches have adapted to suit an arid climate and in so doing have become like a jigsaw puzzle of triangular spikes, often with a vicious thorn at the tip. The gray-blue stems are capable of photosynthesizing and so they do not need leaves to make food. Technically the plant is deciduous because any small leaves that may appear soon fall off and do not contribute to the plant for food or for appearance. Try a hot, sunny, dry spot, perhaps against a wall, to highlight the strange growth pattern. Any soil will do as long as it is free-draining. Transplanting is an art because of the spines and no one would be silly enough to transplant a large specimen.

Colletia = after M. Philibert Collet (1643–1718), a French botanist and author.

Colletia hystrix, syn C. armata

A hefty shrub just over head-high, with rounded, vicious spines. Tiny, white, ice-cream-scented flowers appear in late summer. From Chile. Height x width 6 ft (2 m). ZONE 7.

Hystrix = porcupine-like; *armata* = armed with thorns.

Colletia paradoxa, syn C. cruciata

An angular, spreading bush with blue-gray triangular "leaves," tipped with sharp spines. Clusters of honey-scented flowers deck these weird stems in fall. Native to Brazil and Uruguay. Height x width 6 ft (2 m). ZONE 7.

Paradoxa = paradoxical; *cruciata* = cross or cross-shaped.

Left: *Colletia paradoxa*

Corylopsis

WINTER HAZEL
Hamamelidaceae

In early spring the bare branches of *Corylopsis* are dripping with very pale, lemon-yellow chains of flowers. When you look closely, it is as if they have been threaded together and hung on the bare stems. And as you move closer still, you will notice the subtle, sweet perfume of the flowers, although sometimes you can smell it on the air when you walk past the bush. To some, the scent is reminiscent of cowslips or perhaps primroses. If you saw a *Corylopsis* at this time, you would want one. The problem comes with how to accommodate it for the rest of the year. Yes, the leaves are reasonably attractive, like a cherry or hazel leaf, but the bush often has a sparse look rather than a dense canopy of foliage. Fall color is nothing marvelous, and so we rely on the spring flowers and nice scent for the plant to earn its keep.

The bush usually grows in a big, arching, open umbrella pattern, so it seems to take up a lot of room. In a small garden it is inevitably going to be crowded by other shrubs, diminishing some of its appeal. In a large, woodland garden it is possible to give it enough room to show off its lovely dome shape without constraining it. One possible solution to lack of space is to train a *Corylopsis* against a wall. Those I have seen treated like this are magnificent. Imagine a dense bush 10 ft (3 m) high and half as wide, growing just 1 ft (30 cm) out from the wall and the whole thing teeming with pendulous yellow chains. It is a wonderful sight, and to maintain it all you have to do is secure one or two main stems to the wall and trim the bush after the first flush of spring growth.

There is another exciting way of growing *Corylopsis* to save ground space, and that is by training one as a standard. Choose one strong stem to be the leader and decide how high you want the bush to grow, and then nip the top off and let the branches cascade out from there.

In terms of conditions, the plants are quite easy to please. Any free-draining soil will do as long as it is acidic or neutral. They do prefer a moist climate but, being deciduous, will handle winter cold. Sometimes the flowers can be damaged by a late frost but usually they are sensible enough to delay flowering. Find a sheltered spot with good light or even full sun. There are no serious pests or diseases. *Corylopsis* transplant in the off-season fairly easily at any age and usually do not need any pruning unless you wish to train them to a specific shape.

From a gardener's perspective there is not a lot of difference between *Corylopsis glabrescens*, *C. platypetala*, *C. spicata*, *C. veitchiana* and *C. willmottiae*. Choose a species that grows to the height you want, as the flowers are fairly similar on all except for *C. himalayana* and *C. pauciflora*.

Corylus = hazel; *opsis* = like; thus, like a hazel.

Corylopsis himalayana

The flowers of this species are bigger, fatter and paler than others, and so are easy to recognize. They have a subtle lemon scent that pervades the garden in spring. The gem of the genus as regards the leaf cover and possibly the best for flowering, too, this choice plant is new to cultivation and likely to become a firm favorite. The prominent, bright yellow, pointed buds are full of promise.

Above: *Corylopsis pauciflora*

Right: *Corylopsis himalayana*

Above: *Corylopsis spicata*

Looks good all year, while most in this genus are great for two to three weeks, then very ordinary for the rest of the year. They are ideally suited to a woodland garden away from strong winds. Native to the Himalayas. Height 10–15 ft (3–5 m) x width 6–10 ft (2–3 m). ZONE 8 OR 9.

Himalayana = from the Himalayas.

Corylopsis pauciflora
BUTTERCUP WINTER HAZEL

If you only have a small garden and you want a *Corylopsis*, this is it—a whole lot of flower-power packed into a tiny little bush. Ironically, when you see this dense little bush absolutely laden with flowers you will wonder how on earth it got its name (*pauci-flora* means few flowers). The flowers smell like primroses or *Polyanthus*. Typically it forms a bush wider than it is tall. The leaves, like very small, rough hazel leaves, are nothing special and possibly the least interesting of the genus, but the plant more than makes up for this with its twin attributes of compact size and profusion of flower. From Japan. Height 5 ft (1.5 m) x width 8 ft (2.5 m). ZONE 6.

Pauciflora = not having many flowers.

Corylopsis spicata

The wide-spreading, arching habit of this species takes up a lot of room. The bare stems are decked with chains of pale yellow flowers with intriguing red anthers in the spring. Plant near a path to enjoy the *Primula*-like scent. Native to Japan. Height 6 ft (2 m) x width 10 ft (3 m). ZONE 5.

Spicata = spiked.

Corylopsis willmottiae syn *C. sinensis*

Pale yellow racemes of delicately scented flowers appear in spring on this vigorous, upright to spreading shrub. As with many plants from Asia, it was introduced by E. H. Wilson (1876–1930). There is a version of *C. willmottiae* with soft purple, newly emerging leaves called **'Spring Purple'**, raised by Hilliers Nursery in England. Native to China. Height x width 12 ft (4 m). ZONE 6.

Willmottiae = after Miss Willmott (1860–1934), a famous gardener of the time when the plant was discovered.

Flowers emerge in very early spring and may be frosted-damaged, so it is worth picking a prime site for such a beauty. Glaucous, blue foliage forms a dense canopy whereas most *Corylopsis* tend to be arching shrubs with a rather thin facade of leaves. This wall of foliage tends to weep down, creating a full and lush appearance.

Crataegus

MAY OR HAWTHORN
Rosaceae

These are a large and diverse group of deciduous trees found throughout the Northern Hemisphere. They are usually small, round-headed trees with lobed leaves and tight little heads of cup-shaped flowers in white, pink or red. The scent of the flowers is intoxicating and so well known that we describe other plants as "may-scented."

Being among the showiest trees, resilient and hardy, they are deservedly popular. Hawthorns do best in areas with a definite winter and summer, and tend to fade in warm zones. They handle cold winters, strong winds and even heavy storms. Sometimes you see windswept specimens growing almost horizontally, but they are surviving. They can even cope with city pollution.

Hawthorns grow just as easily in alkaline as acidic soil. In fact, they are one of the standby trees for limestone regions. Heavy clay soil is fine, as is sand or rocky places. There are some pests: caterpillars and other bugs seem to enjoy the taste of this fine plant, but rarely disfigure it because of the jagged leaves and their random placement. The leaf cover does not have an overall pattern one can focus on and so the chewed leaves do not show up. Only the pear slug is capable of defoliating the bush. These nasty beasts are not really slugs at all, although they do look similar. They are the larvae (or caterpillar) stage of a sawfly. The easy way to kill them is to throw dust or dirt at the plant and the "dusty" slugs fall off and die. Diseases such as fireblight can be a problem, too. It is typical of the plants in the Rosaceae family that one must contend with lots of pests. The trunks are gnarly and interesting and the wood is very heavy.

Crataegus = from Greek "kratos" meaning strength, referring to the hardness or strength of the wood.

Crataegus laevigata, syn C. oxycantha
MAY OR ENGLISH HAWTHORN

A European native credited with many of the named forms, when it is more likely they are hybrids between this and *C. monogyna*. In late spring the typical may flowers appear with their fabulous scent. Found in Europe. Height x width 25 ft (8 m). ZONE 5.

'Paul's Scarlet' (syn 'Coccinea Plena') is a tremendous plant with showy, double red flowers and worthy of a place in any garden. **'Plena'** is a choice double white clone.

Laevigata = smooth leafed;
oxycantha = from *oxy* meaning "sharp," because of the thorns.

Crataegus monogyna
SINGLESEED HAWTHORN

A common sight in the hedgerows of England, this small thorny tree is distinctly twiggy and cluttered in winter. Its sweetly may-scented, white flowers appear in late spring in clusters in the axils of the leaves and the whole bush can be covered like snow. Certainly the showiest native tree of western Europe. The fragrance of the blooms is a bonus, as is the scarlet fruit in fall. Small-lobed leaves can sometimes provide a reddish fall color. The tree is often grown to provide food and shelter for birds. If you plant one in a

Left: *Crataegus monogyna*

city garden you will certainly attract birdlife. Height x width 25 ft (8 m). ZONE 5.

Mono = one; *gyna* = female, thus *monogyna* = having a single pistil or female part, resulting in only one seed per fruit.

Cytisus

BROOM
Fabaceae

Brooms thrive in heat and sun, and with the world becoming warmer and water in shorter supply, they could be all the more valuable. The pea-like flowers have all the shapes of a typical legume, with wings and a keel. *En masse* in spring they can be a spectacular sight and have the added bonus of a strong honey, or even a fortified wine, scent.

Cytisus are by nature colonizers, taking over newly turned ground and, as with most pioneer plants, they are generally short-lived. Brooms tend to grow fast and die fast. You can delay this process by pruning them immediately after they flower. If you trim the plant back by around a third of its height when the flowers have faded, the bush will take longer to reach mature height and be less prone to wind-rock, which causes a top-heavy plant to be blown over at ground level. To be more precise, you should look at the growth the plant made last season and cut off nearly all of it, leaving just a finger's length of last summer's stems. The plant will then make vigorous new stems to bear the next crop of flowers. It will become lanky and woody if left unpruned.

Brooms are good for covering dry, inhospitable slopes and other difficult sites. Heavy clay is fine, as are poor, rocky or sandy soils. One of the reasons this is a great colonizing plant is its ability to grow in these poor sites, and in very hot, dry places with not much soil or water. Most colonizing plants need full sun to thrive and this is true for all brooms. Being in the legume or Fabaceae family, it is also capable of acquiring nitrogen from the air and using it as plant food that in turn returns to the soil and is used by succeeding plants. Nitrogen is essential to all plants as the element that turns them green and makes them grow faster. Very few plants other than legumes have the ability to make use of the nitrogen in the atmosphere.

Grown from seed, brooms send down a long taproot and are tolerant of a wide range of soils. These taproots allow them to grow in dry, hot, inhospitable places. Brooms are more willing to grow in alkaline soils than most shrubs. Cultivars grown from cuttings have a more spreading root system and can handle most ground conditions. They do not enjoy having their roots disturbed at all. When you plant a potted broom, take care to spread the roots, as those that have roots circling the bottom of the pot will not live long if their roots are not unraveled.

Above: *Cytisus scoparius*

It is called broom because the flexible stems were bound together to makes brooms, like the traditional witches' brooms.

Cytisus = from Greek "kytisos," for a related medicinal plant.

Cytisus x beanii (C. ardoinii x C. purgans)

A small, semi-prostrate, deciduous shrub with rich yellow, honey-scented flowers in spring. Looks wonderful tumbling over a wall or slope, and is an ideal plant for large rock gardens. **Cytisus x kewensis** (*C. ardoinii* x *C. multiflorus*) is very similar, with more creamy yellow flowers. Both grow happily in limestone or acidic soils. If your soil is acidic, try them in combination with small-flowered blue rhododendrons for a stunning effect. Height 1–2 ft (30–60 cm) x width 3 ft (1 m). ZONE 6.

Beanii = after Mr. Bean (1863–1947), a director of London's Kew Gardens in the 1940s and author of an excellent manual on trees and shrubs.

Cytisus multiflorus, syn C. albus

PORTUGUESE BROOM, WHITE SPANISH BROOM

Known as both the Portuguese or Spanish broom, this glorious white-flowered deciduous plant starts as an upright form, gradually spreading and demanding more space. In late spring and early summer, the heady honey fragrance of the flowers makes it more than worthy of space in your garden. It grows around 10 ft (3 m) high and can be "legged up" (pruning off the lower branches) to make an arching, high shrub to allow perennial plants, such as *Pulmonaria*, some space in the foreground. Native to Portugal and Spain. Height 10 ft (3 m) x width 6 ft (2 m). ZONE 7.

Multiflorus = having lots of flowers.

Cytisus x praecox (C. purgans x C. multiflorus)

WARMINSTER BROOM

A fairly tidy, compact, deciduous broom, ideal for small gardens. The pale primrose-yellow flowers appear in mid to late spring. The heady sweet wine scent is intoxicating on first encounter but can be overpowering when used as a cut-flower. It may need a trim after flowering to keep it dense and bushy as it sometimes becomes top-heavy with the weight of blooms.

There are several clones available, including a rich yellow called **'Allgold'**, and the original hybrid with creamy yellow flowers is now known now as **'Warminster'**, from the town in England of the same name. For all, height x width 6–10 ft (2–3 m). ZONE 6.

Praecox = early, referring to its flowering habit.

Cytisus scoparius

SCOTCH BROOM

One of the great things about scotch brooms is that they flower for months and months, but that is only part of the story. The red and

56

Right: *Cytisus multiflorus*

Below: *Cytisus* x *beanii*

yellow flowers are also delightfully scented in a fruity, pineapple way, and are good for cut-flowers. The scotch broom is despised by many because it has colonized farmland in some regions. But, while I can sympathize with the farmers, I can also see a place for the cultivars of this fine plant. If you live where the plant has never naturalized, you will wonder what all the fuss is about as these easy-care plants are a beacon in early spring, in every shade from yellow to gold, orange to red. The bush itself is an upright, multi-stemmed, deciduous plant, arching out at the tops as gravity takes over. Thin, string-like stems are rich green and capable of photo-synthesizing when and if the leaves fall, as they usually do. So they appear to be evergreen, when in fact the tiny, clover-like leaves often only last a matter of weeks before they fall.

There are many named clones and cultivars, some with bicolor flowers, such as **'Andreanus'** (Normandy broom), with yellow flowers splashed with red. Native to western Europe. Height x width 6–10 ft (2–3 m). ZONE 6.

Scoparius = broom-like.

Daphne

DAPHNE
Thymelaeaceae

Most of us grow one or two daphnes and we think we know what they are, but the genus keeps coming up with surprises. When you consider where they come from it is no wonder that they are so diverse. Daphnes are found across Europe in hedgerows and on mountains, in northern Africa, all through Asia, and into the Pacific. Most are fragrant, and, not surprisingly, these species are the most popular with gardeners. Daphnes vary from hardy and deciduous to more tender evergreens, and they range in height from tiny groundhuggers to tall, upright columns. They are often mountain plants and all of them need good drainage. Most of them like acidic or neutral soil but there are notable exceptions, like *Daphne mezereum*. Ideally they should be given open, free-draining, acidic soil with plenty of compost or humus, but in reality they grow just as well in much tougher conditions and will cope with heavy soils and clays.

One word of advice: if you are ever tempted to shift a daphne, don't, because it will not survive. They have thick, wiry roots without much fibrous material and they hate being moved, so make sure you find the ideal spot to plant them the first time. Buy healthy-looking potted plants for success.

It is hard to be specific about sun, shade or hardiness because of the variation within the genus; we just have to take them one by one.

> *Daphne* = from Greek mythology; Daphne was a beautiful maiden pursued by Apollo. She prayed to Zeus to save her and he changed her into a tree.

Daphne bholua
HIMALAYAN DAPHNE

Daphne bholua tends to be semi-evergreen in mild climates, whereas ideally you want a clone that drops all of its leaves so you can better admire the flowers. However, the fruity sweet scent is so stunning that your neighbors will be coming around to find out what it is and so, even if some of the flowers are hidden by foliage, you will still have its amazing fragrance wafting around your garden. Flowers vary from pure white to pinky purple and often have purple-backed petals with a white interior. They appear very early in spring or even in winter.

An upright, variable shrub from the mountains of Nepal, where it grows on dry slopes, it is usually a tall, upright plant with flexible stems in soft browns and grays. Somehow the stems are prominent even when the bush is covered in leaves. It can be evergreen or deciduous, depending on your climate, and also the seedling variation. After three or four years you will have a small, upright bush about head high, with a neat, columnar habit. After that it gradually loses its shape and becomes more tumbled in its appearance. It grows equally well in a formal small garden and in shady woodland.

The plant seems happy enough in wet or dry climates and in acidic or alkaline ground. From Nepal, Assam and Bhutan. Height 10 ft (3 m) x width 3 ft (1 m). ZONE 8.

Good clones include a very hardy deciduous form called **'Gurkha'**, with rosy pink and purple flowers. **'Jacqueline Postill'** is a semi-evergreen form with large, intensely fragrant, purple-pink flowers. There are pure white clones available, too.

> *Bholua* = a native Nepalese name for this plant.

Daphne x burkwoodii
(D. caucasica x D. cneorum)

A small, deciduous shrub with an upright habit and long, narrow leaves. Plant in a sunny, well-drained border near the house where you can appreciate the sweet fragrance of the flowers. The starry blooms are pinky purple with white faces fading to pink, appearing in rounded heads in late spring. Some of the leaves have a bluish gray hue and there are variegated forms with creamy edges to the leaf, such as **'Carol Mackie'** and **'Variegata'**. Height x width 2–3 ft (60 cm–1 m). ZONE 5.

There is a very good form available called **'Somerset'**, which is a larger plant with bigger purple-pink flowers. Height 5 ft (1.5 m) x width 3 ft (1 m).

> *Burkwoodii* = after the plant breeder Albert Burkwood (1888–1951).

Above: *Daphne* x *burkwoodii* 'Variegata'

Left: *Daphne bholua*

Daphne cneorum
GARLAND FLOWER

This dense little hummock has small, dark green, box-like leaves and small, crowded heads of soap-scented, rosy red flowers in late spring. The garland flower is found in the mountains of Europe growing naturally on rocky, dry, chalky soil, and it is not an easy plant to please in the garden. It is an ideal little shrub for a rock garden or small border as it is semi-prostrate. It does need a cool climate to do well and is temperamental in warm regions. Originates from central and southern Europe. Height 1 ft (30 cm) x width 2 ft (60 cm). ZONES 5 TO 8.

The clones **'Eximia'** and **'Major'** have bigger flowers and larger leaves. There is also a pure white form, **'Alba'**, and a silvery variegated form **'Variegata'**. For all, height 1 ft (30 cm) x width 2 ft (60 cm).

> *Cneorum* = garland.

Daphne genkwa
LILAC DAPHNE

A very unusual plant that is not at all how we imagine daphnes should look. The flowers are not unlike lilac blossoms (*Syringa*) in shape and color, but only have a slight musky fragrance. Nearly all daphnes are neat, tidy bushes, and this one is definitely wayward. It creeps underground, popping up where it pleases and forming a straggly, untidy bush. That said, the bush may be ungainly but the flowers are irresistible. No gardener can ignore blue flowers and here is a fine example. The smoky blue-lavender flowers on the bare stems in spring are tantalizing, and once you have seen them you have to own the plant. The flowers in clusters of twos, threes and fours are long, thin tubes with four large petals splayed out at the end. Flower clusters are at every node of last year's growth, so the more vigorous the plant, the more blooms next spring. You do see variations, as some forms have darker, more richly colored flowers, although no named clones seem to be around. The narrow, green leaves have a purple tinge.

This is a tricky plant to grow and to propagate. Nursery owners have to propagate by root cuttings, an old-fashioned and time-consuming method. In the garden the plant likes a free root run and good drainage to allow it to creep underground and take over more space. A semi-shaded slope seems the ideal spot, but be prepared to wait for it to establish itself and don't be surprised if you don't succeed the first time. Find a semi-shady, free-draining spot out of the wind and weather and hope for the best. It grows on limestone cliffs in China, as do many rhododendrons, but then in cultivation insists on acidic or neutral soil. Given a warm summer climate, it will cope with very cold winters, as you would expect of a native to Korea and northern China. Height 2 ft (60 cm) x width 3 ft (1 m). ZONE 6.

Genkwa = a Korean name for the plant.

Daphne mezereum
FEBRUARY DAPHNE, MEZEREON

A neat little deciduous shrub that doesn't rate a second glance in summer, but is worth its weight in gold in winter. In fact, it needs cold winters to perform. It is one of the first plants to emerge from winter, bearing strident, purple-red, over-ripe-scented flowers. This upright bush has thin, flexible stems and bright green, thin, narrow leaves, often arranged near the tips of the stems with bare stem beneath. The flowers vary from white to pale pink, rich pink and cerise-red, depending on the clone. Flowers are clustered around the top portion of stem, almost like a cone, and are followed by bright red, poisonous berries. It needs limy or neutral soil and a cool climate. A native of Europe, from the Caucasus through to Asia Minor, and therefore very hardy. Height x width 3 ft (1 m). ZONES 5 TO 8.

There are numerous red and white clones and some with larger flowers, as in **'Grandiflora'**, where the flowers are larger

Right: *Daphne genkwa*

Left: *Daphne odora*

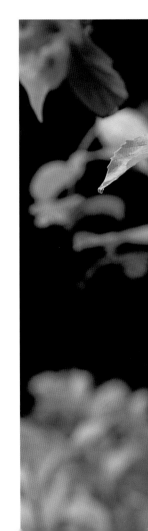

and a darker, richer color on a much bigger bush. Height x width 5 ft (1.5 m).

Mezereum = from "mazaryum," an old Persian name.

Daphne odora
WINTER DAPHNE

In many ways *Daphne odora* is the perfect plant: it has tough, wind-hardy leaves in a rich dark green that look good all year; it is small with a tidy habit and so fits into any garden; and best of all, it has showy flowers with a fabulous fruity scent. Plant breeders are always trying to create this type of garden specimen. This plant even grows in pots. It thrives in acidic or neutral, free-draining soil, but also contends with less-than-perfect conditions, often growing in poor, cold soils at the base of a wall. It does prefer a moist climate, but I have seen it grow well in dry regions.

The clusters of pink flowers have a hint of purple and these flower heads at the tip of each stem appear very early in spring, which can be a problem in very cold regions as the blooms may be frost-damaged. The scent is heavenly, so I suggest you plant one alongside the house so that you get a whiff every time you walk by. It is also a very good cut-flower, albeit small. The tiny twigs of bloom last several weeks and perfume your home.

The only fly in the ointment is the possibility of the plant having a virus. The virus is spread at the propagation stage, when plants are grown from cuttings. Such plants tend to become pale and anemic, the leaves often have a slight twist and the overall leaf cover is less dense. It is possible to buy plants free of known viruses, and it is worth a few dollars more for the peace of mind of having a clean, healthy plant. *D. odora* is from China and Japan. Height x width 2–3 ft (60 cm–1 m). ZONE 7.

There is a white form, **'Alba'**, with a very clean appearance; and variegated forms, **'Aureomarginata'**, with a gold margin, and **'Variegata'**, which has a creamy white margin. **'Leucanthe'** is a more vigorous form with a clean appearance, but the creamy white flowers are less showy and less fragrant.

Odora = fragrant.

Dipelta

Caprifoliaceae

This is a genus of four species of deciduous shrubs from central and western China. Their peeling bark is particularly attractive and they bear charming tubular to bell-shaped fragrant flowers in delicate shades of white and pink.

Di = two; *pelte* = a shield, referring to the bracts protecting the seed case.

Dipelta floribunda

Dipelta floribunda is free-flowering, and sprays can be cut for a vase—but best of all, they are fragrant. The sweet, pollen-like fragrance is delightful. When Ernest Wilson (1876–1930) found this plant growing in the wilds of western China in 1902 he also found *Kolkwitzia amabilis*. The *Dipelta* was very common in the region and so he expected it to be easy to propagate, while the *Kolkwitzia* was scarce and he assumed it would be difficult to reproduce.

It turned out to be the other way round and *Dipelta* has remained a scarce shrub because it is very hard to propagate. Layering seems to be the only sure way and that is not easy because it is such a stiff, erect shrub. Having said that, this plant is a choice specimen, and worth hunting for. You will need lots of room as it grows quite tall and needs plenty of sideways space, too, because it fills out in time. It is not a plant for tidy people or suburban gardens because it is always a bit ungainly. *D. floribunda* is a big, upright, deciduous shrub with strong, erect stems. In fact, it has multi-stemmed, almost cane-like, growths with long, thin strips of pale brown bark constantly peeling away.

It is an unwieldy-looking character and should ideally be planted right at the back of a border where the untidy base of the shrub can be hidden by showier plants. The arching sprays of blossom tumbling out of the uppermost branches are more appealing if the less attractive parts of the plant are concealed. Another alternative is to thin out the weaker shoots at the base and make a feature of the peeling trunks.

The flowers appear in late spring and have a *Weigela* look about them, which is understandable as they are related. Each flower is light pink on the outside of the tube and an orange-yellow in the throat, reminiscent of tiny foxgloves. The seed cases have two wings or bracts protecting the seed case. The neat, simple leaves are thin and slightly hairy. Being delicate, they will not tolerate winds and the plant needs sunlight and shelter to perform at its best. Plenty of warm sun is needed to ripen the wood for maximum flowering. It will grow in semi-shade but will not flower without sun. It is very tolerant of cold winters.

An easy-care plant, it will grow in any soil including lime or chalk, and in very dry regions as well. Despite being difficult to propagate, it is quite happy being moved, and quite large specimens can be transplanted from open ground.

If the plant becomes too woody and messy, you can prune it drastically, bearing in mind that it is the older stems that bear the most bloom. Like *Deutzia*, *Dipelta floribunda* flowers on short side-

Above: *Dipelta floribunda*

growths from last summer's wood, so if it is pruned before it blooms you will be removing a large part of the floral display. A good rule with all shrubs is to prune immediately after flowering, as this gives the plant almost 12 months to grow more stems for next year's flowers. If you were to prune everything in winter, as some people advocate, then you would be destroying the floral display of many fine shrubs such as *Chaenomeles* and *Weigela*. From China. Height 10 ft (3 m) x width 6 ft (2 m). ZONE 6.

Floribunda = with an abundance of flowers.

Dipelta ventricosa

In spring, this species has soft rosy purple flowers with an orange throat and a delicate honey fragrance. Another species collected by Ernest Wilson (1876–1930) in China. Height x width 6 ft (2 m). ZONE 6.

Ventricosa = swollen or inflated, referring to the swollen bases of the flowers.

Dipelta yunnanensis

A rare shrub forming a smaller, more manageable plant that grows fairly upright. The pale, soft yellow flowers have a hint of pink on the outside of the tube and orange in the throat. The scent is subtle and sweet. It often flowers before the other species in early spring and is not such a tall, gaunt specimen as *Dipelta floribunda*, so it appeals more to those of us with a tidy nature.

First discovered by Abbé Delavay (1838–1895) in 1886, and introduced by George Forrest (1873–1932) in 1910. Height x width 6 ft (2 m). ZONE 7.

Yunnanensis = from Yunnan Province, western China.

Left: *Dipelta yunnanensis*

Drimys

Winteraceae

*D*rimys are a group of peppery smelling, evergreen plants from the Southern Hemisphere. You may encounter two of these suitable for the garden and they are worth seeking out. Botanists and gardeners have had difficulty with this group of plants for different reasons. Systematic botanists have included the genus with the magnolia family at times, which means it is one of the most ancient of flowering plants. Also, several members of the genus have been split off into the related *Pseudowintera* genus containing two very handsome New Zealand shrubs. Gardeners have had trouble with *Drimys*, too, because they can be difficult to establish in the garden. They are quite exacting about what they want, insisting on a cool, moist climate and very good drainage.

Drimys = from Greek "drimus," meaning acrid, referring to the taste of the bark.

Drimys lanceolata, syn *D. aromatica*
PEPPER TREE

A striking evergreen shrub with red stems and a hint of red in the leaves. Tiny, white flowers in clusters won't have you dashing for the camera to record the event, but the plant has a lovely peppery scent to compensate. The overall effect is a tidy, upright, reddish bronze bush that we would all be happy to have in our garden if only it were easier to grow. One of the reasons for its obscurity is the difficulty in establishing it as a garden plant. It is one of those Southern Hemisphere plants that is quite likely to turn up its toes and die soon after planting, even if it survives the initial test. At no stage do you feel secure that you have a plant for life. It seems that root rots, such as phytophthora, attack the plant after heavy rain, especially when it is followed by a period of hot, humid weather. So, if possible, give it perfect drainage and perhaps a little shade. I know from experience that the new trichopel fungi will help keep it in good health. Trichopel is a new defense against disease for gardeners. It is based on naturally occurring fungi that fill up the space in a plant's vascular system and don't allow the bad fungi to enter or flourish. It can be applied with a plug after you drill a hole in the stem or as granules into the soil. The cool forests of South Australia and Tasmania are home for this rare treasure. Height x width 6 ft (2 m). ZONES 8 TO 9.

Lanceolata = spear-shaped; *aromatica* = having an aroma, referring to the leaves.

Drimys winteri, syn *Wintera aromatica*
WINTER'S BARK

A large shrub, eventually becoming a dense, evergreen tree, and by far the most well known of the genus. Clusters of ivory-white, waxy flowers like cake decorations appear in summertime. While the flowers are quite pretty, the best thing about them is their delightful jasmine scent. Winter's bark is very happy in some climates and inexplicably refuses to grow in others (possibly because of root rot problems). The overall appearance seems quite tidy as it forms a tall, upright, rounded-top bush or small tree. Closer inspection reveals that it often has an ungainly habit as the branches grow out horizontally, and then drop with the weight before reaching up again towards the sun, so many have a swoop or bow. The leaves are a waxy, dark green above and glaucous blue beneath, and the plant could be mistaken for a rhododendron at first glance. It is reasonably wind-tolerant and sometimes happy in

a wet, maritime climate, but to increase the chances of success it would be best to choose a site with really good drainage. Cool winters and cool summers probably make the best weather combination. It was introduced into cultivation in 1827, but known since 1578 when Captain Winter, sailing in one of Francis Drake's expeditions, used the bitter, aromatic bark to cure scurvy after months without green vegetables. Native to Mexico, Chile and Argentina. Height x width 6–30 ft (2–10 m). ZONES 8 TO 9.

There are several named forms, including **Drimys winteri andina**. This very handsome dwarf form from Chile and Argentina is worth seeking out but hard to obtain, as nurseries find it difficult to build up any number because of the slow growth rate. It is a dense, evergreen bush about 3–4 ft (1–1.2 m) high and wide. **D. w. latifolia** is the form most often encountered in British and Irish gardens. It has broader leaves than other forms and tends to keep a tidier habit. Height 30 ft (10 m) x width 20 ft (6 m).

Winteri = for Captain Winter.

Above: *Drimys winteri*

Edgeworthia

Edgeworthia papyrifera, syn E. chrysantha
PAPER BUSH, MONEY BUSH
Thymelaeaceae

This plant is a herald of spring and known as the "money bush." For many years it was grown in Japan to supply high quality paper for banknotes. Either way it pays handsome dividends. The scent is of rich honey and it is worth siting a bush near your door to appreciate the flowers in an otherwise quiet time of the year. Cut a few blooms for a small vase to enjoy the scent indoors also. Display them on their own, as they are unique and do not blend easily with other flowers. The stems are full of stringy fiber and are so flexible the twigs can be tied in knots without breaking.

For gardeners it earns its keep by bravely flowering when most other shrubs are still tucked up inside their buds. It is always one of the first to show off in the spring—sometimes even in the depths of winter, depending on the zone. When the pom-poms of flowers appear on the bare stems, they look like a peculiar top-knot, as if someone has tied them on. Few of the flower heads sit properly on top of the thick, chunky stems. Most of the blooms sit sideways or hang down from the topmost point. The strongest stems have two or even three flower clusters. These tightly packed heads have new flowers opening every day in pure gold, fading to pale yellow, then to cream and eventually off-white. If you catch the heads at the halfway stage, the outer flowers will have dried to brown leaving a circle of pale yellow flowers with a ring of fresh gold within, and finally in the center are all the pointed buds, ready to open. The flowers open over a period of three weeks or more, so there is plenty of time to enjoy them.

Everything about this bush is a little odd. The stems are thick and almost fleshy-looking. Even the bark is chameleon-like, appearing gray one day and dark brown the next. The bare bush has a unique, rubbery "constructed" look in winter, and the stems have prominent scars where previous leaves have fallen off. In summer, when the bush is covered in leaves, it is a handsome dome of silvery green foliage. The leaves emerge in late spring and are initially covered in velvety silver down making them irresistible to touch.

In many ways this is an easy-care shrub. Find the perfect spot, plant it and forget about it. It is not going to die or be

Above: *Edgeworthia papyrifera*

worried by pests, and it is not fussy about soil type, growing in heavy or light, acidic or alkaline conditions. It has stringy roots like a daphne and so, while it is easily transplanted from pots into the ground, it won't like being shifted at a later date. I know of gardeners who have successfully moved an *Edgeworthia*, but the plants often will not survive such treatment. Digging them up is like digging through rope because of the fiber in the roots. So, make your choice of the best place in the garden and stick to your decision.

While considered to be tender in temperate island climates like Britain's, it is perfectly hardy in more severe climates. As with many other plants, the hot summers ripen the wood, enabling it to survive the colder winters. While it eventually reaches head-height, a 10-year-old bush will only be 3 ft (1 m), so it will fit easily into any garden. You can prune it to improve the shape if you wish, and it will even recover from a drastic pruning. The flowers and the leaves tend to get smaller every year as the plant loses that juvenile vigor.

The bush is native to China but has been cultivated in Japan for so long it is associated more with that country. Height x width 6 ft (2 m). ZONE 6.

The form **'Grandiflora'** has larger flowers, bigger leaves and thicker trunks and rarely exceeds 3 ft (1 m) high and wide. There is also a reddish-orange flowered variety.

Edgeworthia = after M.P. Edgeworth (1812–1881), a botanist employed by the East India Company; *papyrifera* = paper-making.

Edgeworthia gardneri
This exciting shrub is new to cultivation. The flowers appear in late winter or early spring, just below the top circle of leaves. These yellow pom-poms hang on a thread like a ball of string. Although the flowers are bright they are not always obvious and

Above: *Edgeworthia gardneri*

are often hidden among the foliage. They are honey-scented, but the leaves have a stronger "pharmaceutical" smell. A taller, more open bush than its Chinese cousin, it is also evergreen, or almost so, and is more tender. It forms a big bush with gray-green stems and finger-sized leaves. The flexible stems wave in the breeze like bamboo.

Edgeworthia gardneri grows quickly and can become tall and sparse. Cut it back to low stumps in the spring and in no time you will have a dense, tidy bush. It grows naturally on well-drained slopes, but will manage wet or heavy soil and even grows in swamps. Wet or dry climates are fine. Shelter from wind is needed to keep the bush looking its best. Full sun or semi-shade is fine. Native to Nepal. Height x width 10–12 ft (3–4 m). ZONE 8.

Gardneri = after Edward Gardner, a British resident at the court of Nepal in the early 1800s.

Elaeocarpus

Elaeocarpus reticulatus, syn E. cyaneus
FRINGE FLOWER
Elaeocarpaceae

This just has to be one of the best garden trees ever created. *Elaeocarpus reticulatus* is literally festooned with thousands of white bell-shaped flowers in early summer. Move in close to admire the pretty, frilled edge on the bottom of each bell and you are bound to notice the lovely almond scent. A tree covered in flowers, with the attendant bees, is a joy to behold. There is an equally beautiful pink-flowered version and both give rise to brilliant aquamarine-turquoise fruits the size of a small olive. It is tidy, upright and evergreen, and knowing that it won't get too big makes it the perfect suburban garden tree. Neat, narrow, leathery leaves are very dark green with a distinct white, crusty surface: the overall effect is of a nicely rounded, small, dark tree.

Best grown in full sun, this plant will, however, grow under high or distant shade. It's not too fussy about soil or acidity, although it grows best in a moist, well-drained site, and it is capable of handling moderate droughts once established. Plant it directly in your chosen site from a potted or open-ground plant and it will grow quite speedily, giving you a shade tree in five years. The leaves are tough and can tolerate breezy sites, although cold winters can be a problem and it does like warm summers. Its native home is eastern Australia and the genus is widespread, with siblings growing in places as diverse as New Zealand, Thailand and Korea. Height x width 15 ft (5 m). ZONE 8 OR 9.

Elaeo or *elaia* = olive; *carpus* = fruit; *reticulatus* = finely netted.

Another attractive species is **Elaeocarpus dentatus** (hinau), a lovely New Zealand native. It is similar to *E. reticulatus*, with long, thin, dark green leaves and masses of small, white, almond-scented, bell-shaped flowers. Height x width 15 ft (5 m). ZONE 9.

Dentatus = toothed leaves.

Eriostemon

Eriostemon myoporoides
LONG-LEAF WAXFLOWER
Rutaceae

Eriostemon is a handy evergreen shrub with some winning ways. It tolerates drought and wind and yet thrives in wet regions, too. But best of all, it is scented. In fact the whole bush is perfumed with a tangy, almost medicinal, smell. The

Below: *Elaeocarpus reticulatus*

Right: *Eriostemon myoporoides*

white, starry, early-spring flowers have a sharp lemon scent, although it is hard to tell because the whole bush emits such a strong smell. It is typical of the lemon family to have a strong scent, and its pungency is reminiscent of household cleaners. In fact, the odor is very much like the related rue, *Ruta graveolens*.

The long, narrow leaves are tough and leathery in a dull gray-green, again similar to rue. The young stems are the same color, and both leaves and stems have little bumps or glands containing the scent oil. Pale pink buds open to starry white flowers, like little *Choisya*, and they are attractive as cut-flowers.

The plant has a tidy, internal structure, branching into three or four new stems at an almost perfect 45° angle. Older plants occasionally become open and may need a trim to keep them bushy and neat. Give them a light haircut just after flowering. It is naturally a small, dense bush.

Eriostemon will grow in full sun or part-shade. It grows in poor soils, including clays or rocky ground, and, surprisingly, handles poor drainage. It is tough enough to cope with some frost and is therefore a useful addition to borders around the house where constant draughts kill off less-hardy plants. Although it is not in anyone's "top ten shrubs" list, it is effective and you won't regret planting one. It is also ideal for smaller town gardens as it is easily accommodated. There is a selected form, **'Profusion'**, which is a denser, more compact-looking bush with more flowers, as the form name suggests. Native to Australia. Height 4 ft (1.2 m) x width 5 ft (1.5 m). ZONE 8 OR 9.

Erio = Greek "eryon," meaning woolly, referring to the orange stamens (*stemon*) which are woolly; *myoporoides* = like a *Myoporum*, a group of trees from New Zealand and Australia.

Eucryphia

Eucryphiaceae

Blessed with exquisitely sweetly scented, white flowers *Eucryphia* are potential crowd-stoppers. See a bush laden with flowers in high summer and you will want to have one of your own. Part of their appeal is their upright, tidy nature and the fact that they are mainly evergreen. I say "mainly," because in cooler climates some are deciduous. The bold, upright habit is useful for a statement plant and can be used to define or screen a garden. Eucryphias respond to pruning, but this is rarely necessary as they have a good, natural columnar shape. Opposite leaves and opposite stems help to give them a neat appearance. They have a pleasing collection of leaf shapes, sizes and colors, and the leaves of all the species have a slightly viscous or sticky feel to them. They look tough but appearances can be deceptive, as they are sensitive to heavy frosts.

The four-petaled, white flowers have a prominent boss of brown stamens in the middle of the flower, reminiscent of single camellias. Most of them flower from mid to late summer when, apart from hydrangeas, there are few flowering shrubs to be seen. Some gardeners complain that the blooms are short-lived and the plants often take years to come into flower, but I think anything this stunning is worth waiting for. Meanwhile, as you wait for the flowers, the attractive foliage will give you satisfaction.

Left: *Eucryphia cordifolia*

Eucryphias prefer a moist climate free of severe frosts and a well-drained, acidic soil, such as would suit rhododendrons, although some will tolerate lime. They are a bit fussy but it is worth taking the trouble to please them. Ideally choose a sunny, sheltered slope where the roots are shaded and undisturbed because they don't like gardeners digging around them. A mulch is best for weed control and for keeping the roots cool. If you decide to move one, the fibrous root system makes this fairly easy. They do not like wet feet, poor drainage or very strong winds, and are susceptible to some fertilizers (they are best left unfed). They are tolerant of moderately cold winters, but they are not happy in warm, muggy climates and seem prone to root rot when it is humid. Likewise, they are not easy to grow in flat, suburban gardens because of the drainage issue. In hot or dry regions give them some high shade for protection from the hot, baking sun. There are no pests apart from occasional leaf-roller caterpillar or scale—never enough to deter you from growing the plant or have you reaching for the spray can.

Eu = from Greek for well; *kruphios* = covered, referring to the way the sepals form a cap to cover the flower.

Eucryphia cordifolia
ULMO

This evergreen Chilean native has masses of white, sugary-smelling flowers in late summer. The flowers are open and cup-shaped, similar in size to a large *Hypericum*. The central boss of reddish stamens adds a touch of drama. The leaves are wavy-edged, grayish, thick and chunky, and slightly downy beneath. You might almost think it was an evergreen oak on first inspection. It is not as tough and hardy as it looks and will be killed by heavy

frosts. The plant comes from the cooler, wetter parts of Chile and needs a moist climate as well as good drainage. Coping with limy soil and wind, the bush has an upright, columnar habit. Height 20–25 ft (6–8 m) x width 6–10 ft (2–3 m). ZONE 8.

Cordifolia = heart-shaped leaves.

Eucryphia glutinosa
HARDY EUCRYPHIA

Another Chilean native, this time with very dark, almost blackish green, pinnate leaves, so you would be hard-pressed to see any connection with the previous species until it flowered. The white flowers are very similar, appearing in late summer, but they don't last very long and the overall display is brief (although they have a sweet honey fragrance). There are double forms available but I think the single flowers have more charm.

The plant is naturally evergreen and will be so in warm regions. In cooler climates the rose-like leaves turn to beautiful, rich orange-red before dropping in the fall. It is possibly the most cold-hardy species. Unfortunately the leaves are popular with caterpillars and beetles and these pests are capable of ruining the appearance of the bush. Height 20–30 ft (6–10 m) x width 6–10 ft (2–3 m). ZONE 8.

Glutinosa = sticky.

Eucryphia lucida
TASMANIAN LEATHERWOOD

Superb almond-scented flowers smother this bush in summer. The flat, white flowers are about an inch (2.5 cm) across with red-tipped stamens prominent in the middle. *Eucryphia lucida* is a narrow, upright, evergreen shrub that in its native Tasmania is a

Above: *Eucryphia lucida*

Eucryphia moorei
PINKWOOD

A small, upright, evergreen tree or shrub from southeast Australia. This one is different again from others in the genus. The plant has masses of small (1 in/2.5 cm across), pure white, sweetly perfumed flowers in late summer. The leaves are thin and grayish, but this time they are pinnate, with 5–13 leaflets in light grayish green. The leaflets have an unusual pattern, as they grow progressively bigger from the base with the terminal leaflet the largest of all. In many ways this is one of the more garden-worthy of the eucryphias as it is a smaller bush, tolerates more sun, and is not as fussy about site and soil conditions. It is tender, however. Height 10–15 ft (3–5 m) x width 3–6 ft (1–2 m). ZONE 9.

Moorei = from Charles Moore, who discovered the plant in the 1860s.

Eucryphia x nymansensis

The highlight of this plant is the mass of large, white, waxy, honey-scented flowers in late summer that has the whole bush humming with bees. It is the most effective species for cooler Northern Hemisphere gardens. It is a hybrid of *E. cordifolia* x *E. glutinosa* and seems to encapsulate the best of both parents, being hardier than either. The bush often has single as well as compound leaves in glossy dark green. It is evergreen or mostly so. Its *E. cordifolia* parentage allows the plant to be grown in limy soil as well as acidic soil, although like most eucryphias it prefers a good, free-draining site with cool roots and not too heavy frosts. Height 20–30 ft (6–10 m) x 6–10 ft (2–3 m). ZONE 8.

Nymansensis = after the Nymans Garden in Sussex, England, where the first cross was made.

60 ft (20 m) tree. Don't panic, it is not going to grow that big in your garden. In cultivation it is typically a small, upright bush.

It seems every *Eucryphia* has different leaves and *E. lucida* has long, narrow leaves that are gray and shiny. Native to Tasmania, Australia. Height 10–15 ft (3–5 m) x width 3–10 ft (1–3 m). ZONE 8.

'Pink Cloud' is a new form with dainty pink flowers.

Lucida = shining, referring to the leaves.

'Mount Usher' is a hybrid named for the famous garden in Ireland where it was raised. This form shows more *E. cordifolia* parentage, and the white fragrant flowers are often double. Height 20–30 ft (6–10 m) x width 6–10 ft (2–3 m).

Right: *Eucryphia moorei*

'**Nymansay**', a dense, upright shrub or small tree, is laden with single, white, fragrant flowers in late summer. Its dark, glossy leaves are inherited from *E. glutinosa*, although it looks more lush. It can be tricky to please. Height 20–30 ft (6–10 m) x width 6–10 ft (2–3 m).

E. x intermedia is a cross between *E. glutinosa* and *E. lucida*. Some leaves are singles and some are in threes. It is evergreen in a greenish gray, dull finish. Fragrant white flowers. '**Rostrevor**' is a named form from this cross with fragrant white flowers late in the summer. It can also be tricky to grow. Height 15–20 ft (5–6 m) x width 6–10 ft (2–3 m).

Intermedia = intermediate between two species.

Eurya, syn Cleyera

Eurya japonica
Theaceae

This is a small group of evergreen shrubs related to camellias, and usually only one species is seen in gardens, namely *Eurya japonica*. It is not going to be at the top of your shopping list, but it does have some endearing features. In summer, masses of flowers are produced but you probably wouldn't know if it wasn't for their scent because they are so small—tiny greenish yellow, almost opaque, cups. The scent is too strong for some tastes, but is pleasant enough if you don't get

Above: *Eucryphia* x *nymansensis* 'Nymansay'

Left: *Eurya japonica* and *Weigela subsessilis*

too close. Plant it about 3 ft (a meter or so) back from a path. It is a small, neat, upright bush with thick, fleshy leaves about the size of *Camellia japonica*, so it is useful as a screening plant or for any spot where you might use a conifer for shape and density. It looks great up against a wall, where its neat outline and color variation throughout the seasons are highlighted. In summer the leaves have a khaki, greenish brown appearance and in winter they take on rich purple to red-wine shades. This plant is very easy to grow, coping with poor soils such as clay and sand, as long as it is acidic or neutral. *Eurya* handles hot, dry, cold, drafty, windy, cold or shady conditions. It is sometimes considered tender in a fluctuating climate, but any plant native to Korea and northern China is reasonably hardy in regions with hot summers. From Korea, Japan and China. Height 6–10 ft (2–3 m) x 3–6 ft (1–2 m). ZONE 7.

'Variegata' has leaves with a paler center and dark green on the outside.

Eurya = broad, possibly referring to the broad petals (it certainly does not mean large in this context); *japonica* = from Japan.

Fothergilla

Hamamelidaceae

At first glance a *Fothergilla* is nothing special—the leaves look a bit like a hazel or witch hazel and spring brings the white pom-pom flowers. But move closer and you will notice that they are perfumed with sweet, sugary nectar. The flowers are not exactly spectacular and in some climates they appear after the leaves and so tend to be lost among the foliage. These unusual flowers have no petals and are really just a ball of white stamens. Both species in this genus are well-behaved, easily grown shrubs and the more you see of them, the more you will appreciate their attributes. For instance, they fit into any small garden with their tidy, rounded shape. Although they look neat throughout summer, the highlights are spring and fall. At fall time you will be even more amazed when the leaves light up with their hot colors, ranging from golds and oranges through to reds and scarlet, and lasting for weeks at a time. Although they will grow in shade, they need to be in full sun to present their scintillating fall colors.

These tough little deciduous shrubs will survive very cold winters. They are rarely attacked by pests or diseases, apart from an occasional caterpillar. Acidic soil is essential and in theory they will grow in moist sites, but like so many plants from the U.S.A. that are found naturally in wet sites, they do not easily adapt to wetness when planted in a garden setting. They like a moist climate and don't like to dry out, but other than that, any climate from cold zone 5 through to sub-tropical zone 10 will suit them. They are quite robust, but appreciate some shelter, and are easy enough to transplant at any size during winter. They can sometimes be grown from suckers. Both species hail from the Appalachian Mountains. The nearest relatives are *Hamamelis*, or witch hazel.

Fothergilla = after Dr. John Fothergill (1712–1780), an English gardener who gathered the finest collection of plants from the U.S.A. in the early days of the British colony.

Fothergilla gardenii
DWARF FOTHERGILLA, WITCH ALDER

A small, deciduous shrub that fits easily into any garden. It can sucker a little and forms a thicket of upright twigs. In spring, the tips of each stem have round, white, bottlebrush flowers with a fabulous scent of sweet, sugary nectar. This species tends to grow

Right: *Fothergilla gardenii*

in the wetter plains while *Fothergilla major* is found more often in the mountains. It lives in moist sites in the wild and yet prefers good drainage in a garden situation. Choose acidic soil with organic matter, as you would for rhododendrons. Terrific fall colors. Native to southeast U.S.A. Height x width 3 ft (1 m). ZONE 5.

Gardenii = after Dr. Alexander Garden (1728–1791) of Charleston, South Carolina, who discovered it in 1765.

The variety **'Blue Mist'** has very different, glaucous blue foliage that looks great all summer, but the yellow fall color is rather ordinary. It is not as cold-hardy as the species, but has the same flowers and fragrance. Height x width 3 ft (1 m).

Fothergilla major, syn *F. monticola*
LARGE FOTHERGILLA, MOUNTAIN WITCH ALDER

A taller species with a mass of erect stems forming a dense, twiggy bush. The flowers are bigger, white pom-poms up to 2 in (5 cm) long and nicely fragrant in the typical sweet, honeyish style. Fall leaves turn a delightful mix of orange, yellow and scarlet. Native to the Allegheny Mountains, from Virginia to South Carolina. Height 5–10 ft (1.5–3 m) x width 6 ft (2 m). ZONE 5.

'Mount Airy' is probably the best clone available, with large flowers and a good, strong, healthy constitution. A reliable shrub, flowering well every spring and with consistent fall color. Height 5–10 ft (1.5–3 m) x width 6 ft (2 m). ZONE 4.

Major = greater.

Gardenia

GARDENIA
Rubiaceae

This is an exciting group of evergreen shrubs with glossy, dark green leaves and exotically scented blooms. Gardenias are widely distributed, throughout China, tropical Asia and parts of Africa (although a lot of the African species are now in their own genus called *Rothmannia*).

During the Victorian era gardenia blooms were very popular in a lady's corsage, and what perfume could beat it? The fragrance puts many modern perfumes to shame, and it is still the basis of some. The large, white, scented flowers usually only last a day but they come in such numbers that this doesn't matter. They fade to a creamy color before they fall.

Florists' types are usually *Gardenia jasminoides* var *fortuneana* or *G. j.* var *veitchii*, both of which are hardier than the straight species. In Europe these Chinese natives were first cultivated in greenhouses, but many will tolerate light frosts if they get enough summer heat. Many people are more familiar with them as houseplants than as garden plants.

Gardenias have undeservedly gained a reputation for being difficult to grow, but they are surprisingly easy. Be sure to give them a rich, acidic soil with plenty of humus and adequate moisture. They like lots of water during any dry spells to fend off attacks by thrips, red spider mites and whitefly. All these pests

Left: *Fothergilla major*

Above: *Gardenia jasminoides* 'Radicans'

Gardenia jasminoides, syn G. augusta, G. florida, G. grandiflora

CAPE JASMINE, COMMON GARDENIA

Jasmine by name, but not by nature. The only thing this tidy shrub has in common with jasmine is the rich, sweet scent of the flowers. Given a warm, sheltered site it will grow in frosty regions to zone 7, but is usually thought of as a tender plant. The pretty, pure white flowers appear all summer long and you sometimes see it used as a flowering hedge. The flowers have shiny, waxy petals and a clean, rounded shape with radiating petals. It is easy to see why they were popular in corsages as the flowers are a good size without being blowzy: they have a nice neat shape and last several hours without water, and have, of course, a marvelous scent. The plant is native to China and Japan. Height 3–10 ft (1–3 m) x width 3–6 ft (1–2 m). ZONE 7, with warm, sheltered site.

This species is usually grown in its double form, first introduced from China by Robert Fortune (1812–1880) in 1854. Some good double forms, all of which have white flowers, include: **'Florida'**, **'Professor Pucci'**, which has larger double flowers (4 in/10 cm across) and is hardier to the cold. If you want a smaller, spreading version try **'Radicans'**. Height 2–3 ft (0.6–1 m) x width 3–4 ft (1–1.2 m). **'Mystery'**, with its bigger leaves and large, shiny flowers, is popular, too. Height 3 ft (1 m) x width 3–10 ft (1–3 m).

Jasminoides = like a jasmine.

Genista

BROOM
Fabaceae

A mixture of hardy and half-hardy, deciduous shrubs, *Genista* not only look beautiful but the flowers bear a sweet, syrupy scent as well. Ranging from small, tumbling plants to tall, upright shrubs, most have yellow, pea-like flowers in spring or early summer, with a few whites ones for spice. All of them have a sweet, almost intoxicating, scent, like fortified wine. They are often thought of as being evergreen because the stems are usually green and can photosynthesize. We hardly ever notice the leaves clinging to the stems in spring and they seem to fall off at the first sign of stress from drought or cold. Some *Genista* are spiny, too, while the related *Cytisus* and *Spartium* never have spines. Given the right conditions they are very easy to grow and really love hot, dry, sunny environments. They thrive on neglect, or rather on poor, dry, sandy sites. Even clay is acceptable if the drainage is good. Most tolerate alkaline soils and seem to hate fertilizer or rich soils.

As with many legume shrubs, they have deep, searching roots like wire that are difficult to cut with a spade, as they seem to absorb any impact. Once planted you should not try to move them as they will almost certainly die. Ideally plant from pots when still quite small: make sure you unravel any spiraling roots. Grow your own plants from seeds, but chip or soak in very hot water to germinate immediately. Leave the seeds to soak overnight before sowing, allowing them to absorb the water they need. If you sow hard, dry seeds they may take months or even years to germinate.

The plants grow quickly, often too fast, becoming rangy and leggy. Pruning can be useful to keep them compact and possibly extend the life of the plant. If you remove two-thirds of last

like hot, dry conditions and a daily blast with the hose will easily reduce their numbers. Gardenias do well in coastal locations away from strong winds, and in other areas with a moist atmosphere. The ideal setting is filtered sunlight through some leafy trees during the heat of summer, and preferably fully exposed to sunlight in winter.

You often see them looking parched and hungry, with anemic, yellow leaves. Chlorosis, as this condition is called, can have various causes: perhaps the soil has too much lime, or the situation is too wet, or too cold, or the plant is lacking magnesium or iron. A small handful of Epsom salts (magnesium sulfate) or iron sulfate will restore the lush green look. Both chemicals are dangerous to the plant in large doses and so "little and often" should be the motto. Transplant them from pots in the winter or spring, or you can grow them in tubs in cold regions. It is unlikely they will ever need pruning, but they will cope, should you ever feel the need to trim them.

Gardenia = after Dr Alexander Garden (1728–1791), a plant aficionado based in Charleston who encouraged plant hunters like John Bartram and was a correspondent of Carl Linnaeus (1707–1778).

Above and right: *Genista* 'Yellow Imp'

year's growth immediately after flowering the plant stays bushy and is less likely to be blown over. Leggy, top-heavy plants are more prone to wind-rock.

Genista = an old Latin name.

Genista monosperma
BRIDALVEIL BROOM

This is a large, fast-growing shrub and, without a doubt, the most beautiful of the genus. The sweet, sugary scent of the flowers is the most attractive feature and the whole bush has a very airy, open habit. Covered in white down, the new spring stems waft in the

Above: *Genista monosperma*

wind, looking like smoke. The common name confirms its light, ephemeral appearance. Gradually the soft down falls off and the smooth stems appear, a striated silver and green. Clusters of white, pea-like flowers bloom in early spring, or even in winter in warm zones. Each one has a prominent red calyx and this hint of red makes them sparkle. Surprisingly, it is a very good cut-flower.

Genista monosperma thrives in poor soil and hot sun, although it will take sideways shade from high trees or buildings. The more of a summer baking it gets, the more winter-hardy it will be. The plant is wind-tolerant, but the whole bush may be blown over in a storm as it is not always strong at the base. It is often short-lived, as is the way with so many brooms. It pays to have another plant coming on as a replacement; they are easily germinated from seed. It is very difficult to transplant, so it is best to plant young seedlings from a pot or sow the seed in the garden where you want your plant to be. It is not an easy plant to blend with others, but if you can provide a dark backdrop or even a dark ground cover, it looks far more exciting.

Native of Spain and Portugal, where it is a common sight on roadsides. Height 10 ft (3 m) x width 6 ft (2 m). ZONE 8 OR 9.

Monosperma = with a single seed.

Genista lydia
LYDIA WOODWAXEN

A neat dome of a plant, ideal for rock gardens and the tops of walls, where it can trail down. A mass of golden-yellow flowers cover the bush in late spring and the sweet scent is a lovely bonus. Native to the Mediterranean and Balkans regions. Height x width 2–3 ft (0.6–1 m). ZONE 6.

Lydia = from Lydia, in western Turkey.

Genista pilosa
SILKY LEAF WOODWAXEN

Another great ground cover bush, laden with bright yellow flowers in spring that are mead- or honey-scented. It naturally forms a low, dense mound but may need trimming to keep it tidy all year. From western and central Europe. Height x width 2–3 ft (0.6–1 m). ZONE 6.

Two good named clones are: **'Vancouver Gold'**, with a profusion of golden-yellow flowers (height 18 in/45 cm), and **'Lemon Spreader'** (syn 'Yellow Spreader') with lemon yellow blooms (height 12 in/30 cm).

Pilosa = downy.

Genista tenera

One of several *Genista* from the Canary Islands and Madeira, off the coast of Spain. The yellow flowers are so profuse that the bush starts to tumble and arch with the weight of the fragrant, honey-ish blooms. They have a cloying quality, like sweet liqueur. Typical of the genus, this species loves hot sun and dry places, but luckily for us it will cope with moist climates, given good drainage. In fact, they are very easy-care shrubs and seem to flower on and on into late spring and early summer. The gray-green leaves seem longer-lasting and more substantial than most foliage. Height 6 ft (2 m) x width 5 ft (1.5 m). ZONE 8.

Two varieties to try are: **'Golden Shower'**, with its mass of scented yellow flowers in spring, and **'Yellow Imp'**, which has clustered heads of golden yellow flowers lasting for weeks. For both, height 6 ft (2 m) x width 5 ft (1.5 m).

Tenera = soft or tender.

Hamamelis

WITCH HAZEL
Hamamelidaceae

A better name for this plant might be "winter cheer," because there is no more cheerful sight on a late winter's day than a *Hamamelis* in flower. Venture out into the garden and inhale the flowers' perfume—sweet in the air but astringent at close quarters—cut a branch or two and retreat to your warm, cozy fireside, clutching your treasure. It will last for two weeks or more in a vase and you can enjoy the intriguing "curly wig" flowers and scent at close range. The petals look like thin strips of paper attached to a small red cup or calyx. Most blooms appear on bare branches in late winter or early spring. Amazingly, the flowers are untouched by cold and during a frost the petals simply roll up until it is warm enough for them to unfurl.

These long-lived, obliging plants just get better and better every year. Plant them near a path so the early flowers can be admired, or find a dark green backdrop, such as a conifer hedge, to highlight the spidery flowers; against a sunny background they tend to disappear.

Best in leafy, loamy soil, witch hazels will take second-best conditions and still perform well. They prefer a cool, deep, well-drained soil and don't like to dry out, so give them a mulch or provide irrigation in hot climates. Acidic or neutral soil is their preference but they will grow in lime. Full sun is ideal—the more sun, the more flowers and the healthier the plants, but perhaps a little shade is preferable in hot, dry regions. No pests seem to bother them. They are tough, coping with extreme cold, moderate winds and even city pollution.

The best forms and cultivars are grafted, usually onto *H. virginiana* seedling rootstocks. *Hamamelis* are not easy to grow from cuttings and so, although more complicated, the grafting technique is the best option. But it does mean the plants are more expensive. Having grown or bought plants, they are easy enough to transplant during the dormant winter season and even large specimens can be shifted with ease. No pruning is necessary other than to cut stems of flowers in wintertime. They tend to be thicket-type plants with multiple leaders. If space is at a premium, you can train them fan-style against a wall, or you can prune the bushes like grapevines, cutting last year's growth back to two buds after flowering. This makes them bushier and much more compact.

The American *H. virginiana* was called "witch hazel" because the early settlers used "y"-shaped sticks for water divining in the same way the English use *Corylus* or hazel, and the leaves of both genera are very similar. Native Americans used the plant medicinally, and it is still used today on wounds, bites and ulcers. This is another of those plant genera linking eastern America with China and Japan.

Hamamelis = "hama," Greek word meaning together; "mela," meaning fruit, so bearing fruit and flowers at the same time. The seeds take a year to mature and so appear at the same time as the flowers.

Hamamelis x intermedia

This is a name given to a group of hybrids between *Hamamelis mollis* and *H. japonica*, where either one can be the female parent. The flowers are wavy with a subtle, sugary scent (not as strong as *H. mollis* for example). Some popular garden hybrids include: **'Arnold Promise'**, with bright yellow, fragrant flowers on a strong, upright plant; **'Diane'**, one of the best reds and the fall colors are good, too; **'Jelena'** with warm orange-colored flowers and good fall colors. It also tends toward a spreading habit unless trained. For all, height 10–12 ft (3–4 m) x width 6–10 ft (2–3 m). ZONE 5.

Intermedia = mid-way between the parents.

Hamamelis japonica
JAPANESE WITCH HAZEL

A big, deciduous shrub that during the depths of winter has sweetly scented yellow flowers with twisty petals on the bare stems. They have an amazing ability to produce more flowers if the first ones are damaged by frost. Smooth and shiny leaves take on good fall colors. Native to Japan. Height x width 10–12 ft (3–4 m). ZONE 4.

There is a form called **Hamamelis japonica var *flavopurpurascens***, with a pronounced red base to the flower. It is a parent of many red and orange cultivars. Height x width 10–12 ft (3–4 m).

Japonica = from Japan.

Hamamelis mollis
CHINESE WITCH HAZEL

This is the best species for gardens, with the ability to bloom when very young. Good in a vase or in the garden, the delightfully sugar-

Above: *Hamamelis* x *intermedia* 'Jelena'

Above: *Hamamelis mollis* 'Pallida'

scented, rich yellow flowers are much more fragrant than other species. Also, the petals are straight and not curly like some.

Initially a multi-trunked, upright shrub, it becomes rather untidy and wide-spreading in time. Pruning for shape or removing stems for cut-flowers will be necessary to maintain a good framework.

This plant was first introduced from China by Charles Maries (1851–1902) in 1879 and then languished at the Veitch nursery in England for 20 years before being spotted by a curator from Kew and promoted. E.H. Wilson (1876–1930) also introduced it again about this time, rekindling interest in the plant. From China. Height x width 10–12 ft (3–4 m). ZONE 5.

Mollis = downy and soft.

'Brevipetala' has shorter petals, as the name "brevipetala" suggests. From a distance, the flowers look orange, but the petals are actually deep yellow and it is the sepals that are orange. The saccharine scent is a wonderful bonus. Height 10–12 ft (3–4 m) x width 6–10 ft (2–3 m).

'Coombe Wood' is Charles Maries's original form and was named after the Coombe Wood nursery owned by the Veitch family in England. It is a more spreading shrub than the usual upright form we see. It has lovely strongly-scented flowers in bright yellow, and yellow fall leaves. Height 12 ft (4 m) x width 15 ft (5 m).

'Pallida' is probably the most common form seen in gardens, with large, yellow, scented flowers and good fall colors. Height 10–12 ft (3–4 m) x width 6–10 ft (2–3 m).

Hamamelis vernalis
VERNAL WITCH HAZEL, OZARK WITCH HAZEL
A bush with smaller flowers than most other witch hazels, but they still have a good syrupy scent. Being more compact than other species, it is a good choice for smaller gardens. Flower colors include yellow, orange and red and excellent fall colors are golds, orange and butter-yellow. Native to southern and central U.S.A. 'Red Imp' is an especially dark red selection and 'Sandra' is a great foliage plant, with purple-tinged new leaves and brilliant orange and red fall colors. The bright yellow fragrant flowers are pretty, too. For all, height x width 6 ft (2 m). ZONE 4.

Vernalis = of the spring.

Hoheria

LACEBARK, HOUHERE
Malvaceae

*H*oheria are a small group of evergreen and semi-evergreen or deciduous plants from New Zealand. The plants are related to the hibiscus and their flowers all have a pleasant honey scent. They are dense, upright shrubs with a neat, conical habit, becoming small trees after many years. Although naturally evergreen, they are often deciduous in cooler climates and seem capable of surviving frosts. In colder regions they are often grown as a wall shrub to give them extra protection from the cold.

Pale green or gray-green leaves are somewhat like a birch in outline but much thicker, almost fleshy. These handsome leaves provide a backdrop for the clusters of showy white flowers that look a bit like *Eucryphia* or white buttercups. Some of them have more starry flowers with gaps between the petals. They are easy plants to grow, with no special soil requirements. *Hoheria* tolerate moist or dry, acidic or alkaline places. Be careful to spread the roots when planting them out from pots, as they are prone to blow over in the early years. If you prune them to keep them compact and bushy, they are less likely to topple; or you could give them a stake for a year or two. Once established they are quite wind-hardy. A sunny site is best but any well-lit place will suffice, and they do look good planted against a wall.

An occasional light trim is acceptable and they even cope with heavy pruning. The young stems are smooth and brown, and underneath the bark is a fine latticework of fibrous strands. This accounts for the common name of lacebark, as the strands were braided to make rope. Sometimes the plants are attacked by unsightly galls and life-threatening stem borers.

Hoheria = from a local Maori word "houhere," meaning to tie or bind.

Hoheria glabrata
This plant has the most attractive leaves and flowers in the genus, with large handsome, shiny leaves and cup-shaped flowers 1½ in (4 cm) across with a heavy, syrupy scent. This is an unusual tree in its native New Zealand, as it is deciduous in a country where

Right: *Hoheria populnea*

virtually every native tree is evergreen. Being deciduous, it is hardier to cold. Height 20 ft (6 m) x width 12 ft (4 m). ZONE 7.

Glabrata = glabrus or without hairs.

Hoheria lyallii, syn Plagianthus lyallii
LACEBARK

This can be evergreen or deciduous, depending on the coldness of the winters. The sweetly scented white flowers appear in mid-summer and are very similar to *Hoheria glabrata*. The leaves are covered in tiny hairs, while those of *H. glabrata* are smooth. New Zealand native. Height 20 ft (6 m) x width 12 ft (4 m). ZONE 7 OR 8.

Lyalli = from David Lyall (1817–1895), a surgeon and naturalist who sailed to New Zealand and the Antarctic.

Hoheria populnea
LACEBARK

A fast-growing, upright tree from the North Island of New Zealand, where it grows on forest margins and in open fields. Like so many New Zealand natives it has a divaricating juvenile form, or a tangle of stems. Masses of starry, pure white, honey-scented flowers cover the tree and at times hide the foliage in late summer and early fall. The flowers are sometimes cup-shaped and in some cases the petals are reflexed. In the young stage it is a very erect, fast-growing shrub, almost like an Italian poplar, becoming spread out later. The shiny, evergreen leaves are like a cross between a birch and a poplar. Sometime it is semi-deciduous in a cooler region, and has been known to survive cold winters in England. It is also tolerant of drought and very alkaline soils. From New Zealand. Height 20 ft (6 m) x width 12 ft (4 m). ZONE 8.

If you wish to retain the fragrant white flowers but want to try some varieties with different leaf color, look for **'Alba Variegata'**, which has pink new leaves, fading to become two-tone with creamy white margins around the green center. **'Purpurea'** tends to be more purple beneath the leaf and **'Variegata'** is a pleasing variegation with dark green leaves painted in the middle with uneven blotches of gold and paler green, creating a tricolor effect. For all, height 20 ft (6 m) x width 12 ft (4 m).

Populnea = poplar-like.

Above: *Hoheria sexstylosa*

Hoheria sexstylosa, syn H. populnea var lanceolata
RIBBONWOOD

Really just a thinner, smaller-leafed version of *Hoheria populnea*. In summer, it is smothered in starry white flowers that have a very fragrant, rich honey smell. It has a very upright habit and is seemingly more cold-hardy than other species. The foliage often has a weeping habit accentuated by the narrow leaves. New Zealand native. Height 20 ft (6 m) x width 12 ft (4 m). ZONE 7.

Sexstylosa = six styles.

Hovenia

Hovenia dulcis
JAPANESE RAISIN TREE
Rhamnaceae

An attractive deciduous tree with fist-sized heads of tiny yellow-green flowers appearing in upright corymbs (flower stalks) in the axils of the outer leaves in midsummer. While not much to look at, they are nicely fragrant in a fruity way and as a bonus the stems of the corymb are edible, thus the name Japanese raisin tree. I always think of it as

Left: *Hovenia dulcis*

small because it has a light, airy feel but in fact it tends to grow tall and thin with an exaggerated upright look. The structure is quite tidy with sparse branches coming off at a classic 45° angle. If you can look at it from above you will admire the beautiful glossy leaves, similar in size and shape to cherry leaves. You will be impressed, too, with the rich golden-yellow fall color. The stems are smooth and brown, and older trunks have a neat, smooth, gray or white, or sometimes blackish green, appearance, reminiscent of some *Styrax*.

Choose a sheltered position for this tree as it will not tolerate strong winds—the leaves are easily torn and the tree is not super-strong. Ideally, plant one in a gully where you can look down on the leaves and flowers. It needs good drainage and reasonable soil but is not fussy regarding acidity. It grows quite happily in wet or dry climates and is drought-tolerant. Full sun or good light is essential, as it becomes sparse in the shade. It won't need pruning unless damaged by wind, though it responds quite well because of the thin bark. Trees with thin bark regenerate easily from pruning cuts. Height 50 ft (15 m) x width 15 ft (5 m). *H. dulcis* comes from China. ZONE 6.

Hovenia = after David ten Hove (1724–1787), an Amsterdam senator who helped finance Carl Peter Thunberg's plant-hunting trips to South Africa and Japan; *dulcis* = sweet.

Above: *Hydrangea aspera* var *villosa*

Hydrangea

HYDRANGEA
Hydrangeaceae

You may be surprised to find that some hydrangeas are scented. Several of the *Hydrangea macrophylla* cultivars have a delightful spring fragrance, rather like may or hawthorn. And it is not just a delicate air or essence, but a robust and pleasant spring smell. Only the lacecap types of hydrangeas, with their true flowers in the center, have a scent. The mophead blooms, which are made up of sterile flowers, have no scent at all.

Hydra = water; *angeion* = vessel.

Hydrangea aspera var *villosa*, syn H. *villosa*
Hydrangea aspera var *villosa* is the usual form found in gardens, with long, pointed, rough and hairy leaves. Beautiful, pinky mauve, lacecap flowers with a subtle hawthorn-like scent sit nicely on the outer stems from midsummer onwards. This tough deciduous plant survives hot and dry conditions better than most hydrangeas and is very easy to grow as long as it gets enough sunlight. An ideal shrub for the back of a summer border. From China. Height x width 4–12 ft (1.2–4 m). ZONE 6.

Aspera = rough; *villosa* = hairy.

Hydrangea heteromalla
Big, bold shrubs with long, pointed leaves covered in bristly hairs. The big, lacecap flowers appear on the tips of the stems in late summer, with white or near-white outer petals and smoky mauve true flowers within, with a delicious fruity scent. Only suitable for big woodland gardens because of their size. Native to China. Height 10 ft (3 m) x width 12 ft (4 m). ZONE 6.

Heteromalla = having an unequal or varied shape.

Left: *Hydrangea heteromalla*

77

Hydrangea macrophylla

BIGLEAF HYDRANGEA, FLORIST'S HYDRANGEA

These tough, deciduous shrubs are probably at their best in coastal regions, but will grow in sheltered inland gardens. Many of the lacecaps have a scent of spring, like may or hawthorn flowers. Valuable for their big, blowzy blooms and their ability to grow in inhospitable sites such as in shade or damp, almost boggy, ground. Likewise, they are capable of growing in extremes of acidity or limestone ground, with acidic soil giving blue flowers and alkaline soil making the flowers pink or red. Most are very wind-hardy with a few, such as 'Seafoam', able to cope with severe winds. From Japan. Height x width 3–8 ft (1–2.5 m). ZONE 6.

'Nightingale' (syn 'Nachtigall') is surely the best-ever blue lacecap in cornflower blue. One of the many Teller series of lacecaps from Switzerland, named after European birds.

'Opuloides' is a compact bush and therefore ideal for small gardens. Dainty heads of white petals surround a smoky blue interior. They have a nice may-like scent. Happy in sun or shade. Height x width 4 ft (1.2 m).

'Rotschwanz' (syn 'Redstart') is another Teller lacecap with fluted flowers, each with a twist like a propeller. It has rich, dark red, fragrant flowers.

'Seafoam' has big, bold, glossy leaves topped with wide-spreading lacecaps, white on the outside with intense blue, true flowers within. The may-like scent is fabulous. It will grow in dense shade as well as in very windy spots. Height x width 6 ft (2 m).

Macrophylla = with a big leaf.

Hydrangea paniculata

Hydrangea paniculata has big white cones of flower and gardeners are most familiar with the dense triangular heads of the pee-gee hydrangea or *H. paniculata* 'Grandiflora'. While all of them are perfumed with a delicate pollen scent, those with more true flowers have much more scent than the sterile-headed ones. This deciduous species is probably the toughest in terms of cold, but it is, however, the most fragile in windy places, so shelter is the first priority. All of them have creamy white heads, mostly in late

Above: *Hydrangea macrophylla* 'Nightingale'

Above: *Hydrangea paniculata* 'Tardiva'

'Tardiva' is a new cultivar and flowers very late in the summer, so extending the usual flowering season. It has a compact head of sterile and true creamy white flowers. Height x width 6 ft (2 m).

Paniculata = with panicles or clusters.

Hymenosporum

Hymenosporum flavum
AUSTRALIAN FRANGIPANI
Pittosporaceae

A beautiful, evergreen, fast-growing, small tree with simple, glossy green leaves. The clusters of rich honey-scented flowers appear in late spring and each flat-topped flower comes from a spiraled tube. They open as a creamy shade and intensify in color to gold. The tree's tall, narrow habit can sometimes literally be its downfall, as it can grow too fast and be toppled by storms. If it does get blown over, simply resurrect it, cut all the branches off, leaving a stump, and it will quickly regenerate into a bushier plant. Without any trimming it has a handsome, open, tier-like habit but as it gets taller it takes the lovely fragrant flowers further from our noses. It is an exciting plant in narrow borders next to a building as its leaves and overall shape are handsome all year. Apart from potential wind damage, it is an easy plant to grow, accepting almost any soil and sun or part-shade. Wet or dry climates are fine, but not hard frosts. From Australia. Height 15 ft (5 m) x width 6 ft (2 m). ZONE 9.

summer and they are an ideal addition to any sunny border. Originates in Russia, China and Japan. Height x width 5–10 ft (1.5–3 m). ZONE 3.

'Kyushu' is a smaller version with dainty, upright heads with a mix of true and sterile flowers. It is ideal for town gardens as it stays neat and upright. Introduced from Kyushu Island in Japan by Collingwood Ingram (1880–1981). Height x width 5 ft (1.5 m).

Right:
Hymenosporum flavum

'Golden Nugget' is an exciting new form, growing low, dense and bushy. It has a perfect dome of foliage and, being lower, the scented flowers are more accessible. Height 3 ft (1 m) x width 4 ft (1.2 m). ZONE 9.

Hymenosporum = membrane/seeds; *flavum* = yellow.

Illicium

STAR ANISE
Illiciaceae

A small group of evergreen trees and shrubs related to magnolias and once regarded as a part of that family. Although they are not very well known in the garden world, the cooks among you will know the "star anise," *Illicium verum*. These plants have a fragrance that varies from peppery to spicy, and fruity to port wine. Gardeners should experiment more with *Illicium*. They are often regarded as tender and gardening writers usually demand a lot when they are unsure of how tough a plant is. We say it needs good drainage, moist soil, shelter and so on—in other words, perfect conditions. For instance, my first *I. floridanum* I treasured and coddled, as one does with a new prize. I was advised it needed shade to thrive, and it is still struggling in the shade. A year or so later I came across a group of them absolutely laden with flowers at the Biltmore Estate in North Carolina. There they were, in scorching hot sun all day and a picture of health. I am now convinced that all *Illicium* will grow and eventually thrive in full sun. They may look a little sad for a while, but will flower more profusely and eventually surpass a shaded specimen. If in doubt, mulch the roots to keep them cool and moist.

Everyone agrees that *Illicium* are free of pests and disease, and I think before long they will be regarded as easy-care in every other way, too. The leaves are tough and glossy and so they should be wind-hardy. Despite calls for peaty, loamy, acidic conditions, they will handle alkaline soils, although a feed of iron sulfate won't go amiss to keep them green. They also cope with less-than-perfect drainage and clay soils.

These plants are easy to transplant from pots when young. I have never tried moving a larger plant and am inclined to think they wouldn't like being shifted. You can prune them, but it is hardly necessary as they have a good natural rounded shape.

The flowering season seems to vary according to climate. Mostly they flower in spring but it can be midwinter or even late summer. In hotter regions the flowering is often delayed.

Illicium = to attract, from Latin "illicio," meaning allure.

Illicium anisatum

FALSE ANISE, CHINESE ANISE

A fine evergreen shrub with lovely glossy leaves in bright apple-green. It sparkles every day of the year, as if someone has polished it. The wavy-edged leaves are pointed and have a spicy, peppery fragrance. Take a leaf, crush it in your hands and you will be transported to the exotic Spice Islands (as in the spice trade of the 1800s). It has that mystic, spicy quality about it. Small, creamy flowers appear in midwinter and are useful for indoor decoration. They have a strong peppery scent. Depending on the clone, it is a very large, upright shrub or small tree, suitable for full sun, but it

Left: *Illicium henryi*

Above: *Illicium anisatum*

results in failure and it is sensible to give them better treatment in your garden. The tough, waxy leaves have a bronzy purple hue. The plant generally grows to head-height, with a rounded, slightly "tumbly" habit. **'Halley's Comet'** is a selected clone with bright red, fragrant flowers, making it a much more garden-worthy plant. Native to southeastern U.S.A. Height 5–6 ft (1.5–2 m) x width 6 ft (2 m). ZONE 7.

> *Floridanum* = from Florida. An easy name to remember as it came from Florida in the 1770s, courtesy of John and William Bartram.

Illicium henryi

Named for Augustine Henry, an Irishman who worked in China as a customs agent in the late 19th century and an avid collector of plants in his spare time. The starry flowers can be pink to soft cherry red, depending on the clone, and they have a pleasant fruity fragrance. An upright shrub with rich green, glossy leaves, it is happy in sun or shade and generally easy to grow. From China. Height 5 ft (1.5 m) x width 3 ft (1 m). ZONE 7.

> *Henryi* = named for Augustine Henry (1857–1930).

Illicium majus

This new introduction from China has small, opaque to pinkish-red, fragrant flowers in spring, a rigid, upright habit with a strong branch structure, and dull gray-green leaves. Height 6 ft (2 m) x width 5 ft (1.5 m). ZONE 7.

> *Majus* = large.

Illicium mexicanum

A native of Mexico, with large, fragrant, russet red flowers in spring/early summer and handsome, dark green leaves. Height x width 6 ft (2 m). ZONE 7.

> *Mexicanum* = from Mexico.

Illicium parviflorum

A popular, upright bush from the swampy coastal areas of Georgia and Florida. It has creamy yellow scented flowers in spring. Height 6–12 ft (2–4 m) x width 3–6 ft (1–2 m). ZONE 8 OR 9.

> *Parviflorum* = small, or not many, flowers.

can be a small, compact, dense evergreen, happy in shade. In fact, it is one of the best foliage plants around for shade as it always looking lush and healthy.

In cooler regions, the flowers sensibly wait for spring. The small, starry flowers are quite well presented but, being an evergreen, it is easy to pass them by. Because they are a creamy color, they do not make a great contrast with the leaves and are easily missed. Native to Japan and Korea, it is often classed as a zone 8 plant, but Korean gardeners tell me it is much hardier than that. Height 3–15 ft (1–5 m) x width 5–10 ft (1.5–3 m). ZONE 6.

'Pink Stars' is a very lovely clone with lots of fragrant, blush-pink flowers that are larger than usual.

> *Anisatum* = anise-scented, referring to the leaves.

Illicium floridanum
POISON BAY, PURPLE ANISE

The flowers of the poison bay are a rich red-wine color and, to continue the wine analogy, they have a heady port-like fragrance. These starry flowers can be as much as 2 in (6 cm) across but are usually only half this size. In the wild, this plant grows in swamps, but in a garden setting it does best in free-draining soil. This is true of so many shrubs from the southeastern U.S.A. that occur naturally in wet places. Trying to imitate those conditions usually

Itea

SWEETSPIRE
Iteaceae or Grossulariaceae

A small group of shrubs, some of which are deciduous and some evergreen, with honey-scented flowers. Most are East Asian, with one representative from the Appalachians (yet another plant link between Asia and the eastern U.S.A.). They need regular moisture and rich soil. Some of them grow naturally in swampy ground so in general they don't like to dry out. Providing a mulch or irrigation will improve your chances of success. This is not to imply that they are difficult to grow—they just don't like drought. In other regards they are not fussy about the kind of soil they are given. They will grow in full sun and in shade but are most comfortable in a sheltered site away from the worst winds. *Itea* can be a bit temperamental at planting time, so take care when you remove them from the pot. They seem prone to root rots in the first few months after planting, but if they get through this difficult phase they will flourish for years. You can prune them after flowering if you

Left: *Itea ilicifolia*

wish, and they do have a somewhat ungainly habit so a tidy-up may be in order. I have never tried to move an established plant and I am loath to do so, considering they don't even like the transition from pot to soil.

Itea = willow.

Itea ilicifolia
HOLLYLEAF SWEETSPIRE

Many a passerby will think this plant is a holly and not give it a second glance. But if you should see it in flower, you might look again. In fact, it will probably stop you in your tracks to see this so-called "holly" covered in 12 in (30 cm) racemes of flowers. Move close and the sweet honey scent will have you coming back for more. Each individual bloom is a miniature yellowy green star, but the effect of hundreds of them in a long, tail-like raceme is enchanting. It looks as if someone has draped Christmas tree streamers over the bush in midsummer. The stems are a blackish color, and smooth, and the leaves are dark green and toothed, giving them their similarity with evergreen hollies. Introduced in the 1890s from central China by Augustine Henry (1857–1930). Height x width 6–10 ft (2–3 m). ZONE 8.

Ilicifolia = related to the *Ilex*, or holly-like.

Itea virginica
VIRGINIA SWEETSPIRE

The honey-like fragrance of the Virginia sweetspire is just one of its attractive features. Nothing beats the thrill of seeing a garden plant you know well growing in the wild. This is one of those

Left: *Itea virginica*

plants for me. At Merchants Millpond in the northeastern corner of North Carolina, while visiting a *Taxodium* swamp, we came across this little beauty growing in dense shade in very wet ground and in full flower. This day held two surprises: I never expected to find *Taxodium* swamps so far north or this little *Itea* growing in a shady swamp. I have always loved this plant and all the more so since that day. It is a neat, little, arching shrub, sending up new canes from the center of the bush. Smooth, glossy stems take on a reddish tinge if exposed to sunlight, as do the petioles, or stalks, on the alternate leaves. The leaves vary in size. In late spring, long racemes decorate the bush. Creamy white flowers open progressively from base to tip, extending the flowering period, with a nice honey scent to top them off. In the garden, I recommend a better site than swampy shade. Sun or partial shade with reasonable drainage is likely to give more success. Being deciduous, the plant is quite cold hardy and some years has attractive reddish fall foliage.

Itea virginica is not perhaps in the front runners of first-class shrubs, but it does have charm and looks great on a bank. The combination of flower, scent and fall color wins a place in gardens large and small. Native to the southeastern U.S.A. Height x width 3–5 ft (1–1.5 m). ZONE 6.

Virginica = from Virginia

Itea yunnanensis

An evergreen bush, very similar to *Itea ilicifolia*, although the leaves are slightly larger and the sweetly scented, dull white flowers are in longer racemes. Discovered by Abbé Delavay (1838–1895) in 1883, then introduced from Yunnan, China, in 1908 by George Forrest (1873–1932). Height x width 10 ft (3 m). ZONES 7 TO 9.

Yunnanensis = from Yunnan Province in western China.

Jasminum

JASMINE, JESSAMINE
Oleaceae

"Yasmin" was the name given to this plant in ancient Persia (now Iran) and jasmines were most likely part of the Hanging Gardens of Babylon in neighboring Iraq. Most (but not all) jasmines have scented flowers and some are so exquisite they are grown specifically for the perfume industry. Like so many plants in the olive family, they are easy to please regarding soil conditions. If you garden on chalk or limestone, or hard and heavy clay, then look carefully at all the plants in the olive, rose or legume families as the chances are they will cope with your less-than-perfect soil.

Most jasmines are climbers, with a few more shrubby species. The shrubby species usually have yellow flowers and are hardier. They are more or less deciduous in cold places but their green stems create the illusion of being evergreen.

All of the jasmines can cope with hard, packed, heavy soils as well as light sand, and they are indifferent to acidity. They can also tolerate drought, hot sun and generally whatever we care to throw at them. Their waxy leaves make them tolerant of wind as well.

Regarding the climbers, most are scented, some deliciously so, and nearly all of them have white flowers. Jasmines are of course renowned for their scent; they are used for perfume and

Right: *Jasminum humile*

to flavor things such as jasmine tea, and we often describe a scent as being a "jasmine."

Most climbers like their roots in shade and their tops emerging into sunlight. Jasmines thrive in this scenario but it is not as crucial as it is with some other climbers. Their ability to grow in shade can be useful if you want to keep the frost off the more tender species.

Jasmines are easy to transplant when young and it is unlikely that you will ever try to move an established plant. Prune them any way you fancy for shape, or perhaps thin the climbers after flowering.

Jasminum = from the Persian name "yasmin."

Jasminum azoricum
LEMON-SCENTED JASMINE
To my mind this is one of the best jasmines because of its strong lemon scent and because it has a tidier look about it than the other species. The stems and leaves are the same dark green and it rarely looks cluttered, as some of its relatives can. Grow this jasmine if you can for its beautiful scent and for its tendency to flower all year. In cooler climates, this fine evergreen flowers from late summer into fall and has delicious, pure white, starry flowers. It is not very hardy, so find a warm spot for it. From its name you might think this climber hails from the Azores but it is actually from the Madeiras in the Atlantic off northwest Africa, and so it copes well with wind. Height 10 ft (3 m). ZONE 9.

Azoricum = from the Azores.

Jasminum beesianum
ROSY JASMINE
One of the more hardy species that, although semi-evergreen in warm climates (zone 9 and above), is deciduous where it is cold. Rosy jasmine actually performs better in cool regions. Typical jasmine flower clusters appear in late spring to early summer and are cologne-scented. It is unusual in that the flowers are pink or rosy cerise rather than the usual white or yellow of other jasmines. A useful trellis plant. Height 10 ft (3 m). ZONE 8.

Beesianum = after the Bees Nursery in England, to where George Forrest (1873–1932) brought the plant from western China.

Jasminum humile
ITALIAN YELLOW JASMINE
Despite its common name, this bushy, semi-evergreen plant is a native of China and the Himalayas. It was introduced into England by Italian nurserymen during the orangery craze in Victorian England, when every stately home or residence had to have a conservatory with citrus trees.

This jasmine forms a spreading, semi-evergreen shrub with shiny green leaves and bright yellow flowers that have an elusive scent from early spring to late summer. The variety **'Revolutum'** has larger leaves and is more evergreen, as opposed to semi-evergreen. It is more tender, but compensates with larger flowers (1 in/2.5 cm across) and a fruity fragrance. Height 10 ft (3 m) x width 10–12 ft (3–4 m). ZONE 7 OR 8.

Humile = low.

Jasminum mesnyi, syn J. primulinum
PRIMROSE JASMINE
Another yellow-flowered evergreen shrub with arching stems. These can be trained to make a wall shrub or left alone in the open to be a sprawling plant, if your climate is warm enough. It has deep green leaves with three leaflets and showy yellow flowers

with an elusive perfume in late winter and early spring. Sometimes the flowers are semi-double. It seems this plant does not set seed, being sent back from China as whole plants by E.H. Wilson (1876–1930) in 1900 for the Veitch nursery in England. He found the plant in a Chinese garden and it has never been found in the wild. An ideal shrub for covering large slopes, where its arching habit creates a lovely effect. Height x width 6–10 ft (2–3 m). ZONE 8.

Mesnyi = after William Mesny, a general in the Chinese Imperial Army.

Jasminum officinale
COMMON WHITE JASMINE, POET'S JASMINE
Probably the hardiest of the climbing jasmines, it has been grown in old cottage gardens for centuries. It is a vigorous climber, showing off lovely fragrant white blooms from midsummer until the first frost. This is the highly fragrant jasmine used in the perfume industry, and we often describe things as being jasmine-scented. It grows naturally from China right through the length of the Himalayas and beyond. Height x width 10–15 ft (3–5 m). ZONE 6.

Officinale = useful or medicinal.

Jasminum polyanthum
CHINESE JASMINE
This plant sums up gardening for me: half the world's gardeners wish they had a climate warm enough to please this plant and the other half wish they could get rid of it. Love it or hate it, it is hard

Above: *Jasminum polyanthum*

not to be entranced by the delicious fruity scent when the red buds open to a mass of pure white flowers in spring. There must be a few fortunate gardeners who have just the right combination of warmth to grow it and cold to keep it in check.

We once moved to a house with a jasmine growing on a trellis next to the house. When I finally got around to pruning this seemingly rampant vine I discovered that some stems had grown under the house and were about to emerge on the far side of the building and, as I climbed higher, I found parallel stems growing through the attic with the same mission. Exactly how these stems could grow for 60 ft (20 m) or more without light is a mystery, but it gives you some idea of how vigorous this plant can be. Its twining stems can climb trellis or trees and I have seen it used as an exciting ground cover in gardens with unlimited space.

This evergreen was discovered in China in 1883 by Père Delavay (1838–1895). Height 60 ft (20 m). ZONE 8 OR 9.

Polyanthum = with many flowers or free-flowering.

Jasminum sambac

ARABIAN JASMINE, PIKAKE
This evergreen climber is very tender and needs a hot climate, but the big, white flowers and the fabulous jasmine scent make it worth the effort of finding a warm spot for it. It is a spreading, waist-high bush and can be grown in containers. Origin is not certain, possibly tropical Asia. Height 3 ft (1 m) x width 6 ft (2 m). ZONE 10.

Sambac = old Arabic name.

Above: *Kalmia latifolia*

Kalmia

Kalmia latifolia

CALICO BUSH, MOUNTAIN LAUREL
Ericaceae

If you get close to a calico bush in flower you will notice that the blooms are quite pleasantly scented, like perfumed soap. Dark, glossy, evergreen leaves and a neat, rounded shape mean these shrubs look good all year, and in late spring they are stunning, with a mantle of soft, popsicle-pink, fragrant flowers. The fist-sized heads are made up of dozens of flowers, each one looking like the underside of an opened umbrella. These flowers are right on top of the plant and so they are very pretty—they seem to last for weeks without becoming battered or bruised. *Kalmia latifolia* is the state flower for Pennsylvania.

These wonderful plants can be tricky to grow and gardeners have their theories about what they need in order to do well. Some would say they need a cold climate but I would disagree, having seen them growing magnificently in a zone 9 region. Others say they must have a high rainfall, yet I have seen them survive extreme droughts year after year once established. Nearly everybody agrees that *Kalmia* needs an acidic, free-draining soil, which is understandable as they grow naturally in

Above: *Kalmia latifolia* 'Carousel'

the woods and on mountaintops all through the eastern U.S.A. Like most mountain plants, they are wind-hardy, but that is no reason to plant yours in a tough, windy site if you want it to thrive. They will endure extreme cold, being one of the hardiest evergreen shrubs.

In the wild, *K. latifolia* grows in full sun as well as in the shade of big forest trees. I have seen them growing out of the cracks in huge rock faces, which probably accounts for their drought tolerance. For a garden setting I would suggest full sun if you have a cool climate, because they do seem to need summer heat to do well. Typically they become very neat, rounded shrubs and it is unlikely that you will ever need to prune them, although they will survive if you do. These plants are easy to transplant because, like the related rhododendrons, they have a mass of fibrous roots near the surface. Plants with this kind of root system love to have a mulch of bark or woodchips to keep the roots cool and suppress the weeds. Avoid any cultivation, as it damages the surface roots.

There are other similarities to the closely-related rhododendrons; kalmias do not like late frosts and they need deadheading to prevent them putting all their energy into making seeds. They are also prone to vine weevils, leaf spot and leaf blight. Native to eastern U.S.A. Height x width 5–6 ft (1.5–2 m). ZONES 3 TO 9.

Today there are some fabulous cultivars available. The cherry-red **'Ostbo Red'** has a true red flower with a soft pink center and is quite stunning. Another extreme are the chocolate-colored flowers in **'Carousel'**, with really unusual purple-brown spots spattered on a white background. You can just see a hint of white around the edges. For both, height x width 5–6 ft (1.5–2 m).

Kalmia = after Peter or Pedr Kalm (1715–1779), a Finnish pupil of Carl Linnaeus who traveled widely in America; *latifolia* = with broad leaves.

There are also several other species of *Kalmia*, all native to North America, but I don't think any are as exciting as the calico bush. However, you might like to try **Kalmia angustifolia** (lambkill, sheep laurel, wicky). Its small, rosy red flowers appear in early summer and have a soapy scent. It is a small, evergreen bush,

spreading at the roots to form a thicket. You can propagate it by dividing the rootstock. It grows naturally in swamps but is just as happy in dry places, as long as the soil is acidic. The leaves are poisonous to animals, so it is known as "sheep laurel." There is a richer form called **'Rubra'**, with darker, longer-lasting flowers. Height 3 ft (1 m) x width 5 ft (1.5 m). ZONE 7.

Angustifolia = having narrow leaves.

Laburnum

Laburnum x watereri (L. alpinum x L. anagyroides)
GOLDEN CHAIN TREE
Fabaceae

Laburnums are one of the showiest small trees, laden as they are in spring with fantastic chains of golden yellow flowers. These lovely long chains of pea-like flowers are reminiscent of those of wisteria, and show up well against the rich green trifoliate leaves. But if you move closer, you will discover these flowers also have a divine scent. It is like rich honey, or a long-fermented liqueur. The best laburnums are the *L.* x *watereri* hybrids, originally raised in the Waterer nursery in Surrey England, but seen most often is the cultivar 'Vossii', which was bred in Holland. Laburnums have been used for years for avenue planting and are one of the most popular suburban garden trees because they have a tidy rounded shape. They tolerate pollution and poor soil, including heavy clays, and they grow well in acidic or alkaline sites. Being a typical legume bush, they have tough, stringy roots, often twining around the pot when you buy them. Make sure you unravel these roots and spread them out starfish fashion when planting. Laburnums are deciduous and grow well in cold winter climates, and they do like plenty of moisture. They tend to be lackluster in warmer or drier regions. Height x width 25 ft (8 m). ZONE 5.

Below: *Laburnum* x *watereri* 'Vossii'

Right: *Lavandula angustifolia* (*L. stoechas* in the middle).

Lavandula

LAVENDER
Lamiaceae

Lavenders always have an air of the past about them, reminding us of hazy summer days and childhood. These lovely plants are those neat hedges in a neighbor's garden with the showy blue or purple flowers and the wonderful spicy scent enfolded in pillows to aid and enhance pleasant dreams. These Mediterranean shrubs are generally easy-care plants and repay our kindness with a multitude of flowers. Plant books say we should trim them with the shears to keep them tidy, yet whenever I think to do it the bushes are flowering—again. Either they flower for 12 months (in my climate) or else I only think to look twice a year. Whatever the reality, it seems they are constantly in bloom. Even if they never flowered, they would be popular foliage plants for their neat, dense habit. Some species make ideal hedges for herb or cottage gardens.

Coming from the drier coastal parts of the Mediterranean, they naturally like full sun, free drainage and a breezy site. Most are easily grown in any open soil regardless of the acidity. I have seen them growing happily in extremes of acidity and alkalinity, and they will tolerate severe or salt-laden winds. What they hate is shade; cold, wet soil; and constant, dull weather. Generally they like a dry atmosphere and are not easy to grow in wet climates or wet ground, as they get root rot problems. This

seems to be the only thing that attacks them, as pests don't usually attack fragrant herb plants because of the spicy smell. If you live in a wet climate, choose the sunniest and most free-draining site you can find.

Sometimes the bushes get straggly and need a haircut. Ideally they should be pruned a little and often, but as I mentioned they always seem to be in flower when I go to do this and I don't have the heart to cut the flowers off. If your bush has become really straggly, then you may need to prune more drastically. Leave some foliage on each stem as hard pruning to bare wood often leads to the death of the plant. If you prune to an area with some leaves, the bush will then send up new shoots from lower down in the bush and you can prune back down to these at a later date if you want a smaller, more compact plant.

Having chosen a site for your lavender, don't be tempted to shift it. It will almost certainly die. Some people recommend them for containers on patios. I regard this as a poor choice for a lavender, but if you want it in a container, then ensure that the drainage is perfect and the containers do not become waterlogged. It is best not to feed them, as they prefer a poor soil.

Lavender = from "lavare," to wash or bathe, as the herbal extract is used for toiletries.

Lavandula angustifolia, syn *L. spica*
ENGLISH LAVENDER

Called English lavender, this species has been cultivated there since the mid-16th century. Its flowers produce the classic spicy fragrance used for perfume and lavender water. It has smooth,

Left and below:
Lavandula stoechas
'Merle'

slim, silvery-gray leaves on a dense, compact shrub. From mid-summer, small spikes of gray-blue flowers appear on long stalks, giving it an appearance distinct from the other species. From the Mediterranean. Height x width 3 ft (1m). ZONE 5.

Angustifolia = narrow leaves.

'Hidcote' is a fine, compact form developed in the beautiful Hidcote Garden in Gloucestershire, England. Height 24 in (60 cm) x 30 in (75 cm).

Lavandula dentata
FRINGED LAVENDER

Taller than most, growing waist-high or more, with narrow, tooth-edged leaves. The leaves and flowers have a familiar musky lavender aroma. The lavender-colored flowers are in a short cluster atop a long, flexible stem, making them popular for dried flowers. Native to the Mediterranean. Height x width 4 ft (1.2 m). ZONE 8.

Dentata = dentate or tooth-edged leaves.

Lavandula dentata var *allardii*

This is a bigger, more open plant, with gray leaves and much longer heads of flowers spaced along the stem like beads on a string. Again, they have the familiar lavender fragrance. Height 6 ft (2 m) x width 4 ft (1.2 m). ZONE 8.

Allardii = named for Mr. E. J. Allard, Cambridge Botanic Gardens, England.

Lavandula stoechas
FRENCH LAVENDER

Thin, simple, gray-green leaves are small at the base of each stem, gradually getting bigger near the top. The smell is the typical dusty lavender scent. The plant usually becomes a chunky, wide-spreading bush but it can be trimmed to make an orderly hedge. Square flowerheads the size of a finger joint have tiny, purple-black flowers along the four square corners, topped with long, wavy, purple bracts. It is probably the showiest of the various species and will perform better in colder, wetter climates than other lavenders. From the Mediterranean. Height 2–3 ft (60 cm–1 m) x width 3 ft (1 m). ZONE 8.

Stoechas = from Stoechades, a group of islands off the south coast of France.

Ligustrum

PRIVET
Oleaceae

The leaves of the privet have a pungent air about them but the real scent comes from the racemes of tiny white flowers. They look like froth against the dark background and would pass without comment but for the delicious heady perfume. Initially the fragrance is like sweet nectar, but move closer and inhale and it can become heavy and cloying. Unfortunately many people are allergic to the pollen of the flowers. If this is the case, you can give the plant a light trim just before midsummer when the flowers appear. This will remove the offending blooms and improve the shape and color of the plant in the process, but of course you will not have the scent.

Privet is often despised for being so common, but any plant resilient enough to survive central London gets my vote. Often seen as a hedge, a typical privet bush is an upright, dense evergreen with very dark, glossy green leaves. Left to its own devices, the bush becomes wide-spreading and rounded, and some of them become small trees. I have found room in my garden for a single bush of common green privet just for the aroma—I love it.

Privet grows in any soil, except boggy ground. It is very drought-tolerant and even if wilting it will recover. I should also mention that it is cold-hardy, wind-hardy, and tolerates full, hot sun, shade and city pollution. When it comes to tough plants, privet is tops. It transplants easily from pots or from open ground in winter. You can prune it frequently or drastically to bare stumps. In fact, you can prune to any shape you want, so it is a useful topiary shrub. I believe they brighten up a garden and have their uses as a screen or in windy, drafty places.

Ligulare = to tie, referring to stems flexible enough for tying.

Above: *Ligustrum japonicum* 'Rotundifolium'

Ligustrum japonicum 'Rotundifolium'
JAPANESE PRIVET

This is my favorite privet—though some would say the words "favorite" and "privet" are mutually exclusive. It is a nugget-like little plant, knee- to waist-high with very dark, blackish green leaves. These evergreen leaves are rounded and glossy above and have a fascinating twist or kink. Hayfever sufferers need not fear, as the sparse, sweet-smelling flower spikes which start to appear in mid-summer are easily picked off as you walk by. This cultivar is happy in any soil and virtually any situation, but its best use is in Japanese-style gardens or formal situations because it is good for clipping and topiary. Introduced by Robert Fortune (1812–1880) from Japan in 1860. Height 3 ft (1 m) x width 2 ft (60 cm). ZONE 7.

The straight species, *Ligustrum japonicum*, is an excellent hedge plant with larger, camellia-like leaves. There is a form called 'Macrophyllum' that has even more luxuriant blackish green leaves. Both have fragrant flowers from midsummer to early fall. Height 12 ft (4 m) x width 6 ft (2 m). ZONE 7.

Japonicum = from Japan.

Ligustrum ovalifolium
CALIFORNIA PRIVET, OVAL LEAF PRIVET

A common garden plant that is very popular for hedges because of its very dense, dark, oval leaves. The flowers appear in midsummer and have a heavy nectar-like scent. Native to Japan. Height 10–15 ft (3–5 m) x width 6–10 ft (2–3 m). ZONE 5.

Left: *Ligustrum ovalifolium*

'**Aureum**' (syn 'Aureomarginatum'), also known as golden privet, has sparkling green and gold foliage—the oval leaves are heavily edged in gold, and sometimes completely gold. It adds color to dark, shady corners and can be grown in tubs or difficult spots on the shady, dry side of the house. The flowers and fragrance are the same as the species.

Ovalifolium = oval leaves.

Lonicera

HONEYSUCKLE
Caprifoliaceae

*L*onicera are a funny mix of shrubs and climbers that seem to bear little relationship to each other. *L. nitida* is a dense, dark, evergreen shrub used for hedges, while *L. korolkowii* has glaucous blue leaves and small pink flowers. Then there are all the deciduous and evergreen climbers. One thing they do have in common is that they are all very easy to grow and most have the wonderful "honeysuckle" fragrance. Some of the climbers grow too easily, and have become naturalized in warm climates. Loniceras will grow in virtually any ground, be it acidic or alkaline, sandy or clay. Try to ensure the drainage is reasonable, but otherwise don't worry. They are all best transplanted from container-grown nursery plants, and while you could move a shrubby deciduous plant in winter, it would be risky to move the evergreen or climbing ones.

All of these plants can be pruned to keep them tidier, depending on the shape you are trying to create. While most prefer full sun and will cope with shade, a few of the climbers insist on shade, so it is difficult to make hard and fast rules about them. Most are cold- or wind-hardy, but being a diverse group, some are almost tropical in their requirements. Apart from an occasional aphid attack, they are healthy, easy-care plants, especially the climbers. But beware, as these climbers can be tenacious killers of innocent shrubs. The strong vines twine around the stems, constricting the flow of sap until the poor smothered shrub gives up the ghost. Ideally the climbers should

be given a trellis or some independent means of climbing and not be allowed into any nearby shrubs.

Lonicera = after Adam Lonitzer, a 16th-century German botanist and physician.

Above: *Lonicera* x *heckrottii*

Lonicera fragrantissima
WINTER HONEYSUCKLE

There is only one reason to grow this plant, and that is for its sweetly fragrant flowers. It is usually deciduous, but can be semi- or fully evergreen in mild climates, which means the tiny flowers are even less visible. The stems tend to be horizontal and a shiny yellow color. In late winter to early spring pairs of white flowers with yellow stamens appearing along the stems, followed by small red berries. Each curled bud opens up with a keel and two wings, like a pea flower, with a delightful freesia-like scent, ideal for a cut-flower. Prune immediately after flowering to allow the plant to bloom more, as it flowers on last year's wood. Apparently this plant has never been found in the wild, having been introduced from a Chinese garden by Robert Fortune in 1845. Fortune collected many of his plants from nurseries and gardens on the east

Left: *Lonicera fragrantissima*

Above: *Lonicera hildebrandiana*

coast of China, as it was impossible to travel further inland in the days of the opium wars. Height 6 ft (2 m) x width 6–10 ft (2–3 m). ZONE 5.

Fragrantissima = extra fragrant.

Lonicera x heckrottii
(*L. americana* x *L. sempervirens*)
GOLDFLAME HONEYSUCKLE

A vigorous, scrambling climber with dazzling, showy, sweetly fragrant flowers. Seen from above, the flowers form a star of rosy purple tubes opening to golden orange trumpets. The flowering season lasts all summer. Grow in full sun, or in a little shade in warmer regions. Height 10–20 ft (3–6 m). ZONE 5.

Heckrottii = origin unknown.

Lonicera hildebrandiana
GIANT BURMESE HONEYSUCKLE

The magical flowers of this species open creamy white. No one ever seems to notice them, however, because they are captivated by the older apricot flowers which are blessed with a heavenly banana scent. The flowers are large (up to 6 in/15 cm long) by comparison to other species, as seems fitting for such a gigantic

plant. It has lush, green, oval leaves and vigorous stems capable of pulling down any flimsy support with the sheer weight of its growth. This evergreen tropical climber will adapt to frosty climates if given hot, baking summers to ripen the wood. The common name indicates its country of origin, where it was discovered in 1888. It is tricky to propagate, although it will grow from cuttings and root cuttings. Height 60 ft (20 m). ZONE 9.

Hildebrandiana = after H.H. Hildebrand, a plant collector of the late 19th century.

Lonicera japonica
JAPANESE HONEYSUCKLE

Admired by some for its strong, sweetly scented flowers and hated by others as a weed. The long, white, tubular flowers appear over an extended period from spring to the end of summer. They eventually take on a soft yellow color and seem to have more scent at night. This vigorous climber is fine for rapidly covering a fence at the back of the garden. It is evergreen, or almost so, and hails from China and Japan. Height 30 ft (10 m). ZONE 5.

Japonica = from Japan.

Lonicera x purpusii 'Winter Beauty'

The white flowers of this cultivar appear at the end of winter or in early spring and have a subtle honeysuckle fragrance. Berries are rarely produced. Otherwise the plant is very similar to *Lonicera fragrantissima*, being a hybrid between *L. fragrantissima* and *L. standishii*. Height 6 ft (2 m) x width 8 ft (2.5 m). ZONE 6.

Purpusii = named for C.A. Purpus (1853–1941) and J.A. Purpus (1860–1932), German plant collectors.

Luculia

Rubiaceae

This is a small genus of deciduous and evergreen shrubs bearing fragrant panicles of flowers. If you live in a warm climate one of the benefits you can enjoy is the winter fragrance of *Luculia*—a mixture of talcum powder and beautifully perfumed soap. These Himalayan shrubs need summer heat, a

Above: *Luculia grandifolia*

moist climate and freedom from heavy frosts. I have seen them growing in frosty regions, but they are more commonly grown up against a wall for extra heat, otherwise in years with vicious frosts the plants lose all their flowers—or the cold sometimes kills them. If your plants ever get untidy, you can prune lightly after flowering but, better still, give them a severe haircut back to stumps every 10 years or so. Left to their own devices they are usually upright, rounded shrubs. If grown outdoors, they do not seem particularly troubled by pests or disease.

Luculia = a native Nepalese word.

Luculia grandifolia

This species is appropriately named as it has huge, red-tinted leaves up to 14 in (35 cm) long on red leaf stalks, or petioles. It forms a big, bold, upright plant, topped off with huge, white, sharply lemon-scented flowers, the equal of any gardenia. Sometimes the heads are full of flowers, but more often than not they have an almost lacecap look about them. It flowers intermittently through summer and is semi-evergreen. Coming from high altitudes in Bhutan, it can withstand light frosts. Height 10 ft (3 m) x width 6 ft (2 m). ZONE 9.

Grandifolia = large leaves.

Luculia gratissima

The big, round heads of bright pink, talcum-powder scented flowers emerge in the latter part of winter and so can be vulnerable to frosts. Choose a warm, sheltered site with a moist, acidic soil and put a mulch around the roots to keep them cool. Transplant when young and don't try to move them again. It is worth growing these plants just for the foliage because the simple, hand-sized leaves are green with a hint of red and, come fall, they lose a portion of their leaves, becoming rich reds and golds before they drop. The uppermost leaves remain and provide a backdrop for the flowers. **'Early Dawn'** is a particularly good named form. From the Himalayas. Height x width 6 ft (2 m). ZONE 9.

Gratissima = most welcome or grateful.

Right: *Luculia gratissima*

Luculia pinceana 'Fragrant Cloud'

This cultivar is similar to *Luculia gratissima* but with much bigger, purplish pink flowers and longer, darker leaves. The scented flowers appear in late winter/early spring and from a distance smell pleasantly of expensive soaps. However, the fragrance can be overpowering at close quarters. Height x width 6 ft (2 m). ZONE 9.

Pinceana = named for Mr. Pince, a nurseryman from Exeter, Devon, England c.1845.

Magnolia

MAGNOLIA
Magnoliaceae

Magnolias are grown for their wondrous spring flowers. But these large, showy flowers are not the only attribute of this genus, as many blooms are also deliciously scented. Plant them near a path so you can enjoy the scent as you stroll by or, alternatively, cut a few stems for a vase and enjoy the perfume indoors. You will need a substantial vessel to hold these impressive stems, but you will be surprised at how good a cut-flower they

Left: *Luculia pinceana* 'Fragrant Cloud'

Right and below:
Magnolia denudata

can be (though sometimes the perfume is overpowering). As cut-flowers they open and reflex to show the thick, fleshy, inner petals that look like porcelain. In the garden, the petals usually fall off at this stage. The petals and sepals of these fleshy flowers all look the same and are collectively known as "tepals."

Magnolias are possibly the oldest true flowers on the planet, and because they are so large, you would expect the flowers to be pollinated by some large creature, like a bird or a bat.

Instead, they are fertilized by tiny insects that look like thrips, and also by beetles, so it is hard to figure out why they need to be so showy. Magnolias always have just one flower at the tip of a stem, while the related michelias have many flowers in the axils of the leaves.

Magnolias are easy to grow and are surprisingly good city trees; thriving, despite atmospheric pollution and hard, compacted soils. Magnolias perform best in heavy soils. I have a theory that plants with thick, fleshy roots like magnolia and ash trees prefer dense, heavy soils to the lighter, fluffy loams. The roots should not be allowed to dry out when transporting from a nursery to the garden. Generally, magnolias like a moist soil or one that doesn't dry out. They prefer acidic ground and their fleshy roots are capable of searching deep into the soil without ever being a danger to paths or drains. Give them a mulch to keep the soil moist and cool and to prevent any damage to the roots by hoeing or digging.

A few magnolias will cope with lime, namely *Magnolia acuminata*, *M. delavayi*, *M. kobus*, *M.* x *loebneri* and *M. wilsonii*. Sometimes you see pale, unhealthy-looking magnolias. This is usually due to too much lime or a nutrient deficiency such as lack of iron or magnesium. Epsom salts (magnesium sulfate) or iron sulfate will often cure the problem.

While I don't usually like single bushes on a lawn, I make an exception for a magnolia. It is one of the few shrubs that can look good in isolation.

All magnolias flower and grow best in full sun, although they will tolerate some thin shade. Shelter from strong winds is essential for the wellbeing of the plant, but also because the big, fleshy flowers are easily bruised and broken. The only exception to this is the very wind-hardy, evergreen *M. grandiflora* and related hybrids.

Magnolias rarely need pruning, apart from an occasional trim for shape. In the establishment period, you may need to cut off any twin leaders or crossing branches. In general, deciduous magnolias have a good natural shape and an open habit with clean branches and no twiggy growth.

Magnolias are a mixture of deciduous and evergreen trees from China, Japan, southeast Asia, eastern U.S.A. and Mexico. Apart from the species and hybrids listed below, there are some other magnolias with a strong fragrance that might be worth looking for. These include **'Caerhay's Belle'**, **'Claret Cup'** and **'Manchu Fan'**, as well as *M. x loebneri*, *M. sieboldii* and *M. salicifolia*.

Magnolia = named by Linnaeus after Pierre Magnol (1638–1715), director of the Montpellier Garden, southern France.

Magnolia denudata
LILY TREE, YULAN MAGNOLIA

The Yulan magnolia is very upright as a young plant, gradually forming a more rounded small tree as it matures. Beautiful, creamy white, cup-shaped flowers keep a good, upright, tulip shape for a long time before opening out to a flatter saucer shape. The heady fragrance from the blooms wafts through the garden and excites the senses, livening up any spring day. A scintillating combination of lemon and ice, there is a cold, clear feeling as you inhale the scent at close quarters. Because it flowers so early in the spring, the emerging buds are sometimes damaged by frost.

For all the wonderful hybrid magnolias that have been bred over the years, if I could only have one in my garden, this would be it. It is usually the first magnolia in flower in the spring and, I suppose, just like the first strawberries of the season, the first ones are best. But even when you step back and analyze it, *Magnolia denudata* is as good, if not better, than most. Large, hand-sized leaves are almost pear-shaped, broader at the tip, and they emerge just as the last of the flowers are falling. It is surprising more named forms have not been selected. Mostly it comes "true" when grown from seed, and there is very little variation in flower size or color. The few named colored forms around are now thought to be hybrids such as **'Purple Eye'**, which has flowers with lavender at the base, and **'Forrest's Pink'**, with pink blooms. From eastern China. Height 30 ft (10 m) x width 15 ft (5 m). ZONE 5.

Denudata = bare or naked, referring to the flowers appearing on naked branches before the leaves emerge.

Above: *M. x soulangeana* 'Rustica Rubra' and *Rhododendron arboreum*.

Magnolia grandiflora
BULL BAY MAGNOLIA, SOUTHERN MAGNOLIA

Huge, white, terminal flowers endowed with an intoxicating lemony perfume decorate this big, bold tree in midsummer. Each flower is short-lived, but there is a succession of flowers over weeks or even months. It is one of the more unusual magnolias as it is evergreen and, even more surprising, it is wind-hardy, even coping with coastal gales. The big, glossy leaves are protected by the shiny top surface and the felted undersides. A coating of fawn-brown indumentum (thick hairy covering) protects the emerging leaf from dehydration. From the southern states of U.S.A. Height x width 70 ft (20 m). ZONE 6.

The hybrids **'Freeman'** and **'Maryland'** (resulting from a cross with *Magnolia virginiana*) are smaller, more compact bushes with similarly fragrant flowers but I think they lack the impact of *M. grandiflora*. Height x width 30 ft (10 m).

Grandiflora = large flowers.

Above: *Magnolia grandiflora*

Magnolia x soulangeana (*M. denudata* x *M. liliiflora*)
SAUCER MAGNOLIA

A wonderful group of hardy hybrids suitable for small gardens, with flamboyant flowers on bare branches in early spring. The scent, elusive in the garden, is very pleasant at close range and smells of ice-cream and clean white linen. Initially the plants are narrow and upright but after many years they can become enormous wide-spreading trees.

The flowers are like tall tulips, rich, purplish red at the base fading into pale purple and white towards the tips. They have a diffused look, as if the color has run like a dye. The petals are white within, but you won't see this unless you pick them. They make surprisingly good cut-flowers and even large branches laden with blooms can be cut to last two weeks successfully in a vase. Like all magnolias, the flowers are terminal and face skywards, looking superb against a conifer hedge or a heavily clouded sky. The stems are brown and smooth, apart from the little white bumps called lenticels, the breathing holes for the stems. Height 25 ft (8 m) x width 15 ft (5 m). ZONE 5 TO 9.

Many beautiful forms are available, including:

'Alexandrina', a good form for small gardens, keeping a tidy, upright shape for many years. The fragrant white flowers are purple on the outside.

'Lennei' has very dark purple flowers in a tidy, tulip shape. It is justifiably popular and named after P. J. Lenné, director of the Prussian Royal Gardens in Berlin in the 1840s, when this hybrid first appeared. It is more resistant to late frost than many others.

'Rustica Rubra' (syn 'Rubra') has smaller, more rounded, soft purple-red flowers. For all, height 25 ft (8 m) x width 15 ft (5 m).

Below: *Magnolia stellata*

Soulangeana = after Etienne Soulange-Bodin, who first bred these hybrids in a garden near Paris in 1820.

Above: *Magnolia wilsonii*

Magnolia stellata

STAR MAGNOLIA

Surely the best and most compact magnolia for small gardens. Smooth, bare, gray stems are covered in lovely tactile, gray, furry flower buds during winter, opening to wide, flat, starry flowers in spring. The tepals are spaced slightly apart, thus the star effect, and they have a nice lemony scent. In time it becomes quite a large bush, but it is only going to be 6 ft (2 m) high and wide after 10 years, so it is easy enough to fit into a smaller space. The star magnolia hails from Japan. ZONE 5.

Stellata = starry.

Magnolia wilsonii

An unusual magnolia with nodding flowers, each with a red center. The lemony scent of these flowers is glorious and they are easy to reach, unlike many magnolia flowers which sit high on the tips of tall stems. It is an ideal woodland garden plant, enjoying some shade and shelter. Native to western China. Height 10–12 ft (3–4 m) x width 6 ft (2 m). ZONE 7.

Wilsonii = after E. H. Wilson, who found the plant in western China.

Mahonia

MAHONIA
Berberidaceae

ll mahonias are evergreen, most are hardy, and the foliage is stupendous. And all this is topped off with terminal spikes of flowers. Not only are the flower heads big, bright and beautiful, they are presented in a unique way—like a child's posy—and some have a lovely perfume. They even have fascinating bark and trunks, as well as purple-blue berries.

Being one of the most cold-hardy evergreens, mahonias have become a standby for many gardeners, but that is not to imply that they are dull. They are certainly not boring and should not be restricted to cold regions or the difficult spots in which we

Left: *Mahonia* x *media* 'Charity'

see them placed. Mahonias are good enough to be in the forefront of any garden. Some make excellent groundcovers, while others are fine architectural plants.

Of all the places in your garden where you might plant a mahonia, the one situation they don't like is a windy position. The tough-looking leaves are easily bruised by strong or regular winds. And you might not want to plant the very spiny ones near a path. They are easy to transplant and even large plants can be moved in winter, if cut back a little. Most regenerate well from pruning but it is rarely necessary. Mahonias are closely related to *Berberis*, as shown by their ability to interbreed. (It is very unusual for two genera to cross and successfully produce viable seed.) Like the *Berberis*, some species are host to a rust disease, otherwise they are easy-care plants.

Mahonia = after Bernard M'Mahon (1775–1816). Of Irish birth, he became famous in America as an author and nurseryman. A friend of Thomas Jefferson, he helped sponsor the Lewis and Clark expeditions across the U.S., yielding *Mahonia aquifolium*, among other exciting discoveries.

Above: *Mahonia japonica*

Mahonia aquifolium
OREGON GRAPEHOLLY

The leaves of this mahonia take on a reddish purple tinge in the colder months and then in spring the stems are topped with fragrant, pollen-scented, canary-yellow flower spikes. This low-growing, spreading bush is a terrific groundcover for sun or shade in areas with deciduous shrubs to provide a visual backdrop. It will keep down the weeds and provide winter interest. Native to western North America. Height 2–5 ft (60 cm–1.5 m) x width 5 ft (1.5 m). ZONE 6 TO 9.

Aquifolium = sharp-pointed leaves.

Mahonia japonica

A wonderful foliage, fragrant and flowering plant. The pinnate leaves with their spiky edges are a shiny dark green all summer and take on hints of red and yellow in winter. The racemes of late winter or spring flowers arch out and droop away from the center of the crown and are nicely honey-scented. A terrific architectural plant near buildings, it eventually grows around head-high in a nicely rounded fashion. A Chinese native, mahonia has long been grown in Japan and was assumed to be from that country. Height 6 ft (2 m) x width 10 ft (3 m). ZONE 7.

Japonica = from Japan.

Mahonia x *media* (*M. japonica* x *M. lomariifolia*)

A group of hybrids with handsome foliage and brilliant fragrant flowers. Multi-trunked, upright bushes with beautiful pinnate leaves, the contrast between the older, darker leaves and the lovely bright green new foliage is a highlight of any spring garden. Bright yellow spikes of flowers are sweetly scented and very showy. The bell-like flowers are popular with bees and gardeners alike. Some plants, like **'Lionel Fortescue'**, have upright flower spikes, and others swoop down, like **'Charity'**. Height x width 10 ft (3 m). ZONE 8.

Media = intermediate, as in between two species.

Mandevilla

Apocynaceae

A group of South American vines or climbers with fabulously scented flowers. Sweet, heavy and heady, their gardenia-like scent overwhelms you and compels you to inhale some more. Long, arrowhead leaves are opposite along the red new vines. Pick one off and you will notice the milky sap. Most of the Apocynaceae have milky or oil-like sap that can be poisonous.

Like most climbers, these plants like their roots in shade and tops in sun, but they are not as insistent about this as some. Mandevilla will grow in shade in a hot climate, but most gardeners will need to give them maximum heat and sun to thrive and flower well. In cool regions, grow them in tubs, with perhaps a small trellis for support. Then grow them outdoors in summer and over-winter in a conservatory. Shelter from cold or tearing winds is essential. This genus tends to be deciduous in cool regions, but they will retain most leaves if it is warm enough. Both the following species transplant easily from pots, but don't be tempted to shift them again later. They do well in poor or hard, compacted soil and even tolerate short droughts. Use this to advantage by growing one near the house in poor, dry soils under the eaves. It will also be close enough for the scent to be enjoyed. Another possibility is to send it up a small tree, perhaps a birch. It is safe to winter-prune, with the flowers appearing only on new growth.

Mandevilla = after H. J. Mandeville (1773–1861), a British diplomat based in Buenos Aires, Argentina who introduced the plant in 1837.

Mandevilla laxa, syn *M. suaveolens*
CHILEAN JASMINE

Luckily this is the hardiest and most common of the genus. Clusters of pure white, gardenia-scented, trumpet flowers appear in the axils of the leaves on the new growth and open in succession,

Mandevilla laxa

Above: *Mandevilla splendens*

extending the flowering season from summer into early fall. This plant is from Peru, Bolivia and Argentina. Height 10–20 ft (3–6 m). ZONE 8 OR 9.

Laxa = loose or lax.

Mandevilla splendens

This plant is appropriately named, with its strongly fragrant, ostentatious, shocking-pink trumpets as big as a coffee cup. When this vine flowers in summer, everybody notices. Its dark, evergreen leaves are big, bold and glossy. Native to Brazil. Height 10–20 ft (3–6 m). ZONE 9.

The hybrid **'Alice du Pont'** is similar, with huge, pink, scented trumpets with five spiraled petals. Sometimes called *M. x amoena*, it has big, glossy, contoured leaves in pairs along the brittle stems. Choose the hottest spot you can find, as the plant is tender. Height 10–20 ft (3–6 m). ZONE 9 OR 10.

Splendens = shining or bright.

Meliosma

Sabiaceae

Acapricious group of plants of which some are deciduous and some are evergreen. Just to confuse us even more, some have simple single leaves, while others are blessed with fabulous pinnate leaves. The uniting theme is the plumes of tiny, creamy white flowers. Although not wonderful to look at, they are deliciously honey-scented. So the plants are definitely worth growing for the combination of wondrous scent and handsome leaves.

You are likely to encounter them only in botanic gardens, but I'm sure any gardener who found a space for one of these gems would not regret it. Although they are potentially large shrubs or trees they are usually much smaller in cultivation and

would fit into most gardens. Give them freely draining acidic or neutral soils. They can be a bit tricky to transplant, so handle them carefully when planting or transplanting. Find a sheltered spot away from strong winds in full sun, or at least good light. They will thrive in hot summers and tolerate cold winters.

Meli = honey; *osme* = odor, thus honey-scented.

Meliosma cuneifolia, syn *M. dilleniifolia* subsp *cuneifolia*

This deciduous shrub has leaves like a sweet chestnut and in summer the erect panicles of creamy flowers are packed in like sardines. The scent is heavenly, like hawthorns (*Crataegus*). One of the hardier species. Introduced from western China by E.H. Wilson (1876–1930) for the Veitch nursery in 1901. Height 15 ft (5 m) x width 10 ft (3 m). ZONE 8 OR 9.

Cunei = wedge-shaped; *folia* = foliage.

Right: *Meliosma myriantha*

Meliosma myriantha

A choice shrub with single leaves like the sweet chestnut and panicles of small, off-white, almost greenish yellow, honey-scented flowers in summer, followed by showy red berries. Also introduced for the Veitch Nursery, only this time by Charles Maries (1851–1902) in 1879. Native to China, Japan and Korea. Height 15 ft (5 m) x width 10 ft (3 m). ZONE 9.

Myriantha = multi-flowered.

Meliosma oldhamii, syn *M. pinnata* var *oldhamii*

In the wilds of China and Korea this is a tree, but it is usually only a shrub in cultivation. The big, handsome, pinnate leaves are like a *Euodia* and in early summer the showy plumes of sweetly fragrant white flowers look like billowy candy floss. Height x width 6–15 ft (2–5 m). ZONE 8.

Oldhamii = after Richard Oldham (1838–1864) of Kew Gardens, England, who collected the plant in Korea.

Meliosma veitchiorum

This plant is currently top of my "lust list." ("Wish list" just does not describe how much I crave this plant.) When you see the huge, 30 in (75 cm) long pinnate leaves you will understand. When the plant is big enough, you will be blessed with 18 in (45 cm) long panicles of sweetly fragrant, creamy white flowers in late spring. Resembling a cross between an *Aralia* and *Mahonia*, the leaves are richer and more handsome than either. Even the stems and buds are exciting. It eventually forms an upright tree, but is usually so slow-growing it will not require much space. Introduced by E. H. Wilson (1876–1930) in 1901 from western China. Height 6–15 ft (2–5 m) x width 10 ft (3 m). ZONE 8.

Veitchiorum = after the Veitch Nursery in England.

Michelia

Magnoliaceae

Everyone has heard of magnolias and they are rightly very popular with gardeners. What if I told you about a group of "evergreen magnolias" that are even more exciting? Michelias are basically the same as magnolias, with two important differences. One, they are all evergreen and, two, they have lots of flowers per branch rather than just one at the tip of each branch. As michelias have a flower bud at the base of every leaf, produced the previous summer, they produce many more flowers. All michelias are scented, each with a different perfume, and although it seems unfair to compare, they put magnolias to shame when it comes to fragrance.

Michelias are very easy to grow if you have the right climate. Most need a mild zone 9 to 10 range, although they will grow in warm, sheltered parts of zone 8. Like so many plants, they will tolerate colder winters if they have scorching hot summers. I was reminded of this when I saw several "tender" michelias growing in Korea, where they have horrendously cold winters. They vary in their need for sun and their ability to handle wind. Most do best in full sun and certainly flower better in a sunny site. They will tolerate shade and grow quite well, but with reduced flower power.

The plants are happy in any acidic or neutral soils as long as the drainage is adequate. They not only cope with heavy soils but thrive in them, which seems to be true of all magnolias. They

Above: *Meliosma oldhamii*

seem to grow willingly in impoverished soils, although, like most plants, will benefit from an occasional feeding. The roots of both michelias and magnolias have a distinctive smell, like rope, and tend to be thick and wiry with no apparent hair roots. They are easy to transplant from pots and need no special attention. Pruning is rarely necessary as they have such a good tidy, upright shape, but should you ever need to, they tolerate severe pruning, just like magnolias.

An occasional caterpillar chews at the leaves, but never seriously enough to make treatment necessary. Diseases seem to be non-existent, apart from infrequent black spot on the leaves after prolonged periods of rain. Magnolias are also attacked by the same black spot.

Michelia = after Pietro Antonio Micheli, a botanist from Florence, Italy.

Michelia alba
PAK-LAN

A tall, evergreen, conical tree with glossy, grass-green, hand-sized leaves with a tropical drip-tip. In spring and summer, you will be captivated by the sweet gardenia-like scent of the spidery, off-white flowers. Walk in any garden at flowering time and you will wish you could bottle such a scrumptious aroma. It is easy to see

Above: *Michelia doltsopa*

so excited about this plant. It is difficult to propagate and often has to be grown by layers. Potted plants transplant well, and small, open ground plants can be moved until about head-height.

First introduced from western China by George Forrest (1873–1932) in 1918, it also grows to the west through the Himalayas. Height 20–50 ft (6–15 m) x width 15–50 ft (5–15 m). ZONE 8 OR 9.

The leaves of the cultivars do vary, with some having very dark, blackish leaves and others being just plain green. The size of the flowers and the number of petals also vary from cultivar to cultivar. All are fragrant.

'**Silver Cloud**' has paler, smoother leaves and bigger flowers with many long petals. They can look rather untidy when seen up close. It needs more shelter that some others. Height 20–50 ft (6–15 m) x width 15–50 ft (5–15 m).

'**Rusty**' has furry buds and a reddish brown reverse to the leaf. It has a darker leaf color and is more wind-hardy. Height 20–50 ft (6–15 m) x width 15–50 ft (5–15 m).

Doltsopa = a Nepalese name.

why this plant is revered in Asia. In fact, it has only ever been found in temple grounds and is now thought to be a man-made hybrid. Height 30 ft (10 m) x width 15 ft (5 m). ZONE 9.

Alba = white.

Michelia champaca

CHAM-PAK

Very similar looking to *Michelia alba*, the only difference being the flower size, color and scent. It has smaller flowers with more compact petals in soft apricot to orange and a more basal, oily scent. It comes from deep, warm valleys in Tibet and Yunnan, China. Height 30 ft (10 m) x width 15 ft (5 m). ZONE 9.

Champaca = native Chinese name.

Michelia doltsopa

Michelia doltsopa is one of the most exciting plants in cultivation, with masses of hand-sized, white, deliciously cinnamon-scented flowers lasting over a period of two months from late winter to spring. It is initially an upright, evergreen shrub becoming a big, wide-spreading tree in similar proportions to *Magnolia grandiflora*. It has rich, dark green, glossy leaves with a definite valley down the middle and a tropical drip-tip. Quite happy in heavy, wet soil in valley bottoms and near water, and it does need a moist climate to do well. Some michelias live in very poor soil but *M. doltsopa* likes deep, fertile soil to encourage strong growth. Grow in full sun and don't crowd it with other trees, as it does best in isolation, where you can view the long-lasting floral display. Give it plenty of room and shelter, as it is very vulnerable to wind.

In cooler climates the tree is very sensible and starts flowering later in the spring and the plant drops its spent flowers, so the tree looks tidy when in flower. Add the cinnamon scent that wafts around the whole garden and you begin to see why gardeners get

Michelia figo

BANANA SHRUB, PORT WINE MAGNOLIA

Michelia figo is grown for its phenomenal port wine fragrance. Step up close to smell the flowers and the scent often disappears, which is most odd. But catch a whiff of this on the breeze and it can set your soul alight. Although nearly all michelias have a fabulous scent, this one has to be the best. Some say it smells of bananas, and others say strawberries.

Given this beautiful fragrance, it seems only fair that the flowers are rather miserable to look at. They are small, about the size of an almond, and a funny gray color with a hint of purple. They never truly open and seem to be in permanent bud mode, and if it were not for the scent you would dismiss them as worthless. Blooms appear throughout spring and summer and the scent is usually more noticeable in the evening, but can bowl you over at any time of day.

Below: *Michelia figo*

Right: *Michelia yunnanensis*

The bush itself is a dense, evergreen shrub with small, thumb-sized, glossy, apple green leaves. It is handsome enough; a shrub growing just over head high with a conical shape. With age, a specimen will grow into a small tree.

It loves to be in shade and hates the hot sun where the leaves tend to be bleached and turn anemic yellow. Most books say it will not take heavy frosts but I have seen it growing in Korea, tolerating quite harsh winters. Perhaps the hot summers bake the wood to prepare it for this cold. Try and find a spot for it, if only in a conservatory. It is quite happy in a large container and easy to transplant later should you find a niche in the garden. There are some hybrids between *M. figo* and *M. doltsopa*. The flowers are an improvement on *M. figo* but they are nowhere near as showy as *M. doltsopa* and, although scented, they lack the knockout fragrance of

either parent. Native to southeast China. Height 10–15 ft (3–5 m) x width 10 ft (3 m). ZONE 9 OR possibly 7 TO 8, depending on summer heat.

Figo = the name for the bush in China.

Michelia maudiae

This species thrills me every spring with its collection of thin, upright flowers. Pointy green buds open in succession, making the flowering season last for quite a few weeks. The creamy white flowers have a strong scent of icing sugar that can make you catch your breath. The tropical-looking leaves look tough, but as they are easily bruised by strong winds, a sheltered, sunny site is essential. Ideally, plant it down a slope so that it can be admired from above. The big, bold, evergreen leaves are glossy dark green above

Above: *Michelia maudiae*

and a glaucous blue-gray beneath. Although handsome in its foliage, it is the sort of plant you hardly notice until the flowers come in early spring. Native of eastern China, around the Hong Kong region, and it is quite hardy for a plant from this region. Height 10–15 ft (3–5 m) x width 10 ft (3 m). ZONE 8 OR 9.

Maudiae = named after B. Maude, author of botanical works.

Michelia yunnanensis

In terms of scent, perhaps *Michelia figo* is ahead, but this is a close second. The scent of cinnamon and ice-cream pervades the garden at all times, unlike the elusive scent of *M. figo*. Without a doubt, this is the toughest of the genus. I have seen them planted on a clay slope seemingly deprived of moisture, or planted in shade among tree-root competition, and they not only survive, they thrive. They are seemingly indestructible, growing in wet or extremely dry regions, and cope with full, hot sun or dense, dry shade. The hotter the summer the more winter frost they will endure, but shade can also be used as a means of frost protection.

The dark, blackish green leaves are a picture of health no matter where they are planted. It is also the most garden-worthy of the genus in terms of shape. Only *M. doltsopa* beats it for numbers of flowers, and then only just. The flowering season starts in spring and lasts for around five weeks and a large bush has literally hundreds of blooms. It can be grown in pots and could be a substitute for the ubiquitous *Ficus benjamina* as an indoor plant.

I am biased in favor of this plant because I believe my nursery grew the first plants outside China. There is a lot of seedling variation and the flowers vary from cup-shaped blooms about 1 in (2.5 cm) across to flatter flowers 3 in (8 cm) across. Some have perfect cup or round flowers and others are more starry and open, like a *Magnolia stellata*. Native to China. Height 6–12 ft (2–4 m) x width 6 ft (2 m). ZONE 8, and possibly 6 OR 7 with enough summer heat.

Yunnanensis = from the Yunnan Province of China.

Myrtus

MYRTLE
Myrtaceae

Myrtles are a group of evergreen shrubs and small trees with neat, little, aromatic leaves, and some have the advantage of fragrant flowers. They are very easy to grow and, being evergreen, have many uses in gardens large and small. Any soil, including alkaline and impoverished ground, will suffice. They love the sun and can cope with heat and drought, as well as wind and even coastal conditions. Myrtles can be used as a screening plant, and some make good hedges. The larger ones are ideal specimen trees. They are easy to transplant, although I wouldn't move them again once planted. You can trim them as a hedge or prune them drastically should you ever feel the need, they will quickly regenerate.

Myron = perfume.

Myrtus communis

COMMON MYRTLE

A dense, evergreen bush with neat, pointy leaves and a spicy aroma when brushed or plucked. Lots of white, brush-like flowers lasting several weeks appear in the later part of summer and

Below: *Myrtus luma* 'Glanleam Gold'

Above: *Myrtus communis*

Right: *Myrtus luma*

smooth pink and fawn-brown trunks, constantly peeling to provide the twin colors. You can make interesting shapes by training the tree with multi-leaders and making a character specimen. If you want a more formal shape, simply keep and train a single upright leader. If you have room for only one tree in your garden (and the right climate), this one should be near the top of your wish list. Native to Chile. Height 15 ft (5 m) x width 10 ft (3 m). ZONE 8.

'Glanleam Gold' is an eyecatching variegated form with a creamy margin to the leaves, which even have a pinky tinge when they emerge. Height 15 ft (5 m) x width 10 ft (3 m).

Luma = a Chilean name for this plant.

Oemleria

Oemleria cerasiformis, syn Osmaronia cerasiformis, Nuttallia cerasiformis
OSO BERRY
Rosaceae

There is only one *Oemleria*, and a handsome plant it is, too. Plant one near a path just to enjoy the lovely almond perfume of the flowers. The new leaves and the flowers emerge simultaneously in early spring, creating a lovely contrast of fresh green and clear white. The new leaves are tiny at this stage and the flower stalks and calyxes are the same fresh apple green. Nice shiny brown stems are a feature, too. The upright habit and the dainty, pendulous flowers are reminiscent of *Ribes* or currants, and you may be surprised to hear that its closest relative is the genus *Prunus*.

The male and female flowers are found on separate plants and obviously you need both to get a crop of plum-like, purple fruits. Although I must confess it is not in the forefront of gardeners' "wish lists," it is a useful shrub for larger woodland and informal gardens. Full sun or part shade is fine and it is happy in any soil. It does sucker a little, and is thankfully not too invasive. Equally at home in wet or dry climates, this robust

they, too, have a spicy smell. This upright shrub is beautiful with its shimmering, shiny foliage and, being from the Mediterranean, it will grow near the sea and tolerate wind, hot sun and drought. Surprisingly perhaps, it even handles moderate frosts and has been grown in England for centuries. Sometimes you see them clipped and trained or even used for topiary, especially the subspecies *M. c. tarentina*. Height 10 ft (3 m) x width 6 ft (2 m). ZONE 8.

'Flore Pleno' is a double-flowered form and **'Microphylla'** has neater, smaller leaves, while **'Variegata'** has leaves with a creamy white margin. For all, height 10 ft (3 m) x width 6 ft (2 m).

Communis = common.

Myrtus luma, syn M. apiculata, Luma apiculata
A fantastic small tree that is ideal for city gardens. It is evergreen, tough, has neat, little, blackish green leaves and masses of white, scented flowers in midsummer. The blooms may be small but they appear in such profusion that they put on a great display, and the scent is spicy and peppery. Each flower is a small cup with a set of bristly white stamens within. But for me the highlight is the

Above: *Oemleria cerasiformis*

shrub is easy-care. You will not have to coddle it in any way; just plant it and forget about it until you see the spring flowers. Native to California. Height 10–12 ft (3–4 m) x width 6 ft (2 m). ZONE 6.

Oemleria = after Augustus Oemler, a German botanist who sent plants home from his travels in America in the 1840s; *cerasiformis* = cherry-like.

Osmanthus

Oleaceae

If you fancy a holly (*Ilex*) with a scent then you are going to like *Osmanthus*. But if hollies are not your ideal plant, then let's hope the zing in the scent of these plants can still appeal to you. An easy way to tell these apart from hollies is that they have opposite leaves while *Ilex* have alternating leaves. Tough, resilient, evergreen shrubs with handsome, shiny leaves—that is how I picture *Osmanthus*. However it is the olfactory rather than the visual senses they appeal to. To say the scent is heavenly is an understatement. They all have fabulous perfumes which vary from species to species. The best two are *O.* x *fortunei* and *O. fragrans*. Plant one along the side of your house where you need a robust shrub or perhaps something to disguise part of a building, or obscure a view. They will grow in all those difficult places, such as where it is drafty, or too hot in summer and cold and damp in the winter—somewhere you need a tough customer to cope with the vagaries of the weather. As you will have gathered, these plants are tough, tolerant and trouble-free. Whatever is thrown at them by way of wind, drought, wet, cold, sun or shade seems to have no impact. They prefer to be in full sun, and will have a thinner leaf cover in shadier places. Slow-growing, long-lived, easy-care, evergreen shrubs such as these are indispensable.

Caterpillars sometimes take a chew of the new foliage, but they are never brave enough to tackle the older leaves and usually move on to something more tender and tastier. Any soil including alkaline is fine, as you might expect from a member of the olive family. Oleaceae include ash trees, *Forsythia* and *Syringa*, all of which do well in alkaline soil.

Above: *Osmanthus* x *fortunei*

When you see the thick mass of roots you will understand why they are easy to transplant and why they thrive in any soil. You can even grow them in large tubs. *Osmanthus* are fantastic patio plants with their compact nature and wonderful perfume. You can clip them into whatever shape you want. Even severe pruning to bare stumps is acceptable; they will quickly recover. Plant one on a patio or near the entrance to your house and you will enjoy the scent every time you walk by. With the exception of *O. americanus*, all are Asian in origin.

Osma = fragrance; *anthos* = flowers.

Above: *Osmanthus delavayi*

Osmanthus americanus

This has shiny glossy leaves and small, greenish white, sweet-smelling flowers in early summer. Found from Virginia to Florida, this sole American representative in the *Osmanthus* genus grows to 30 ft (10 m) in the wild but is more likely to be height 10 ft (3 m) x width 6 ft (2 m) in a garden setting. ZONE 7.

Americanus = from America.

Osmanthus delavayi

Considered to be a garden treasure because it is easy to grow, evergreen, and fits in any garden—but most of all because it has sweet yet lemony fragrant flowers. Tiny, holly-like leaves with serrated edges are a dark blackish green on a dense, compact bush reaching waist-high and maybe twice as wide after 10 years or so. With such a tidy habit it is unlikely to ever need pruning.

Best in full sun, it copes with heat and drought as well as cold winters. In spring, the clusters of white flowers appear along the stems, highlighted by the dark foliage. Lasting for several weeks, the blossoms are intensely fragrant and prolific. An ideal shrub for any small garden where you need a tidy, tough evergreen and would enjoy the bonus of fragrant flowers. Height 3–6 ft (1–2 m) x width 6–10 ft (2–3 m). ZONE 7.

Delavayi = after Jesuit priest Jean-Marie Delavay (1838–1895), who sent seeds from China to a French nurseryman, Vilmorin, who cultivated the plant.

Osmanthus x fortunei
(O. fragrans x O. heterophyllus)

Most people assume this is a holly, and it does look remarkably similar. But its special attribute is a gardenia-like scent so powerful that it is recognizable over 100 yards away. That was my first experience of this plant, and I knew immediately I had to have one of my own. So, if you need a big, bold shrub that is happy in wet or dry climates and has a scent that will drive you wild, this is it. Height x width 6 ft (2 m). ZONE 8.

Fortunei = after Robert Fortune (1812–1880), who found the plant growing in a Japanese garden in 1862.

Osmanthus fragrans

KWAI FA, FRAGRANT OLIVE, SWEET OLIVE

This is the gem of the genus, and how appropriate that the most sweetly scented of all these fragrant plants should be called *fragrans*. It is cherished in China and Japan, its twin homelands, for its exquisite scent, a mixture of ripe peaches and pineapple. In China, flowers are added to tea to improve the scent. Fortunately for us, the plant is inclined to flower twice a year, in spring and again in late summer. Often described as tender, this plant will tolerate quite cold winters if it has hot summers to ripen and harden the wood. Left to its own devices it is a large, upright shrub or small tree. The new leaves are bronzy and older ones are paler and less rigid than those of other species and have fewer spines. There are two forms, the usual white-flowered one and **Osmanthus fragrans aurantiacus**, with showier apricot or orange flowers. Height 6–15 ft (2–5 m) x width 6–10 ft (2–3 m). ZONE 7.

Fragrans = fragrant.

Right: *Osmanthus fragrans* in center.

Osmanthus heterophyllus

FALSE HOLLY, HOLLY OSMANTHUS

This is a great foliage plant, typically 10 ft (3 m) high with a neat, round, columnar shape. You can clip it occasionally to keep the shape or prune it drastically should the need arise. The hidden flowers open in fall and would be missed but for the fruity scent (which eludes some people). The leaves are small with sharp spines, and they come in various shapes and colors. Some are rounded and almost smooth, others have sharp spines; there are even unusual dagger and trident shapes. It is hardy and grows more or less anywhere. A Japanese plant, introduced by Thomas Lobb (1817–1894) in 1865. Height 6–10 ft (2–3 m) x width 3 ft (1 m). ZONE 6.

Above: *Osmanthus heterophyllus* 'Variegatus'

Some cultivars to consider are: **'Aureomarginatus'**, a variegated clone with deep yellow margins surrounding the dark green inner leaf. **'Gulftide'**, a compact shrub with twisted, sharp, spiny, green leaves. **'Myrtifolius'**, a smooth leaf version. **'Purpureus'** has shiny leaves that are almost a blackish red. There appear to be two forms available—one has spiked edges and the other has smooth leaves. **'Variegatus'**, with pale, gray-green leaves edged in creamy white. For all, height 6–10 ft (2–3 m) x width 3 ft (1 m).

Heterophyllus = having leaves of diverse forms.

Oxydendrum

Oxydendrum arboreum
SORREL TREE, SOURWOOD
Ericaceae

The scented flowers of sorrel are most welcome in late summer when few other flowers from woody plants want to show themselves. Long chains of creamy white bells, like *Pieris* or lily-of-the-valley, are deliciously fragrant, rich in honey and popular with bees. Not only are they delightfully scented but they last a long time and even the spent flowers look attractive for ages. Then, come fall, the scarlets and reds of the fall leaves will have you wondering why this plant isn't more popular. Not only is it pretty as a small tree, but it fits easily into any garden with its well-formed, almost rounded, shape.

The sorrel tree is in the rhododendron family and, like them, has numerous fine roots near the surface and needs a moist spot with good drainage. Acidic soil is essential, too, and a mulch of bark will help keep those surface-feeding roots cool and healthy. They are sometimes attacked by phytophthora root rot, just like rhododendrons.

It may not be as robust as a cherry tree, but if you succeed with it, it will provide you with more interest throughout the year with the combination of flowers, perfume and fall foliage. Seedling plants do vary in leaf color and flower size, and selected

named cultivars would be useful addition so gardeners could get the very best forms.

The plant is very cold hardy, yet equally at home in warm zones 9 and 10. Full sun results in more flowers and better fall color but it will grow in a semi-shaded woodland garden.

As it is the only plant in the genus, there seems to be no reason to call it a "tree tree" (*dendron* = tree; *arboreum* = tree). However, it was originally called *Andromeda arborea* (*Andromeda* being the old name for *Pieris*), and so *arborea* had to stay. Under the international rules for naming plants, if a new name is decided upon for a genus, the existing name for the species must remain. Native to eastern North America. Height 10–20 ft (3–6 m) x width 6–12 ft (2–4 m). ZONE 5 TO 9.

Oxy = sharp; *dendron* = tree; *arboreum* = tree, making it a "sharp tree tree."

Above and left:
Oxydendrum arboreum

Paeonia

PEONY
Paeoniaceae

We all know about the herbaceous peonies with their delicious blowzy flowers in spring. Then one day you discover "tree peonies." It is hard to believe they are closely related to the humble buttercup and were once included in the Ranunculaceae family. They now dominate a family of their own. The term "tree peony" is a bit of an exaggeration as they are usually only head-high shrubs. They have an open and rather stiff habit reminiscent of *Rhus typhina*. As they are deciduous, they are very cold hardy, and yet they thrive in heat and dry conditions. While herbaceous peonies need winter cold to perform, these tree peonies have no need of the cold. You can grow them in wetter climates, but try to find them a free-draining, hot spot. They are not fussy about acidity, growing equally well in acidic or alkaline soil. Partial shade is acceptable but, more importantly, they need shelter from strong winds, as their beautiful foliage is delicate. Some of them have fabulous ferny foliage worthy of a space in the garden even without any flowers. These flowers are incredible but sadly rather short-lived, but that is part of what makes them desirable. Knowing you will only see the flowers for a few days each year makes them all the more alluring.

When you buy these shrubs in pots or as bare-root plants, you will see they have thick, fleshy roots that should be kept moist until planted. Plant them in a favored spot and don't be tempted to shift them again. Once they are planted you'll probably never need do anything else for the plants, although they might appreciate a mulch or a feed occasionally. You are unlikely to ever need to prune them, but they will tolerate some thinning or pruning if you think it necessary.

Paeonia = after Paeon from Greek mythology, who was a physician to the gods and said to be the son of Apollo.

Paeonia delavayi
TREE PEONY

A wonderful plant worth growing just for its fabulous ferny foliage, let alone its perfumed flowers. The dark chocolate red flowers have a rich, fruity scent and tend to arch out on long stems, often face down. As most of these plants are grown from seeds there is a lot of variation, and the flowers differ in size and color from apricot to red, purple and maroon. I have grown this in hot, dry as well as warm, humid climates, and it is happy in either. I have even planted one on a hot, bone-dry clay bank and it is completely happy. From China. Height x width 5–8 ft (1.5–2.5 m). ZONE 5.

Delavayi = after the great plant collector, Jean-Marie Delavay (1838–1895), who collected literally thousands of plants in China when working there as a missionary in the latter half of the19th century.

Right: *Paeonia delavayi*

Left: *Paeonia lutea*

Paeonia lutea

YELLOW TREE PEONY

The popular form most often seen in gardens is *Paeonia lutea* var *ludlowii*, collected by Ludlow and Sherriff in Tibet in the 1930s. The flowers are nearly twice the size of *P. lutea* at 5 in (13 cm) across. Big, gleaming, yellow cups appear above the new leaves in the spring and they have a subtle fruity fragrance. This is one of the most beautiful, yellow-flowered shrubs you will ever see. Like *P. delavayi*, it is worth growing just for its foliage, but this bush is more compact and the flowers sit up and are nicely presented, so it is better suited to smaller gardens. I think most gardeners would prefer this showier species. Originates from China and the Himalayas. Height x width 3–6 ft (1–2 m). ZONE 5.

Lutea = yellow.

Paeonia suffruticosa

MOUTAN, TREE PEONY

The moutan or tree peony has been grown in Chinese gardens for centuries. The straight species (if such a thing still exists) is pink. Having been hybridized for centuries, however, it is hard to know what is the true form and what is not. But there are many cultivars, from white to pink to rich reds, and double flowers as well as singles. The flowers sit proudly on top of the plant in spring, at least most of them do. For me the singles have more style and present better, sitting properly on top of the bush, while many of the blowzy doubles become so top-heavy that the bloom lists sideways. The colors often fuse into the white or pale parts of the petals. The ripe fruity fragrance of the flowers is especially appreciated when they are used for floral displays indoors. The hybrids appreciate a little shade in the heat of the day. Native to China. Height x width 3–6 ft (1–2 m). ZONE 5.

Suffruticosa = somewhat shrubby; *moutan* = from Meu-tang, the king of flowers in Chinese mythology.

Perovskia

Lamiaceae

This whole bush is aromatic, with a strong scent of sage. At first, you may think you are looking at a *Salvia* or perhaps some strange lavender, and you would be on the right track as they are all in the same family. The seven or so *Perovskia* come from the hot, dry regions of central Asia through to the western Himalayas. Although naturally native to hot, arid places they are easy to grow in wet or dry climates, providing the drainage is perfect. Very acidic or even very alkaline soil is fine. Choose as hot and sunny a spot as you can find, perhaps in a mixed or perennial border. Sometimes grown in rock gardens or on the tops of walls, it looks wonderful with a background of thunderclouds or a late evening sky or, failing that, a conifer hedge. These deciduous shrubs can be scruffy in winter and need a regular haircut to keep any semblance of order. They are not the tidiest of plants even in their prime in midsummer. The upright stems are reluctant to branch and are topped with long panicles of smoky lilac flowers.

Perovskia = after M. Perowsky, a governor of the obscure province of Orenberg in central Russia.

Perovskia abrotanoides
AFGHAN SAGE

A bushy shrub that keeps a low, compact habit with upright stems and gray-green, feathery, ferny foliage and smoky blue flowers in summer. The whole bush has a strong sage or camphor smell. An excellent plant in mixed borders, but also quite stunning on its own in a rock garden or on a wall. Native to Afghanistan. Height x width 3 ft (1 m). ZONE 5.

Abrotanoides = like an *Abrotanum*, or southernwood.

Perovskia atriplicifolia
RUSSIAN SAGE

This plant is a useful addition to the late summer garden scene. A sage-like scent is given off by the plant and the silvery white stems of shooting, upright growths have vivid, violet-blue, hooded flowers in long vertical panicles. Small, rather simple, oval leaves are covered with soft gray hairs. The bush looks quite sparse, requiring an annual prune in winter to keep it well formed. Height x width 5 ft (1.5 m). ZONE 6.

The cultivar **'Blue Spire'** is an improved form, with frilly-edged leaves and bigger, better blue flowers. Height x width 5 ft (1.5 m).

Atriplicifolia = leaves like an *Atriplex*, a saltbush.

Below: *Perovskia atriplicifolia* 'Blue Spire'

Philadelphus

MOCK ORANGE
Philadelphaceae

Some *Philadelphus* have a fabulous fragrance and others are sadly lacking in this respect. They do vary in the degree of their scent, and it is worth seeking out plants with the stronger perfume. It always seems a travesty to plant a rose or *Philadelphus* with no scent. My childhood garden was heavy clay soil over limestone, which does not suit many shrubs, but we did have a thriving *Philadelphus* or "mock orange," one of the few shrubs to actually enjoy a high pH or limy soil. Yet it is equally happy in very acidic conditions. *Philadelphus* are also a standby for drought-prone regions, so I can say with confidence that this plant will grow more or less anywhere. They are very hardy to cold and cope with a breezy site. They love sun—the more the better—but will grow in semi-shade. So they are easy-care plants with no need to stake or water, and no pests and diseases to bother them.

Flowers are white, although a few have a subtle pink or mauve center. Blossoming in early summer, long after most shrubs have finished flowering, they fill a niche in this often quiet time. Plant them in a herbaceous border where they blend easily with the perennials. They look equally good in dense shrubbery to lighten the effect of the darker evergreens.

The flowers appear in early summer on last year's wood, so if you feel the need to prune them, do so immediately after flowering to get as much new growth as possible for next year's blossom. They will not object if you forget to prune them and my own preference is to leave them alone for five or six years and then give them a severe haircut. They have dull gray stems and a rather messy, twiggy nature, so the bush has no redeeming features when it is not in flower. They transplant readily and you can move an established bush in winter if you really need to. Just cut back the stems to facilitate the move.

Philadelphus are good cut-flowers for home gardeners but they are not available in shops, as they do not travel well. They are a great complement to roses in the garden as well as in a vase.

One of the best things about *Philadelphus* is that the flowers remain white and don't fade, blotch or burn, even in strong sunlight. So many white blooms, like rhododendrons and camellias, look sublime with the first flush of flowers and then retain a portion of muddy, scarred or bruised flowers. Not so *Philadelphus*, whose flowers are either perfect or else they fall off cleanly.

Philadelphus are native to North America, both its east and west coasts, and to Mexico, China and Eastern Europe. Most are very hardy, deciduous shrubs, with a few evergreen types.

Philadelphus = after the king of Egypt, Ptolemy II, Philadelphus (308–246 B.C.).

Philadelphus coronarius
MOCK ORANGE

A big, arching shrub with flowers that have one of the most heavenly scents on earth; slightly citrus-like, definitely a sharp, almost icy, lemon scent.

Even without the showy flowers it would be an essential garden ingredient for its scent alone. It is going to take up lots of space, but will earn its keep in late spring when laden with blooms. Despite its airy, seemingly lazy habit, the bush is quite

well formed overall, with a rounded shape. Each flower is made up of four petals forming a pure white cup of scented bliss. The wood is brittle if pushed or broken and yet the plant is quite wind-tolerant and hardier than it looks.

With its dense, twiggy habit, you would imagine it would look rather scruffy when it loses its leaves, but somehow the bush just disappears and you will only notice it again the following season when, reliable as ever, it is smothered in flowers. Native of eastern Europe. Height x width 6 ft (2 m). ZONE 5.

The cultivar **'Aureus'** is a great little plant to brighten up a shady corner. The bright yellow foliage gradually greens as summer progresses and it is ideal for shade, where it will retain its yellow color better. It is more likely to burn and scorch in hot sun. The flowers do not show up well, being white on yellow, but the scent is still as enjoyable as the species.

Coronarius = used for garlands.

Philadelphus 'Manteau d'Hermine'

This plant is ideal beside a path or at the front of a border, where you can enjoy the flowers and the subtle lemon fragrance. Creamy white, double flowers appear in early summer, but what sets this cultivar apart is its dwarf habit, making it suitable for cramped places or limited garden space. Height 2 ft (60 cm) x width 3 ft (1 m). ZONE 5.

Right: *Philadelphus*
'Virginal'

Philadelphus 'Virginal'

Everyone says this is the best double, and I have to agree. In early summer, the big panicles of snow-white double flowers appear and they are wonderfully full with a strong lemon and ice-cream fragrance. 'Virginal' has been around a long time and it is still hard to beat. The leaves look luscious compared to many: they are rounded and heart-shaped, with a very distinct point. Height 6–10 ft (2–3 m) x width 3–6 ft (1–2 m). ZONE 5.

Poliothyrsis

Poliothyrsis sinensis
Flacourtiaceae

W hat is good about this plant? The flowers are the main attraction, appearing in mid to late summer, a time when few other woody plants want to put on a show. And the big 8–12 in (20–30 cm) plumes of creamy, frothy flowers give off a musky fragrance. The leaves, too, are quite large, about hand-sized, with sawtooth edges and a reddish tinge, and they are much enhanced by the fall color. Even in winter the tree looks quite handsome, with clean, smooth stems and a neat, tidy structure.

This species should be more popular, but despite the postive characteristics described above, other factors that might limit its popularity include the shape and needs of the tree. It is a very upright, deciduous tree, almost lanky and prone to wind damage. Add to this the need for a free-draining soil, plenty of

Above: *Poliothyrsis sinensis*

sun, shelter and the number of places it can be grown are significantly reduced. That is not to say we should not try to grow it if we have a large garden, and there must surely be a place for it in our city parks. Given a warm summer climate, it is capable of growing in quite cold regions. Young potted plants transplant easily in winter, but I suspect larger specimens cannot be shifted so readily.

One of the many plants introduced from China by Ernest Wilson (1876–1930). Height 30 ft (10 m) or more x width 20 ft (6 m). ZONE 7.

Polio = many; *thyrsis* = densely branched, perhaps in reference to the many branched panicles of flower; *sinensis* = from China.

Prostanthera

MINT BUSH
Lamiaceae

These are known collectively as the "mint bushes" because of their strong, pleasant mint smell whenever you touch or brush past them. Not only is the scent from the leaves stupendous, the sheer flower power is amazing. Each hooded flower is quite small but their huge numbers make up for what they lack in size.

Being native to Australia, these plants love heat and sun, and soon become leggy and sparse if shaded. Really good drainage is essential and place in acidic or neutral soil. It is the sort of bush you plant and forget about, partly because it is easy-care and

partly because it hates being moved. These dense, evergreen shrubs cope with breezy places but can be toppled by strong winds if they get top-heavy. In colder regions, grow one next to a wall for the extra heat and rain-shadow effect. (Invariably, one side of a wall is drier than the other because of the rain coming with the prevailing wind.) It is a showy plant for those narrow borders around the house, where you want a modest flowering shrub that won't keep trying to block the windows.

There are no obvious pests, but unfortunately it is prone to dying for no apparent reason. This is usually due to cold, wet soil or wind rock, when the root structure has been damaged by wind.

Proste = appendage; *anthera* = flowers, as the anthers have spurs or appendages.

Prostanthera cuneata
ALPINE MINT BUSH

One of the hardier species of this genus and a little gem of a plant. The bush only grows around waist-high and has glossy, wedge-shaped leaves that give off a fresh minty fragrance. In summer, its hooded white flowers with purple spots in the throat look like charming little faces, with big white bibs where the lower three petals are longer than the top two. From Australia. Height 3 ft (1 m) x width 5 ft (1.5 m). ZONE 8.

Cuneata = wedge-shaped.

Prostanthera rotundifolia
ROUND-LEAVED MINT BUSH

A big, dense, minty-smelling shrub that should be trimmed after flowering to keep a tidy shape. Masses of purple-pink flowers

Left: *Prostanthera cuneata*

Above: *Ptelea trifoliata*

This species is happy growing in any soil and, given enough sunlight, will perform in virtually any climate and any place. The plant is a native to the eastern parts of North America, from Ontario down to Texas and northern Mexico. Height x width 12–25 ft (4–8 m). ZONE 2.

There is a form, **'Aurea'**, which has soft yellow leaves. Height x width 12–15 ft (4–5 m). And an upright form called **'Fastigiata'**. Height 12–20 ft (4–6 m) x width 6–12 ft (2–4 m).

Ptelea = from the Greek word "ptao," referring to the winged fruit;

trifoliata = having three leaves.

Pterostyrax

Pterostyrax hispida
EPAULETTE TREE
Styracaceae

Don't be put off by the name, as it is a silent "p"; just think of it as *terostyrax*. It is a peculiar plant: I rave over it for two weeks of the year and the rest of the time I hardly notice it. Some people choose to prune the plant so you can walk underneath to better admire the drooping panicles of white-fringed, honey-scented flowers. These probably do last for two weeks, just. But the plant impresses twice, when it first comes into flower, with its chains of epaulette-like blooms, and then when the leaves turn to gold in the fall.

It is a resilient bush. I planted my first one close to a swamp in wet, heavy soil, and subsequent seedlings have come up even further into the swamp, so it is very happy in wet soil growing next to black birches, *Betula nigra*, which also love "the wet." It seems to handle drought, too. It will take any soil texture, as well as extremes of acidity and alkalinity. Young plants transplant easily in winter, but they are best left alone and not moved again.

There are no pests of any note, although the plants can be short-lived or prone to dieback in mild, moist regions. Somewhat surprisingly, *Pterostyrax* will grow quite happily in smoggy cities. This is often the case with deciduous plants with peeling bark, like plane trees, but I am not sure if there is any connection. *Pterostyrax hispida* has stems that resemble parchment both in color and the way they shed old bark. The young stems

smother the bush in early summer. Native to Australia. Height x width 6 ft (2 m). ZONE 8 OR 9.

Rotundifolia = having round leaves.

Ptelea

Ptelea trifoliata
HOP TREE, STINKING ASH
Rutaceae

Ptelea is regarded as the most highly scented hardy tree, which is no small recommendation. It does not rate highly in plant books or catalogs, but there are two or three reasons you might want to grow this large shrub or small tree. It makes a worthwhile addition to a large garden, especially as it is cold hardy and highly perfumed. Clusters of tiny, greenish white flowers appear in midsummer and develop into exciting hop-like fruits (no good for making beer, unfortunately). These starry flowers are delightfully scented, like honeysuckle. The leaves of this deciduous small tree are somewhat like a three-leafed maple and the fall color is a clean gold, contrasting well against the shiny, blackish-brown stems. Not only are the flowers scented but the bark, leaves and young fruits release a strong and pungent but pleasant aroma rather like incense when bruised.

Above: *Pterostyrax hispida*

are smooth and upright when young, and the plant becomes a wide, spreading, small tree in time. Left to its own devices, the bush is often multi-trunked, which may suit you, but if you want a tidier, single-stemmed bush you will have to do some early training. The structure of the plant and the way the stems emerge from the main trunk is very symmetrical, and even the flowers are beautifully precise in their presentation.

Like most of the *Styrax* family, a place out of serious winds is essential. Try and find a spot with full sun or good light, because the plant will be rather sparse if too shaded and will not color as well in the fall. It deserves a place in a large woodland garden. I cannot say that it sets the garden alight, but it does have a certain charm. It can also be used as a lawn specimen or shade tree, as well as a shade provider for rhododendrons.

Native to Japan and China. Height x width 15 ft (5 m). ZONE 6.

Pteron = a wing; *hispida* = bristly: a *styrax*-like plant with winged seeds that happen to be hairy.

Pterostyrax corymbosa is less common and less attractive than *Pterostyrax hispida*. It has smaller oval leaves and panicles of fragrant, white flowers in early summer, followed by winged fruits. From Japan. Height 15 ft (5 m) x width 10 ft (3 m). ZONE 6.

Corymbosa = clustered or arranged in corymbs.

Pyracantha **hybrids**

FIRETHORN
Rosaceae

Much as I would like to, I cannot claim that the flowers on a *Pyracantha* are stunning to look at. They do, however, have a heady scent rather like hawthorns and you are sure to notice them as you walk by if they are planted on a wall close to a path. The corymbs, or flat-topped clusters, of white flowers are not unlike some of the less photogenic *viburnums*. But it is what the flowers lead to that is important, because as a berry plant *Pyracantha* has to be one of the finest, especially when you see a plant trained against a wall absolutely packed with bright orange berries.

It is a typical rose family plant, growing in virtually any soil. It handles heavy clay, alkaline soil, and all the so-called difficult sites with ease. The drawback with Rosaceae is that they are prone to pests and diseases, and *Pyracantha* is no exception. The leaves are attacked by all sorts of bugs and in some cases devastatingly so. In some regions it is impossible to grow them because of the pests. Apple diseases such as fireblight, canker and scab are all waiting to attack.

Apart from the pests, it is a resilient plant content in all kinds of weather. Its tough, chunky growth pattern makes it very stable and not liable to succumb to storms. Winter cold is no problem, and it will grow from zones 6 to 10. It loves full sun but will take a certain amount of shade. It will never need coddling or watering and is easy to transplant when young. It is too bony and cumbersome to shift again later on, and does not like this treatment anyway.

Pyracanthas make superb hedges—they are nice and dense, and thorny enough to deter pedestrians and animals, which is useful where you want to prevent foot traffic. Bright green, glossy leaves and a fairly tidy natural shape all help, and it is

quite happy being clipped. The plant flowers on second-year wood, so be careful just to trim off the stems that have already flowered or you will be cutting off flower buds.

A good, robust plant for a general border and for difficult sites, it is especially useful to city gardeners. You are most likely to encounter cultivars when buying *Pyracantha*. Look for the newer cultivars that are resistant to disease, for example, **'Navaho'**, **'Shawnee'** and **'Teton'**. The wild species grow from southern Europe, across Asia and into China. For all, height x width 6–10 ft (2–3 m). ZONE 6 OR 7.

Pyr = fire; *kanthos* = thorn, thus the common name "firethorn."

Rhododendron

RHODODENDRON
Ericaceae

Some gardeners are astonished to find that many rhododendrons are fragrant. Even more surprising is that there are three groups of quite differently scented ones (four if you include mollis azaleas, which are technically rhododendrons, see page 117). All these fragrant rhodos have common needs. They want a free-draining, acidic soil with a cool root run. Hot, dry soils, or cold, wet ground are often fatal to them. A mulch of wood chips or bark is essential to their well-being, keeping the roots cool and moist with the added bonus of reducing weeds.

Below: *Pyracantha* cultivar in flower.

Right:
*Rhododendron
arborescens*

The more light they receive, the better they will flower, as long as their roots are shaded and cool. A dollop of acidic fertilizer in spring will boost growth. Rhododendrons are easily planted and can be shifted at any size if you choose the cooler months. Their mass of fibrous roots just below the surface allows even huge specimens to be shifted to a new location.

Most rhododendrons have a good natural shape and rarely need pruning. They can be hard-pruned if necessary: do the whole bush and not half, because only the tall half will grow well at the expense of the shorter, pruned side. It also pays to deadhead them after they flower by flicking off the spent flowers with a finger and thumb action. They put a lot of energy into producing thousands of seeds and if you leave them on the plant, it will inevitably mean a poorer flowering display the next spring.

Rhododendrons hate wind, especially hot or salty winds. Surprisingly, they will tolerate short spells of strong wind much better than constant, monotonous winds. The leaves of a rhodo in a windy or dry site will have unsightly brown edges. Many are attacked by powdery mildew, leafhoppers and thrips, although the *R. maddenii* group tends to be resistant to most of these. Weevils can be a pest and may even ringbark and kill young plants. Root rots caused by wet soil or root damage can also kill them, sometimes seemingly overnight. A healthy plant can be dead within a week if the roots become waterlogged, or if torrential rain is followed by hot, sultry weather.

Rhodo = from the Celtic "rhodd" or "rhudd," meaning red; *dendron* = tree.

Rhododendron arborescens, R. calendulaceum, R. prinophyllum (syn R. roseum), R. prunifolium, R. vaseyi and R. viscosum

The first rhododendrons to be discovered by western gardeners were the deciduous, summer-flowering American rhodos. These small, upright bushes grow naturally in the swamps and hills of the Appalachian Mountains. Most have small, dainty, tubular or

Left: *Rhododendron viscosum* and *Lobelia tupa* behind.

Left: *Rhododendron* Loderi 'Fairyland'

trumpet-shaped flowers with a sweet heavenly scent. Although a wonderful sight in woodland gardens, they do not really suit small town gardens. Height x width 6 ft (2 m). Most are very cold-hardy to ZONE 4 OR 5.

Fortunei series: *Rhododendron griffithianum, R. decorum* and *R. fortunei*

The Fortunei series of evergreen rhododendrons is named for Robert Fortune (1812–1880), an intrepid plant collector sent to China in the 1840s. This series includes *Rhododendron griffithianum, R. decorum* and *R. fortunei*, all with that typical smooth, oval leaf we associate with rhododendrons. *R. decorum* and *R. fortunei* are dense, well-formed bushes, ideal for gardens, and it is easy to keep them around head-high, while *R. griffithianum* does tend to become leggy and open, although it compensates with beautiful peeling, smooth trunks. The flowers all have an intoxicating fragrance and are typically bell-shaped in tidy heads, usually in whites and creams. Hybrids such as the **Loderi series** and **'Van Nes Sensation'**, **'Lalique'** and **'Mrs A.T. de la Mare'** have this heritage and are blessed with a garden-filling scent. Try them as a cut-flower and you will be delighted. They last up to three weeks in a vase and release their heady fragrance indoors as well. It is a flowery, lemony scent and you can smell the nectar. These rhododendrons are mostly from western China and the Himalayas. Height x width 6–12 ft (2–4 m). ZONES 6 TO 9.

Left: *Rhododendron* 'Mrs A. T. de la Mare'

Maddenii series: *Rhododendron edgeworthii, R. formosum, R. crassum, R. polyandrum* and *R. nuttallii*

If you have the luxury of a zone 9 or 10 climate you will be able to grow Maddenii rhododendrons. Even a zone 8 region, if you have hot summers to ripen the wood, will allow you to find a niche for these fantastically fragrant bushes. The Maddenii series includes *Rhododendron edgeworthii* and *R. formosum*, the parents of

Above: *Rhododendron* 'White Waves' (*R. nuttallii* x *R.* 'Lindal')

Vireya rhododendrons: *R. herzogii, R. jasminiflorum, R. konori, R. superbum*

Having said there are four groups of fragrant rhododendrons, to be truthful, there are five. The last group is the fragrant species of the vireya or subtropical rhododendrons from Borneo, Malaysia and New Guinea. These waxy-flowered beauties need a warm zone 9 or conservatory conditions. Most of them will grow in planters and remain compact enough for this to be possible. They come in a fabulous range of hot colors from orange to red, strong pinks and gold with a few subtle whites and soft pinks. It is usually the flowers with the subtle colors that have the scent. In some it is an overpowering carnation-like perfume. Not only are they beautiful and scented but they flower two or three times a year, sometimes in a burst and sometimes on and on. As they originate near the equator they are not influenced by day length, and flower whenever it suits them. Being from the highlands they are hardier than one might expect of a tropical plant. Height x width 3–6 ft (1–2 m). ZONE 9 OR 10.

Above:
Rhododendron maddenii

R. **'Fragrantissimum'**, as well as the intoxicating *R. crassum, R. polyandrum* and *R. nuttallii* and all the resultant hybrids of these. The Maddenii types fit into two categories: very early spring-flowering and very late season flowering, blooming up to midsummer. The early-flowering ones, known as the Ciliicalyx series, usually have smaller, slightly hairy leaves and often have an open, sparse habit. Their heads of smallish flowers are usually white, perhaps with a hint of pink or cream, and are highly scented with a cinnamon fragrance. Most in this group are tender, needing shelter, as both the bush and the flowers are quite prone to frost damage.

The more typical Maddenii types flower after the main rhodo season, up to midsummer. Most of this group, such as *Rhododendron crassum* and *R. maddenii*, have large, bronzy, shiny leaves topped off with tidy heads of big, scented, trumpet-shaped flowers. The bigger, more open *R. nuttallii* has the largest flowers of any rhodo, resembling huge white lilies with a yellow throat. Their lemony ice-cream scent is fabulous, but you will need a sheltered gully to protect the plant from wind and frost. The large, bullate (rough) leaves are reason enough to grow this wondrous plant, not to mention the beautiful peeling, mahogany-colored bark, equal to *Acer griseum*. Height x width 6–10 ft (2–3 m).

Rhododendron spp.

MOLLIS AZALEAS, DECIDUOUS HYBRID AZALEAS
Ericaceae

Technically, azaleas don't exist and have for a long time been classified as rhododendrons, but every gardener still calls them azaleas. Sometimes their fall color is attractive, but in late spring you remember why you planted them. More than just floriferous, they are fragrant—and not just with a gentle hint of fragrance, but with a knock-out, sensational perfume like an expensive scented soap. Walk through a dell of azaleas in flower and you will come away with a big, beaming smile.

The plants come in two distinct styles; the smaller, evergreen types flower in early spring and are often used as indoor plants, and then there are the taller, deciduous azaleas, known as mollis azaleas, that I want to talk about. Ideally suited to a large woodland garden, these big, rounded, deciduous shrubs are rather dull, twiggy plants for most of the year. But in spring, the flower-power and range of colors are stunning, with big, bold flowers smothering the bushes. Some have subtle shades of soft

pink, whites and pale yellow, but it is the hot colors—the bright oranges, gold and reds—that grab our attention. There is nothing subtle here, more of a blazing trumpeting of flower. And then, suddenly, it's all over for another year and the plants are ignored for another 11 months. Don't ignore them completely though, as they do appreciate a feed and a mulch of wood chips or bark to keep their roots cool and moist. They have a mass of fine, fibrous roots near the surface of the ground, and in hot soils they tend to dry out and lose a portion of these roots. Irrigation is a possible savior here, but a climate with year-round rain is their preference.

People talk about rhodos and azaleas needing shade, when what they really need is shaded roots to keep them cool. That is why they should be in a woodland garden where they are sheltered from hot, drying winds. They are quite happy in full sun, and in fact the more sun they get, the better they flower.

Azaleas are rather fussy about the soil as well as the site, and it is worth going to the trouble to satisfy them. An open, free-draining, acidic soil is ideal, and they will not tolerate lime or heavy, wet soils. A liberal dose of acidic fertilizer in spring will help to keep them happy all year. One of the advantages of their fibrous root system is that they can be dug up at any age and transplanted, providing you move them in cooler months when they are dormant. While azaleas don't like wind or hot, dry climates, they can survive very cold winters.

Most azaleas have a good natural shape and do not require any pruning. If your bushes get too big or straggly you can cut them back hard to stumps in late winter and they quickly regenerate to make a dense, bushy plant. You will lose the flowers for the following spring but it is worth the sacrifice long-term.

Mollis azaleas do suffer from some pests and diseases, but not as many or as badly as their evergreen cousins. Powdery mildew is probably their worst problem and it seems to attack some varieties much more than others. Some varieties can be covered with gray mould almost as soon as the leaves emerge and are sometimes defoliated. Others, like the Melford series, seem to be reasonably resistant. Cold, wet soils or prolonged heavy rain can lead to root rots, as can any damage to the root system by weeding or hoeing around the root base. This is another reason to mulch the soil, so that you can keep weeds to a minimum without resorting to mechanical means of clearing them.

The deciduous or mollis azaleas are a complex group of hybrids based on *R. japonicum*, *R. molle* and *R. occidentale*. Height x width 6–10 ft (2–3 m). ZONE 5 OR 6.

Ribes

FLOWERING CURRANT
Grossulariaceae

Whenever I see the name *Ribes*, I think of food and delicious scents and jams. The *Ribes* genus includes blackcurrants and redcurrants. Ribes have lovely scented flowers and some have aromatic foliage. It is a large and varied group, with evergreen and deciduous shrubs from both hemisperes. As well as the edible blackcurrant, it includes the popular flowering currants. Most are very hardy, easy-to-grow shrubs handling any soil, including alkaline, and heavy clays. They are best grown in an open, sunny site although they will put up with shade from buildings as long as there is enough light. Breezy to windy sites are fine, and if you pick the wrong spot at first, they are easy to move when they are dormant. Most of them have a suckering habit, sending up new stems close to the crown, but these are never invasive.

Ribes = an old Arabic name for these plants.

Ribes odoratum
BUFFALO CURRANT, CLOVE CURRANT
A deciduous North American species forming an open bush with a lax, arching habit. Grown primarily for the scented yellow flowers in spring, these golden-yellow little bells hang below the stems and have a spicy, clove-like scent. The shiny green leaves turn rich reds and purple in fall. *R. odoratum* is from central U.S.A. Height x width 6 ft (2 m). ZONE 5.

Odoratum = scented.

Ribes sanguineum
FLOWERING CURRANT
This upright, deciduous shrub looks very much like a black- or redcurrant bush in its growth habit. The trifoliate leaves are a typical currant shape and have the currant's distinctive, pungent smell. Happy to fit any role in your garden, this easy-care plant can be relied upon to put on a good show every spring.

The fragrant pink flowers come in panicles, pushing upwards and eventually tumbling with the weight of bloom. They appear with the new leaves in spring, but they are showy enough not to be hidden by them. If anything, the leaves enhance the flowers by providing a lovely contrast. In cold climates the flowers have the stage to themselves as the leaves wisely wait for warmer weather. The flowers of the wild species are pinky red, while some clones are a much deeper red. **'King Edward VII'** is probably the best known of the darker clones. Cut a few for an unusual floral arrangement.

The plant is hardy, growing to zone 6 and yet very happy in warm zones, too. It seems to prefer cold, heavy soils and copes with lime. It needs full sun to thrive and will put up with breezy sites. Give it a prune every three years or so just to restore some vigor to the plant, and prune immediately after flowering. Discovered by Archibald Menzies (1754–1842) in 1793 and later introduced into cultivation by David Douglas (1799–1834). Native to western North America. Height x width 6 ft (2 m). ZONE 6.

There are some charming hybrids called **R. x gordonianum** (*R. odoratum* x *R. sanguineum*) with hanging racemes of flowers in a mix of red, copper and yellow. Height 6 ft (2 m) x width 8 ft (2.5 m). ZONE 6.

Sanguine = blood, referring to the red flowers.

Ribes speciosum
FUSCHIA-FLOWERED GOOSEBERRY, CALIFORNIAN FUCHSIA
This is the gem of the genus as far as I am concerned. It is a beauty, decorated in spring with charming fruity-smelling, red, fuchsia-like flowers at every node. Although much thinner than a fuchsia,

Left: *Ribes sanguineum*

they have that typical "up and down" look considered unique to a fuchsia and the same whiskery anthers appearing below the skirt. The flowers also hang down and the flowering display lasts for a month or more. It is only when you look at the leaf that you see that they are very different from fuchsias, with small, gooseberry-like leaves in a *fleur-de-lis* style. Bright apple green, new leaves are bristly at first, becoming smooth and shiny with age. It is ever-green, or almost so, and the contrast between the two types of leaf is most appealing. The stems are bristly, with three sharp spines at every node, so take care how you handle this plant.

This interesting shrub is ideal for training up against a wall as it likes hot, dry, sunny places. Put it on the side with least rain and the most sun. It hates to get wet feet and I have had to treat it like an epiphyte by planting it in an open-ended cylinder because of my wet climate. This crafty technique keeps arid-loving plants alive in wet regions, providing the plant is kept stable. By keeping the base of the trunk above ground level the plant is able to sur-vive because the crown can breathe. When the plant is happy it starts to sucker a little. From California. Height x width 3–6 ft (1–2 m). ZONE 7.

For something different, search out **Ribes laurifolium**, a dense, evergreen bush with leaves like an "improved" *Viburnum tinus*. It is a fabulous ground cover shrub. Originates from China. Height 2 ft (60 cm) x width 3 ft (1m). ZONE 8.

Speciosum = beautiful, special.

Above: *Ribes speciosum*

Romneya

TREE POPPY, MATILIJA POPPY
Papaveraceae

This genus contains only two species and they are both good choices for fragrance, as their showy white flowers are beautifully honey-scented. These flowers, like white poppies, have a boss of yellow stamens and their crinkled petals look like crepe paper but are deceptively tough. They only open during the heat of summer and are undeterred by scorching sun or wind.

I think romneyas are amazing shrubs, but they are quite demanding in their needs. I don't think there is a climate too hot for them, but it can easily be too cold. They also prefer a dryish atmosphere, although they will grow in damp climates providing the drainage is perfect. Think hot and dry, like their homeland in southern California and northern Mexico, and you won't go wrong.

It is an exaggeration to call them "tree poppies," as they are soft shrubs at most. They are a kind of sub-shrub and best treated as a perennial in cooler climates. Cut them down in winter to re-emerge in the spring, as they tend to be deciduous in cold regions and evergreen elsewhere. *Romneya* are one of those tricky plants you either have as weeds, or you don't have at all. They are a bit like mint in that they like to romp and sucker through the ground. If you try to contain them, they get moody and die. They are more than happy growing in old rubble and similar rough sites, but if you treat them too kindly by giving them nice rich loam, they are likely to die. They're not fussy as regards acidity or alkalinity, just remember good drainage is essential.

The trident-like, blue-gray leaves give the clue that they are suited to a sunny climate and used to coping with drought. In fact, the plants must be in full sun or they fade away. Romneyas love being near the coast, but will grow inland as well, given those essential ingredients of sun, warmth and drainage. They are reasonably robust and cope with wind, although strong wind can make the plants tumble.

These plants would probably be more common if they were easier to propagate. They are very tricky to root from stem or branch cuttings and so are traditionally grown from root cuttings. As they are suckering plants, you would think just pulling up a runner would work, but more often than not they die. In fact, even transplanting from pots purchased from a nursery is tricky. They never look very enticing in a garden center and are purchased more on the basis of reputation than their visual impact. Take extreme care when planting and have a site prepared with open, gravelly soil. Don't disturb them once planted until at least three years later, when you might be tempted to give a runner to a special friend to try. Don't ever fertilize them or attempt to shift to another spot. Being such unique-looking plants they don't blend easily with others and look best in a drift, growing on a sunny slope where room is not at a premium. Tidy gardeners need not apply.

Romneya = after Thomas Romney Robinson (1792–1882), an early 19th-century Irish astronomer who was director of the Armagh Observatory. He was also a poet, a priest and a great orator.

Romneya coulteri
CALIFORNIAN TREE POPPY

This is the more lax of the two *Romneya*, often tumbling and flop-ping over like a perennial plant. Smooth flower buds open to huge, white, scented flowers with a heady pollen fragrance that seems to intoxicate bees. If you cut the stems while in bud, the flowers will open in a vase and last for several days as a spectacular table dec-oration. Each stem ends in one large flower, but as the plant gains strength the bigger stems divide near the top and have six or seven flowers, with the central one opening first. Eventually, super-

strong stems emerge that have more than one flower off each divide, providing more than a dozen blooms per stem. Native to California and northern Mexico. Height 3–6 ft (1–2 m) x width 3–10 ft (1–3 m). ZONE 8.

Coulteri = after Irishman Thomas Coulter (1793–1843) who discovered the plant in California in 1844. His herbarium collection became the basis of the Trinity College Herbarium in Dublin, Ireland.

Romneya trichocalyx

Although the stems are thinner than *Romneya coulteri*, this species has a more bush-like appearance. The easy key to its identification is the hairy flower buds. *R. trichocalyx* is thought to be more cold-

hardy and the flowers are less fragrant, but still with that honey-like scent. Native to California. Height 3–5 ft (1–1.5 m) x width 3–6 ft (1–2 m). ZONE 8.

There is a hybrid called **'White Cloud'**, but don't worry too much about which one to choose, because they are all lovely. All are around the same size and hardiness.

Trichocalyx = having a hairy calyx.

Rosa

ROSE
Rosaceae

Somehow roses are the epitome of fragrant plants. Whenever anyone offers us a rose, we automatically sniff it, assuming it will have a perfume. Walk into any garden when the roses are in bloom and that top-of-the-nose perfume goes straight to your brain in a heady way. A few minutes later, the scent has disappeared, as if your scent-detectors have been overpowered or even anesthetized. And yet many roses have little or no scent, and we are disappointed, grumbling at rose breeders for "breeding out all the scent," and insisting that only perfumed roses are worth growing. However, roses can be grown simply

Left: *Romneya trichocalyx*

Right: *Romneya coulteri*

for their wonderful flower shape and colour, for their foliage or their fruits (known as haws or hips). Some are even grown for their beautiful thorns.

Roses grow naturally all over the Northern Hemisphere, from the Arctic Circle south to hot regions like Mexico, North Africa and India, and all across Europe, Asia and North America. It is very hard to generalize about this genus because of this variety of habitat. We can say that they are easy to grow, but not always easy to grow well. Although most can cope with acidic or alkaline soils, as well as heavy ground such as clays, they are prone to numerous pests and diseases.

Almost all roses need full sun and prefer a sheltered site, and they are all encouraged by a feed of animal manure or compost. Modern hybrid roses can be difficult to blend with other plants and are happiest in beds and borders devoted totally to them. However, the more old-fashioned roses are much easier to meld with other plants and are usually more robust and not so demanding of our disease-eradicating skills.

Rosa = from Celtic "rhodd" or "rhudd," meaning red.

English roses

There are, of course, hundreds of hybrid roses with lovely scents, especially in the hybrid teas. Because there are so many to choose from, for fragrance, color and foliage, I have concentrated on the species roses and some venerable hybrids and forms. Worthy of special mention, however, is the newer breed of "English Roses," bred with the intention of creating bushes able to withstand average garden conditions. Not everyone wants to be out spraying and tending their roses every weekend. Not only are they more robust

and less likely to have pests or diseases common to the hybrid teas and the floribundas, but they have been bred for fine blooms and most importantly for scent. Most are repeat-flowering plants and have blowzy, old-fashioned-looking blooms. David Austin of Shropshire, England is the greatest exponent of the art of breeding these fine plants. The most successful have been the yellows and pinks, while some of the reds and darker colors still seem prone to disease. Height x width 6–10 ft (2–3 m). ZONE 6.

Above: English Rose 'Abraham Darby'

Rosa x *alba*, syn *Rosa* x *alba* 'Maxima', R. 'Alba Maxima'

WHITE ROSE OF YORK, JACOBITE ROSE, GREAT DOUBLE WHITE ROSE

These are tall, arching shrubs with a bluish cast to the leaves. They are grown for the lemony scent of the white to soft pink flowers, which appear in spring and early summer, and also because they are so tough and adaptable. You can grow them almost anywhere, even in shade, which is an anathema to most roses. They resist dis-

Above: English Rose 'Mary Rose'

'**Alba Plena**' is the double white form and '**Lutea**' (syn var *lutea*) the double yellow. '**Lutescens**' is the single yellow and '**Normalis**' (syn var *normalis*) the beautiful single, creamy white form. Native to western and central China. For all, height x width 20–40 ft (6–12 m). ZONE 7.

Banksiae = Named after the wife of Sir Joseph Banks (1743–1820), the founder of London's Kew Gardens.

Rosa bracteata
CHICKASAW ROSE, MACARTNEY ROSE

A bristly, thorny, spring-flowering rambler rose for an informal situation. The glossy evergreen leaves look good all year and the bright new leaves provide a pleasant contrast with the old. Best of all, the "fried egg" white flowers have a boss of yellow stamens. Thankfully you can inhale the lemony scent without having to get too close to the spiny stems. Prune occasionally as desired for shape, but this rose is not too vigorous and can be left untouched for years. Also free of pests and diseases. This rose hails from China. Height x width 5–10 ft (1.5–3 m). ZONE 7.

Bracteata = having prominent bracts.

Rosa x centifolia
CABBAGE ROSE, PROVENCE ROSE

Some say this fine old rose dates back to the days of Roman emperors and Cleopatra, while other researchers say they were brought into cultivation about 200 years ago. Either way, these full, almost cluttered, flowers, which appear in summer, are appealing and have a fruity, old-fashioned rose scent. The scent is always stronger on hot days and the petals are used for rosewater and potpourri. The mass of jam-packed petals overlap like leaves on a cabbage, hence the common name. Even the leaves are scented, both "on the air" and if crushed. Initially an upright bush

ease and are simple easy-care plants. They were taken as an emblem in England by the House of York during the War of the Roses in the 15th century and later by the Jacobites around 200 years later. The flowers are squat and wayward but still delightful and their pure, sweet fragrance is heavenly. Height x width 12 ft (4 m). ZONE 4.

Alba = white.

Rosa banksiae, syn *R. banksiae* var *alba*, *R. banksiae* 'Alba Plena'
DOUBLE WHITE BANKSIAN ROSE, LADY BANK'S ROSE

First introduced from China in 1807, it has been popular ever since. This lovely old rose has winning ways—it is thornless and in late spring is laden with pretty little, white, violet-scented flowers. Another advantage is its resistance to diseases and bugs. Grow one up through an old tree or, better still, allow it to clamber over an old tree stump where the branches can drape down with cascades of flowers. You can prune it drastically or leave it unconstrained, depending on the setting. There are two white and two yellow forms, including a double form of each.

Above: *Rosa bracteata*

Above: *Rosa damascena*, the damask rose.

Left: *Rosa rugosa* 'Roseraie de l'Hay'

just over waist-high, they tumble and arch with the weight of foliage and flowers. Numerous delightful cultivars are available, including **'Fantin-Latour'** and **'La Noblesse'**. Height 3–5 ft (1–1.5 m) x width 5 ft (1.5 m). ZONE 4.

Centifolia = 100 leaves, referring to the mass of petals.

Rosa damascena

DAMASK ROSE

In summer, this bush often arches over with the weight of its blooms. The cluttered informal heads in white, pink, red or purple come with a fantastic fruity perfume. The cultivar **'Tringini-petala'** (and some others) are grown for attar of roses, the essential oil extracted from rose petals. Originates from the Middle East. Height x width 3–6 ft (1–2 m). ZONE 4.

Damascena = after the city of Damascus, Syria, from where it was supposedly brought home by the Crusaders.

Rosa pimpinellifolia, syn R. spinosissima

BURNET ROSE, SCOTCH ROSE, SCOTS ROSE

A somewhat ungainly but delightful rose covered in tiny, thin thorns. In early spring and summer the single, creamy white or rosy pink flowers appear freely with a simply delicious scent—a mixture of lilac and sweet rose. The reddish chocolate stems push out their new growths at the stem tips and the tiny, serrated leaves are charming, but the *pièce de résistance* is their tiny buds. Each new side growth is topped with a miniature bud opening to a soft rosy pink, or in some cases creamy white, and a richer color within. Easy to grow in full sun and any soil, and free of pests. It is a dense thicket and suckers moderately. It grows from eastern Europe through Asia. Height 3 ft (1 m) x width 6 ft (2 m). ZONE 3.

Pimpinellifolia = leaves like a pimpernel.

Rosa rugosa

HEDGEHOG ROSE, JAPANESES ROSE, RAMANAS ROSE, SEA TOMATO

An upright, suckering shrub growing over head-high given good conditions. The stems and contoured leaves are covered in bristles and spines and the sweet-smelling flowers, in pinks and rich wine-reds, can be simple singles or complex doubles. They appear from spring into summer and the scent is so rich and fruity, we invariably inhale a second draft. Grow the plant in hard conditions such as heavy clays to reduce the height to a more manageable level, the better to appreciate the flowers. It also grows on pure sand and surprisingly takes semi-shade. In fact, it is one of the toughest roses around, coping with severe cold, strong winds and even coastal conditions. Several cultivars exist, including my all-time favorite, **'Roseraie de l'Hay'**, a richly scented, purple-red, double-flowered rose. This rose comes from Japan, Korea and northern China. Height 3–6 ft (1–2 m) x width 8 ft (2.5 m). ZONE 2.

Rugosa = wrinkled or corrugated.

Rosmarinus

Rosmarinus officinalis

ROSEMARY

Lamiaceae

The species name *officinalis* is a useful one to learn because it means "herbal." Literally it means "of the shop," which translates to pharmacists as being useful, edible or herbal. This fine Mediterranean plant has been grown since ancient times, and with its aromatic foliage and flowers it is a stalwart of culinary herb and cottage gardens, not to mention seaside gardens. Commonly known as rosemary, it has been greatly popularized in name and song.

A typical rosemary is an upright, multi-stemmed shrub around head height, with stems clad in tight, dark green leaves in a rotating bristle fashion. These thin, spiky leaves completely encase the stem from base to tip, and through spring to early summer, and sometimes again in the fall, near the tips there are small, blue flowers like mini-foxgloves in a long cone.

Sometimes the bush becomes woody and sparse and may need thinning or pruning to encourage rejuvenation. As long as you are not too ruthless, the bush will quickly recover. Being evergreen, it is perfect for any border, creating an accent by being so upright. Full sun and maximum heat are the best recipe for this plant and, like so many Mediterranean plants, it can cope with drought, although it is equally content in wet climates if the drainage is good. It is not at all fussy about soil or acidity and transplants quite easily as a container-grown specimen. It will not take kindly to being shifted once in place. It is much easier to root some cuttings, even by putting them directly into the ground where you would like a new plant. Like so many smelly bushes, it is free of bugs and pests. It can be damaged by severe frosts when young, but if kept in a dry soil is less likely to succumb to cold.

Rosemary is very useful as a bold shrub for seaside gardens, for windy places, and in large tubs near the house to use for Mediterranean flavoring. It can also be used as an informal hedge in a herb garden. Rosemary has for centuries been used in meat and chicken dishes and also in the manufacture of Eau de

Left: *Rosmarinus officinalis* 'Prostratus'

Above: *Rosmarinus officinalis* 'Tuscan Blue'

Cologne and so it is a very familiar scent. Native to the Mediterranean. Height 3–6 ft (1–2 m) x width 3–5 ft (1–1.5 m). ZONE 8.

'Prostratus' is a form with a completely different habit, and if planted at the top of a wall, it will hang down for over 3 ft (1 m). The leaves are shorter and the overall habit is smaller and neater. While it is somewhat tender, when grown on hot walls this should not be a problem. It is not an easy plant to keep weed-free in a flat garden as its growth is not dense enough to suppress the weeds. Draped over a wall is the ideal setting. Height 6 in (15 cm) x width 3 ft (1 m). ZONE 8.

'Tuscan Blue' is an upright form with deeper blue, showier flowers that often appear in winter as well as summer. It has a tidier habit, but is slightly more tender than the species. Height

x width 3–6 ft (1–2 m). ZONE 8. There are numerous other named cultivars said to be better than the wild rosemary.

Ros = dew or spray; *marinus* = sea, because this plant often grows naturally on sea cliffs where it is drenched in sea spray.

Ruta

Ruta graveolens
COMMON RUE
Rutaceae

This is an amazing little evergreen plant and is unusual in many ways. For a start, it has blue foliage, which is almost unique in the plant world. The named form **'Jackman's Blue'** is an especially good blue color. If you brush past rue, it gives off a pleasant but strong odor that is acrid and overpowering if you crush the leaves. Apparently the crushed leaves of rue were strewn around in courtrooms in olden times to disguise the smell of the prisoners. Last but not least, it is a valuable little shrub for sunny borders. The ferny foliage is very handsome and in high summer little brushes of rich yellow flowers appear on the tips of the stems.

Some people are allergic to the foliage and come out in a skin rash if they touch it, so take care where you plant it. It is a great border plant as it only grows knee-high and is ideal for those little spots that are difficult to fill. It loves hot, dry, sunny conditions typical of Mediterranean plants, as it comes from southern Europe. Any well-drained soil will do and it is especially happy in alkaline soil.

While it is generally a tidy little plant, it will accept a light trim in the spring before the new growth starts. The leaf color is more intense when the plant is grown in full sun and not overly lush or too well fed. Rue is the center for the Rutaceae family, which includes oranges and lemons as well as *Choisya*. It is sometimes known as the "herb of grace." From southeastern Europe. Height x width 2 ft (60 cm). ZONE 5.

Ruta = from the Greek "rhyteé," meaning obscure;
graveolens = strong smelling.

Right: *Ruta graveolens*

Salvia

SAGE
Lamiaceae

Salvias have been in cultivation for centuries as culinary herbs, for medicine and for ornament, and yet new species and cultivars are becoming available all the time. Most have some aromatic air about them, from the pleasant kitchen sage through to spicy-, acrid- or even musty-smelling leaves.

Salvias grow across such a wide number of territories in Europe, Asia, and North and South America that it is not surprising new ones are being discovered or rediscovered all the time. Many of them are herbaceous perennials and some are shrubby or woody. Nearly all of them are heat-lovers and cope with drought and hot climates. That is not to say wet-climate gardeners cannot grow them, they just have to be more diligent about providing good drainage and maximum light. Having said that, some of the larger species will grow in shade in warm zones. It is such a large genus that it is difficult to make hard-and-fast rules. Typical of the Lamiaceae, salvias cope with both acidic and alkaline soils and seem almost to prefer poor soils providing the drainage is free. All salvias are easy to transplant and propagate. Some are cold-hardy and some are not. Some are evergreen, some are hairy-leafed to handle wind, and a few are wispy and delicate. Flowers usually appear from midsummer onwards in terminal spikes and each flower has two big petals forming the lower lip and a hooded top. Salvias certainly add a dazzling array of colors to borders, with anything from hot reds to true blues, smoky mauves, lilac, pinks and even yellows and near-black. The leaves are always opposite on distinctive square stems.

Salvia = from the Latin "salvare," to save, meaning safe or unharmed.

Right: *Salvia gesnerifolia*

Above: *Salvia officinalis* 'Purpurascens' and *Daphne odora.*

Salvia elegans
PINEAPPLE SAGE

A large, dense, soft-leafed shrub with neat, heart-shaped, very pointed opposite leaves making a neat patterned bush. Crush a leaf and enjoy the strong pineapple scent or wait until summer to enjoy the long panicles of red flowers. From Mexico. Height 5 ft (1.5 m) x width 7 ft (2 m). ZONE 8.

Salvia gesnerifolia is very similar.

Elegans = beautiful or choice.

Salvia involucrata 'Bethellii'
ROSYLEAF SAGE

A rather sparse shrub with a subtle sage scent. It has dull, hairy leaves and from late summer to mid fall terminal cones gradually release the tubular flowers in a shocking pink, cerise color. It is evergreen in warm zones but can be cut to the ground in cold climates to re-emerge the following spring. It will grow in sun or part-shade and is a useful plant in light woodland. Originates in Mexico. Height x width 3 ft (1 m). ZONE 8 OR 9.

Involucrata = wrapped or covered, referring to the cap on the flower head.

Salvia leucantha
MEXICAN BUSH SAGE

An open, soft shrub with long, narrow, furry leaves and arching spikes of soft purple flowers. Plant a group of them at the front of a border for late summer color. The flowers and leaves have a musty sage scent. Native to Mexico. Height x width 3 ft (1 m). ZONE 8.

Leuca = white; *antha* = flowers.

Salvia officinalis
COMMON SAGE, PURPLE SAGE

This common or garden sage has been popular for centuries and is a useful, dense, shrubby plant for a sunny border. The leaves have the distinctive sage smell that we associate with cooking. The scent is much stronger when the leaves are crushed. The long, felted leaves are usually deep green but there are some interesting leaf

colors. **'Icterina'** has leaves that are gray-green splashed with gold. The leaves of **'Purpurascens'** are soft, velvety and purple, with matching purple flowers. **'Tricolor'** has leaves that are a peculiar mix of green, cream and purplish pink. The species is from the Mediterranean. Height 2–3 ft (60 cm–1 m) x width 3 ft (1m). ZONE 5.

Officinalis = useful or medicinal.

Salvia x sylvestris (S. nemerosa x S. pratensis)

A low, dense plant topped with beautiful long spikes of purple or blue flowers in early to midsummer. Becomes a permanent shrub in warm climates but regarded as a temporary plant in colder climates, as the cold can kill it. There are lots of lovely named clones in blues and pinks, but all have the soft sage fragrance. Height 2–3 ft (60 cm–1 m) x width 3 ft (1 m). ZONE 5.

Sylvestris = of the woods.

Right: *Salvia involucrata* 'Bethellii'

Right: *Salvia* x
sylvestris

Santolina

Santolina chamaecyparissus
LAVENDER COTTON
Asteraceae

Sometimes known as "lavender cotton," this low-growing shrub is a perfect ground cover for a sunny site. You only need brush past the plant to get the aroma and it has a very strong camphor scent if crushed. It is a Mediterranean plant, long cultivated in herb gardens for its strong scent. It creates a low, tumbling mound with contours like a rolling hillside. Just give it plenty of sun, heat and good drainage and the plant will do the rest. It is dense enough to suppress any weeds, providing you start with the ground free of deeply rooted perennials. It is an evergreen bush in a true silver color with thin narrow leaves hugging the stem like some kind of pipe cleaner. The leaves are covered in a white felt, protecting the bush from hot sun and drought. Yellow, disk-like flowers last two months in high summer and appear way above the plant like antennae.

Left to its own devices it spreads and tumbles but you can use it to make a neat little hedge if you clip the bushes regularly. The plant can also be used to hang over walls and is even better blended with heathers and conifers for color variation. It is a plant that bushes up nicely if trimmed on a regular basis and surprisingly will shoot up again if you cut it back to stumps. Some people recommend clipping it all the time to prevent flowering, suggesting that the creamy yellow flowers don't blend with the silver foliage. I rather like the haphazard nature of the flowers.

So, *Santolina chamaecyparissus* needs plenty of sunlight and heat and the drainage must be good, otherwise it is not fussy about ground conditions, growing as well in limestone as it does in acidic soil. Actually, it grows better in poor, impoverished soil than it does in rich, well-fed sites. It does not like wet feet, but it will cope with humid climates providing it has good free drainage. It becomes thin and sparse if shaded by other plants and even in a sunny site will need an occasional prune to keep it dense. It takes wind and grows quite happily in coastal sites.

Above: *Santolina chamaecyparissus*

It is an easy plant to propagate from cuttings. But don't be tempted to move an older plant because it will probably die. Native to the western and central Mediterranean. Height 1 ft (30 cm) x width 3 ft (1 m). ZONE 7.

A smaller, denser form called **'Nana'** is ideal for hedges and rock gardens. Height x width 1 ft (30 cm). There are new forms with bright lemon-yellow foliage and others with deep green leaves called **'Lemon Fizz'** and **'Lime Fizz'** respectively.

Santo = Latin "sanctum," meaning holy; *linum* = flax;

chamaecyparissus = with cypress-like foliage.

Sarcococca

CHRISTMAS BOX, SWEET BOX
Buxaceae

If I showed you a *Sarcococca* you would think it was rather ordinary, but this bush has at least three outstanding qualities. In late winter or early spring the flowers emerge and the scent is divine—a sweet, "top of the nose" scent. Its shiny, dark green leaves look as if they have been specially polished and, being evergreen, it looks good all year. Another wonderful attribute is that it grows in dense shade, and we should treasure every plant willing to grow where few plants want to be. Any one of these qualities should be reason enough to grow one or more of these fine shrubs, but it seems that gardeners want more… they want pretty flowers. With *Sarcococca* they are so small and hidden you could be forgiven for asking, "What flowers?" But what they lack in size and color, they more than compensate for with their marvelous sweet fragrance.

It always amazes me that when gardeners are desperate to find a plant to grow in dry shade and I suggest *Sarcococca* or *Aucuba*, or perhaps *Mackaya*, they say no thanks. They want showy flowers, too.

As you will have gathered, I'm a bit of a fan of *Sarcococca*. I love easy-care, tough plants that will fill a difficult role. This one

is more robust than most, coping not only with shade but dry shade, and with any climate, any soil, in fact anything but hot sun. You only need to spread the roots out at planting time, otherwise leave the plants to their own devices. It is possible to move older plants in winter if you find a better spot but why not just buy more of them? They look good in drifts and make a fine ground cover. You can trim them with shears if you want to create a smooth-topped appearance, but generally no pruning is necessary.

All of the species in this genus hail from China and East Asia. The red berries would look at home on many a *Pyracantha*, *Sorbus* or *Cotoneaster*.

Sarca = from Greek "sarx," meaning flesh;

kokkos = berry; therefore, fleshy berry.

Sarcococca confusa
A low, dense bush with pointed, glossy leaves. In early spring the creamy, sweetly fragrant flowers appear, followed by black berries. From China. Height 2–3 ft (60 cm–1 m) x width 3 ft (1 m). ZONE 5.

Confusa = confused.

Sarcococca hookeriana var digyna
This is an erect shrub and in comparison to most it has pale, almost camouflage-wear, khaki-colored leaves. Some forms have narrow, lance-like leaves and others are almost oval. The fragrant white flowers arrive in early spring and are violet-scented. Native to western China. Height 6 ft (2 m) x width 3 ft (1 m). ZONE 8.

Hookeriana = from Sir Joseph Dalton Hooker (1817–1911), botanist, plant

hunter and later, Director of Kew Gardens; *digyna* = two styles.

Sarcococca hookeriana var humilis, syn S. humilis
This is the opposite to the above variety, being at times very low-growing, almost ground-hugging, with long, narrow, blackish green leaves. It also has white, violet-scented flowers in spring, followed by black berries. It is native to western China and the Himalayas. Height 18 in (45 cm) x width 3 ft (1 m). ZONE 6.

Humilis = small or dwarf.

Sarcococca ruscifolia
This is the most likely *Sarcococca* that you will find for sale and the sweet violet fragrance of its flowers are the best of the genus. Its shiny, blackish leaves and tight, compact habit make it a perfect little shrub for those difficult spots we all have in our gardens. The flowers are produced in early spring and are followed by red berries. From China. Height x width 4 ft (1.2 m). ZONE 8.

Ruscifolia = having leaves like a *Ruscus* or butcher's broom.

Schima

Schima wallichii, S. khasiana, S. superba
Theaceae

This rare genus is related to camellias, and so, unsurprisingly, the flowers have a wonderful tea fragrance. It is an evergreen tree and the handsome leaves have an exotic look about them, but I always feel it should have bigger and brighter flowers. Thought I shouldn't complain about such an easy-care, pest-free shrub. After all, it tolerates city pollution, poor, heavy soil, drought, and (in some cases) cold winters.

Above: *Sarcococca ruscifolia*

Right: *Schima
superba*

It is a rather confused genus and botanists are busy trying to put all the *Schima* into one species. But to gardeners the variations are too great. For instance, *S. superba* and *S. wallichii* have smooth, oval, finger-length leaves while *S. khasiana* has corrugated leaves that are twice as long.

However, naming details aside, the structure of a typical *Schima* is tidy and often multi-trunked, with a very upright, almost columnar shape in the early years. It does become broader at the top with age and finally loses its lower branches, but it is possible to keep it clothed right to the ground as a dense shrub rather than becoming a tree. Prune or trim as you see fit, though they have a good natural shape. The stems are smooth and the leaves are usually presented in a semi-circle, like a hand. It is an ideal bush for woodland gardens, adding substance with the simple outline and glossy, evergreen foliage. You can also use it as a dense backdrop

plant. The only drawback with planting it away from the path is that you will miss out on the cup-shaped, scented, white flowers in midsummer to fall. They look more like a *Eucryphia* than a camellia. To cultivate a robust *Schima*, give it full sun for maximum heat, adequate shelter and an acidic, free-draining soil. The leaves are reasonably tolerant of wind, but the bush is vulnerable to storm damage in the early years. Winter is the problem: like so many plants, if it receives hot summer temperatures it copes with more winter cold. Originates along the Himalayas, western China, Vietnam and Taiwan, even into Borneo. Height 30 ft (10 m) x width 10 ft (3 m). ZONE 8 OR 9, but can survive colder zones if given enough summer heat.

Schima = from Greek "skiasma," meaing shadow or shelter, referring to the plant's thick canopy of leaves.

Skimmia

Rutaceae

Skimmia are well-known shrubs, popular for their tidiness rather than their scent. However, many of them have delightfully citrus-scented flowers. Again, the family provides a clue, as many Rutaceae plants (such as oranges) have a strong perfume. Even the leaves of some species have a pungent odor. Certainly they are neat evergreen bushes and seem so handy, even utilitarian. But don't ignore the lush dark, leathery leaves, the brilliant red berries and the oft-neglected scented flower clusters. They are ideal for narrow borders around the house, those troublesome spots with too much shade, poor heavy soil or sneaky winds. They are tough, tidy and resilient, and *Skimmia* are bushes that will never need trimming. Another bonus is that they grow happily in shade but will also grow in sun in cool climates. They often look pale or anemic when grown in hot sun. They also grow in alkaline as well as acidic ground. They cope with city pollution and they handle wind and coastal conditions.

Easy to transplant when young, *Skimmia* don't move well later on. A plant's family often indicates what conditions it will tolerate, and in this case we know they won't like being shifted, as *Choisya* and other plants in the Rutaceae family all resent being moved.

I think of *Skimmia* as the cold-climate version of *Raphiolepis*, but they are not always happy in warm, humid climates (zone 10 or more). Small, yellowish or red buds open to fragrant off-white flowers in the spring followed by radiant red berries. Although you notice the flowers, it is really the resulting berries that stand out. Most plants are either male or female, and so both are needed for a crop of berries. The males seem to have the better scent, but obviously the females are required in order to enjoy the berries. First introduced in 1850 by Robert Fortune (1812–1880), from plants he found in Chinese gardens. The original clone is now named after him.

Skimmia = adapted from "shikimi," the Japanese name for these plants.

Skimmia x confusa (*S. anquetilia* x *S. japonica*)

A dense, compact, evergreen plant and the best for flowers and lemony fragrance—it even has spicy aromatic foliage. The creamy white clusters of flowers appear in spring. Several named clones exist, such as **'Kew Green'**, a male clone with larger flower heads. This plant has previously been called *Skimmia melanocarpa* and *S. laureola*—so everyone is confused. Height 3 ft (1 m) x width 4 ft (1.2 m). ZONES 7 TO 9.

Confusa = confused.

Skimmia japonica
JAPANESE SKIMMIA

Always a joy in winter when the lustrous red holly-like berries may be the only color in the garden. Good, robust, dense evergreen with the added feature of citrus-scented, creamy white flowers in spring, contrasting with the little red flower buds, especially in the male clone **'Fragrans'**. Height 3 ft (1 m) x width 4 ft (1.2 m). ZONES 7 TO 8.

Japonica = from Japan.

Left and far left: *Skimmia japonica* showing both the creamy white spring flowers and the bright red winter berries.

Right: *Spartium junceum*

Spartium

Spartium junceum
SPANISH BROOM
Fabaceae

There is only one species in this genus, but what it lacks in kin it makes up for in dynamism. It is a remarkable shrub with dazzling flowers. They have a strong, old-wine scent, fantastic shape and a unique countenance. Its lovely fluted stems shooting skywards are so distinctive that they add a vertical dimension to any border or garden scene. The real leaves are tiny and soon fall off, so it is the green stems that sustain the plant. Being leafless, hard and waxy, the bush is supremely wind hardy. Plant in the hottest, sunniest spot you can find and, indeed, any place that doesn't remain damp. It handles drought with ease, as well as any variety of soils—acidic, alkaline, sand, clay or rock... this plant doesn't care. In fact, it is probably better served with a poor site.

They should be planted young and never moved again. Just make sure you spread the roots at planting time and perhaps stake it until the base is secure. From then on it is indestructible. Prune back after flowering to keep the plant lower and stop it from getting top-heavy. This will extend the life of the plant as, like many legume bushes, it is inclined to be short-lived if allowed to reach maximum height in a short time. It is sometimes a difficult plant to blend into a traditional garden, but instead of trying to make it blend, why not make use of its exciting vertical aspect to add drama to your garden.

Anytime between spring and fall the reed-like stems are smothered in brilliant, golden-yellow, pea-like flowers. Some seasons it blooms twice. Take time to cut a few stems for a vase so you can enjoy the knock-out perfume in your home as well. They look very much at home in arid places, as you would expect, being native to Portugal and Spain. Height 10 ft (3 m) x width 6 ft (2 m). Happy in any climate from ZONE 6.

Spartium = from Greek "spartos," meaning cord or rope, referring to the stringy stems; *junceum* = rush-like.

Staphylea

BLADDERNUT
Staphyleaceae

Its large, upright, rather rangy habit originally put me off this plant, and I always felt I could use the garden space for something showier. Now that I realize it has fragrant flowers—with perfume reminiscent of dry spices, or perhaps almonds—I think I should show them more respect.

Staphyleas are native to eastern North America, Europe, and through to the hot and dry parts of Asia and China. They are all similar in habit, forming an upright, airy bush with new canes or

Above: *Staphylea colchica*

Above: *Syringa oblata* var *dilatata*

watershoots appearing lower down to replace the older spent wood. The leaves, with their pale green leaflets, are similar to those of ash trees. In cold climates the flowers appear before the leaves, but in warmer zones they both appear simultaneously. The five-petaled, waxy flowers are small, but when clustered together in long racemes they are quite lovely. They do earn a place in a large woodland garden but rarely qualify in an urban setting where space is at a premium.

These hardy, deciduous shrubs are easy to grow in any soil, any climate—indeed anywhere that is not too windy. They are especially valuable for gardeners on limestone soil, where it is a struggle to find shrubs capable of thriving. You can transplant at any size, prune heavily if necessary, and do just about anything you like to them.

The flowers are more profuse in regions where summers are hot, and are followed by strange, inflated, bladder-like seed pods, giving them their common name "bladdernut." These opaque structures have two or three compartments and look more like jellyfish than anything belonging to a plant. Children think they are fun to "pop" between their fingers. The name comes from the Greek "staphlye," for bunch or bunches of flowers. Of all the bushes that could have earned this name, why did *Staphylea* qualify I wonder?

Staphyle = Greek, for bunch or bunches of flowers.

Staphylea colchica

A stiff, upright plant with neat, striated, gray-striped, smooth stems. The pale leaves have three to five shiny leaflets. The panicles of pure white, almond-scented flowers appear in late spring, followed by big green bladder pods. **Staphylea pinnata** is similar. Native to the Caucasus, Europe. Height 10 ft (3 m) x 6 ft (2 m). ZONE 6.

Colchica = from Colchis, former name for the Caucasus.

Staphylea holocarpa 'Rosea'

This is the *Staphylea* you are most likely to see in gardens, as it has the best flowers. In most species the flowers are white, but this form has delightful pink-tinged blooms with an almond fragrance. It also has a bonus of bronzy-colored new leaf growth. From western China. Height 10 ft (3 m) x width 6 ft (2 m). ZONE 6.

Holocarpa = whole fruit.

Syringa

LILAC
Oleaceae

Lilacs are a worthy addition to any mixed border or shrubbery and for all of them the flowers have a sweet, fruity fragrance. They like alkaline or neutral soils and cold winters, although they will cope with very hot summers as long as they have had a proper winter. Lilacs are deciduous shrubs, thriving from North America and Eastern Europe right through to Asia, often growing in severe climates with extreme cold or drought and baking hot summers. They need good drainage, full sun and preferably some shelter, although this is not essential.

Being deciduous, they can be shifted when the leaves are off without any difficulty. Generally they form a good upright, slightly open shape and don't need any pruning but should you need to restrain them, they can be thinned after flowering. Some will tolerate, and regenerate from, more rigorous pruning.

Syringa = from the Greek "syrinx," meaning pipe or tube, which could refer to the tubular flowers or to the hollow stems that were once used for tobacco pipes.

Syringa x hyacinthiflora (*S. oblata* x *S. vulgaris*)

An upright shrub, becoming more spreading with age. Large cones of flowers with a fruit fragrance appear in spring in colors ranging from white to pink and purple. The heart-shaped leaves have the typical clean look that we associate with lilacs. They often have a bronzy tinge when they first emerge and it is one of the few lilacs to have any fall color, with hints of purple. Height 6–12 ft (2–4 m) x width 3–10 ft (1–3 m). ZONES 3 TO 8.

Hyacinthiflora = bearing flowers like a hyacinth.

Syringa meyeri 'Palibin', syn S. *palibiniana*
DWARF KOREAN LILAC

An amenable shrub ideal for small gardens and even for patios. The fruit scent is good, but not remarkable. However, two things set this plant apart. First, it is small enough to grow in any garden and, second, it is quite happy in warm, mild climates. The neat little rounded leaves have a smooth, clean appearance that lasts all summer. The surprisingly large panicles of flowers to 4 in (10 cm) long appear mid-spring. Each individual flower is a tiny tube of lilac-pink, and the overall effect is very ornamental. Height 3–6 ft (1–2 m) x 3 ft (1 m). ZONES 4 TO 9.

Meyeri = Named for the famous American plant explorer, Frank Meyer (1875–1918), who spent many years in the colder regions of China and Korea, searching mostly for edible plants.

Syringa oblata

A hardy, upright shrub with fragrant fruity-scented flowers that, true to its origins, needs hot summers and cold winters. Given the right conditions, it is a handsome, clean-leafed bush, often with a hint of purple in the leaves and in spring bears lovely lilac-blue flowers in wide, showy panicles. Native to China and Korea. Height 6–10 ft (2–3 m) x width 6 ft (2 m). ZONES 4 TO 8.

Oblata = widened, referring to the broad leaves.

Syringa x prestoniae (*S. reflexa* x *S. villosa*)
PRESTON LILAC

This beautiful group of hybrids are handsome, upright shrubs or small trees with cones of fruit-scented flowers appearing in late spring to early summer. They are super-hardy and, being late-flowering, have a low risk of frost damage to the flowers. They come in a variety of colors, from pink to lilac to deep purple. Height 10–12 ft (3–4 m) x width 6–10 ft (2–3 m). ZONES 2 TO 8.

Prestoniae = after Isabella Preston (1881–1965), of Ottawa, Ontario, who developed the plants in the1920s.

Syringa vulgaris
COMMON LILAC, FRENCH LILAC

This lilac demonstrates that "vulgaris" means "common" or "plentiful" not "vulgar," for although it is common, it has the most exquisite flowers and sweet, fruity perfume. Typically a tall, upright bush or small tree with gray stems and a tidy habit, it needs no pruning apart from shaping in the early years. Lilacs do not have a central leader, as they produce twin buds on the top of each stem and so naturally fork into two shoots. The smooth, heart-shaped leaves add to their manicured appearance, and it is one of those rare plants that looks as luxuriant at the end of summer as it did at the beginning. It is almost the perfect boundary bush as it is unlikely to upset your neighbor, and will be appre-

Right: *Syringa vulgaris* 'Souvenir de Louis Späth'

ciated by both parties. Lilacs don't get too big or cast too much shade and they don't have messy leaves or flowers; all in all they are quite well behaved.

Lilacs like heavy soil including clay, and full sun to ripen the wood and produce more flowers. Most plants for sale are grafted on lilac seedlings or onto privet. Remove any suckers that may arise from the rootstock or they will take over the plant. Flowers appear late spring and early summer in big terminal cones 4–8 in (10–20 cm) long. They come in singles and doubles in colors ranging from white to cream, purple-pink to red. There are literally hundreds of cultivars. Originates in eastern Europe. Height 12–20 ft (4–6 m) x width 6–12 ft (2–4 m). ZONES 4 TO 8.

Vulgaris = common.

Tecoma

Tecoma stans
TRUMPET BUSH, YELLOW BELLS, YELLOW ELDER
Bignoniaceae

I have no idea why, but some gardeners don't like yellow flowers. This plant is no exception, until I tell them that the flowers smell like the finest quality chocolate or cocoa beans. After inhaling the heady brew, they are hooked. The opposite leaves are vaguely reminiscent of *Sambucus* or elderberry, giving it one of its common names. Good forms have lovely rugose leaves, much better than any elderberry. *Tecoma stans* vary considerably from seed. Some have thin, smooth leaves, a sparse habit and pale yellow, smallish, trumpet-shaped flowers while others have handsome contoured leaves and bigger, more richly colored flowers up to 2 in (5 cm) long. And then there is their divine scent! You will be drawn again and again to partake of this ambrosia. To say this is one of my favorite plants is an understatement.

Most of the tecomas come from Central and South America and are upright bushes. They seem to want to head skywards no matter how you prune them. In their wild state, they form a large, open bush or even a small tree up to 20 ft (6 m) high, but they are more usually around 10 ft (3 m) high and wide. Content to grow in heavy or difficult alkaline soils as well as acidic, as long as the drainage is good, they are equally happy in wet or dry climates. They may need extra summer moisture in some areas to keep up the lush growth. Site them in as hot and sunny a spot as you can find and make sure it is sheltered. The shrub is made up of soft, pithy stems, easily broken by strong winds.

It is evergreen, or nearly so, although in cold regions it will be deciduous. It doesn't really matter because it puts out strong, whippy growths in late spring and the flowers appear on the tips of these new stems. In theory it is not frost hardy, but if you can get a rootstock established it may be possible to treat it like *Erythrina crista-galli* or a *Buddleja*, where a stout central trunk is the permanent plant, and last summer's growth is cut back to the trunk by frost or by pruning every winter. You can prune it any time during the cold season when the bush is looking bedraggled, as it can do. In hot climates, it keeps a better winter coat and will flower nearly all summer. In cool regions, on the other hand, it seems to need to accumulate heat for the first half of the summer before it can bestow its gaudy flowers on us in late summer. Wherever you live, it still has a long flowering season compared to most shrubs.

It is native to Arizona and Texas, down through Mexico to Peru. Height 10–20 ft (3–6 m) x width 10–15 ft (3–5 m). ZONE 9.

Above: *Tecoma stans*

Tecoma = an abbreviation of the local Mexican name "tecomaxochitl";

stans = erect.

Ternstroemia

Ternstroemia gymnanthera
Theaceae

Although there are many *Ternstroemia* (mostly in the tropics) only one is commonly found in gardens. Small, white, soap-scented flowers appear midsummer, hanging on long, hooked appendages. Showy red berries follow the saucer-shaped blooms.

This dark-leafed relative of the camellia is grown for its shiny, leathery leaves and because it is evergreen and hardy. We always need compact evergreens to provide body and shape in the garden and it is nice to have options other than conifers and rhododendrons. This rugged, dense bush is an ideal alternative. The leaves are rounded, on a reddish petiole, or stalk, and are often crowded towards the tips of the stems, with an area of bare branch beneath. The leaves seem to change color with the seasons, being greener in summer and taking on an almost wine color in the winter; even the new spring leaves have a bronzy look.

You can prune these plants to whatever shape you desire, as they quickly regenerate from any trimming. The plant is rather unusual in that it will grow and even thrive in shade. So it is happy in sun or shade, wind or weather, and any soil will do as long as it is not alkaline.

It is easy to transplant the first time, but does not like being moved again. It is sometimes considered tender in marginal climates but as it hails from Korea, Japan and China it is hardy in regions with hot summers. Height x width 3 ft (10 m). ZONE 8.

> *Ternstroemia* = after Christopher Ternstroem, a Swedish botanist and student of Linnaeus. He sailed to China in 1735 to botanize and died on the return voyage in 1738; *gymnanthera* = naked flower.

There is a form called **'Variegata'**, with creamy white leaf margins, turning rosy in winter.

Above: (from left) *Indigofera decora*, *Ternstroemia* 'Burnished Gold', *Ternstroemia gymnanthera* and *T.* 'Variegata'.

An even better form is **'Burnished Gold'**, named by J.C. Raulston (1940–1996), founding director of the J. C. Raulston Arboretum in North Carolina. The new leaves are a lovely coppery gold and an exciting color variation for the garden.

Teucrium

GERMANDER
Lamiaceae

Germanders have tough, sage-scented leaves and are typical Mediterranean plants—give them full hot sun and terrible soil and they will be happy. They do seem to grow better in poor sites and, apart from loathing wet feet, are indifferent to soil. Breezy sites are fine, as are even downright windy places near the sea. Cold winters are not a problem, but cold, wet winters are, so in these climates find a dry wall to plant them against.

> *Teucrium* = Teucer, a king of ancient Troy.

Teucrium chamaedrys
WALL GERMANDER
A neat, little, evergreen sub-shrub with a sage-like smell. It is ideal for a ground cover in a sunny spot. It has small, bright green, hairy leaves and soft purple flowers all through summer. It is often considered to be a herbal or medicinal plant, as the soft leaf tips can be brewed to make an aromatic tea for rheumatism, fevers and skin disorders. Native to Europe and southwest Asia. Height 1–2 ft (30–60 cm) x width 2–3 ft (60–90 cm). ZONE 5.

> *Chamaedrys* = an old name for germander, meaning low to the ground; *chamae* = dwarf or on the ground.

Above: *Teucrium fruticans*

Teucrium fruticans
SHRUBBY GERMANDER, TREE GERMANDER

An upright, evergreen, or should I say "evergray," shrub. The new leaves are almost white, being covered in dense hairs, and they mature to a dull gray. You will notice the strong, pungent smell of the leaves when trimming, but even brushing past will give you a whiff of the medicinal scent.

The pale lavender-blue blooms are shaped like *Salvia* flowers, but they are fairly small and easily missed. They appear in summer over quite a long period. The form **'Azureum'** has showier darker blue flowers.

Above: *Teucrium fruticans* as a hedge.

It is a dense, multi-stemmed bush, seemingly trying to grow in every direction at once and usually succeeding. It can be overly vigorous and although it makes a good, dense hedge in a dry climate, it tends to grow too fast and need too much trimming in moist regions. It is best given a spring and fall prune, and can usually be cut back quite hard if necessary. It grows easily from cuttings if you need new plants. Don't be tempted to shift older plants because they will not survive the move.

It grows in extremes of alkaline or acidic soils and is supremely tolerant of windy sites, so ideally suited for difficult spots where other plants refuse to grow. Alternatively, it is a great contrast plant with its bold, silvery gray cast. Try one against the dark green of a typical conifer and see how good it can be. It can be hit by severe frosts in wet climates, but is much hardier if grown "dry" to harden the wood. Originates from the western Mediterranean. Left to its own devices it grows to height x width 10 ft (3 m). ZONE 8.

Fruticans = shrubby, to distinguish this bush from the many perennial species in the genus.

Tilia

LIME TREE, LINDEN TREE
Tiliaceae

Lindens are stately deciduous trees growing all across the Northern Hemisphere and they are frequently seen as shade trees, especially in the streets and squares of big cities. In summer, most have fragrant, creamy, cup-shaped flowers with a scent like honey. Each flower has a long, whitish bract that acts later as a wing to disperse the seeds. The scented flowers are a narcotic to bees and *Tilia tomentosa* is even toxic to them.

Most limes are probably too big for the average-sized garden but that doesn't prevent us from enjoying them in the city. They are beautiful, big, bold trees with a neat outline and handsome heart-shaped leaves. One of the reasons for their popularity is that the leaves look almost as good in late summer as in the spring. If you find yourself having lunch under a lime, try a leaf in your sandwiches. The edible leaves make a pleasant change from lettuce.

The fall color can be yellow or gold, but cannot be relied upon. Some of them have the annoying habit of secreting a gooey honey-like substance that drips onto cars and benches beneath the trees. This happens when they have been infested with aphids and so it is essential to select the species resistant to attack from these bugs. Some *Tilia* have a tendency to throw up a mass of suckers around the base of the tree, spoiling the clean-trunk effect we desire on large trees. Again, choose the right species to have clean-bole trees for planting.

Also called basswood, limes have long been a favorite of woodworkers as the pale easily-worked timber is ideal for small, hard items like wooden shoes and statues. They like plenty of water and a good, deep soil although they are not fussy about acidity or alkalinity. They are very hardy, coping with continental climates with extremely hot summers and devastatingly cold winters. A breezy climate is fine, but not strong winds. Often grown from seed, good forms need to be grown from layers, cuttings or by grafting onto a rootstock.

Tilia = an ancient name for the tree, frequently referred to by the Roman poet Virgil (who may have used its bark for paper).

Right: *Tilia tomentosa*

Tilia x euchlora, syn T. dasystyla
CRIMEAN LIME
A hybrid of doubtful origin, but a superb tree for campus and street planting. It should be the first choice for city planting, as it doesn't attract aphids and therefore has no dripping honeydew. The yellowish white, honey-scented flowers are borne in midsummer. The big, bright, shiny green leaves and slightly pendulous habit add up to a magnificent tree. Height 70 ft (20 m) x width 50 ft (15 m). ZONES 3 TO 8.

Euchlora = dark green.

Tilia x moltkei (T. americana x T. tomentosa)
The most desirable of all the large lime trees, still with the typical fragrant honey-scented flowers in summer. This noble tree has dense, dark green leaves with a slightly weeping outer canopy, adding considerably to its appeal. It does not grow too fast or too large. Height 70 ft (20 m) x width 50 ft (15 ft). ZONE 4.

Moltkei = after the 19th-century German general, Helmuth Moltke, who planted the first specimen at Späths Nursery in Berlin.

Tilia tomentosa
EUROPEAN WHITE LINDEN, SILVER LINDEN, SILVER LIME
A beautiful big tree with a nice clean outline and smooth-topped leaves, felted-white below. In a breeze these white faces shimmer, thus the name "silver lime." The honey-scented flowers are toxic to bees. Look for the clone **'Sterling'**, which is more resistant to pests. Native to southern and eastern Europe. Height 100 ft (30 m) x width 70 ft (20 m). ZONE 6.

Tomentosa = hairy.

Trachelospermum

Apocynaceae

Apocynaceae is a peculiar plant family and is commonly known as "dog's bane," probably because nearly all the members of its family are poisonous. Most exude a sticky, clear or milky sap if a leaf is removed, so take care not to get any on you if you are pruning this plant. It is not deadly but can be a skin irritant. Hopefully I have not put you off this plant already, because if you are looking for a self-clinging, evergreen climber with fragrant flowers, you have just found it. Hardy, evergreen climbers are a scarce commodity so let's not be hasty in dismissing this plant.

It is typical of the Apocynaceae family, with opposite leaves and a banded line around the node; the new stems are bright green and furry initially, while the older wood is brown. Evergreen, glossy leaves the size of a finger joint are pointed at the tips. People say that *Trachelospermum asiaticum* has the smaller leaves but on a trip to Korea we saw plants of both *T. asiaticum* and *T. jasminoides* with tiny, medium and large leaves, and the local botanists insisted leaf size had nothing to do with differentiating the two species. There are many other species but only these two seem to be in cultivation.

These plants are rambling and scrambling at first and then eventually they get the message to climb and cling tightly to concrete, timber or tree trunks, using tiny sucker roots. I gave

mine some netting to creep through, as I was not confident that it would cling on for itself. It scrambled for two years, seeming to prove that my fears were well founded, and the next time I looked it was tenaciously clinging to the concrete wall. Before long it had completely smothered an area 6 ft (2 m) x 6 ft (2 m), hiding the boring old concrete almost completely. They are certainly happy in full sun or a little shade, but in dense shade they fade away. Like so many climbers, they put up with terrible soil, including heavy clays and limestone. Climbers always have to cope with poor soil because in the wild they have to make do with whatever they encounter, finding a niche at the base of trees and often in shade. *Trachelospermum* also handle wet or dry and hot or cold climates and the waxy leaves tolerate windy sites too. No pests dare attack them, one of the advantages of their being poisonous perhaps. The plants are easily established when young, but should be left alone once put into the ground. In a garden

situation, use them to cover walls, especially near an entrance where you can enjoy the sweet scent as you walk by. Do not attach one to a timber surface that you may want to paint at some later date, as you will regret it. Once the tenacious roots are attached they are reluctant to come off.

Trakelos = neck; *spermon* = seed, referring to the shape of the seeds.

Trachelospermum asiaticum

This is a seemingly directionless, wandering, scrambling type of plant. I have seen it growing on the tops of windswept mountains, clinging to rocks as if for sustenance. Given a helping hand it makes a fine climber for a patio wall. Flowers emerge in late spring in the axils of new leaves. The sweet scent is superb as you pass by, but if you linger the smell becomes rather cloying. These flower clusters open in succession, giving a long season of blooms. Thin, orange tubes topped with five outspread flat petals in soft

Above:
Trachelospermum asiaticum

apricot are reminiscent of the English primrose or *Polyanthus* in shape. As the flower fades, the petals curl a little and give the impression of a spiral wheel, almost like rotary hoe blades, and this increases the starry effect. There are white clones available, too. Height x width 6 ft (2 m). The plant is from Korea, China and Japan. ZONE 6, but can be zone 8 or even 9.

Asiaticum = from Asia.

Trachelospermum jasminoides
CONFEDERATE JASMINE, STAR JASMINE

While this plant is scented like a jasmine, it is not as rampant. Leaves on cultivated versions of *Trachelospermum jasminoides* are usually larger than those of *T. asiaticum*, and perhaps a little thicker and fleshier. The older leaves often take on a purple bronzy tinge in winter. It flowers late spring to early summer, exactly the same time as *T. asiaticum*, and the blooms are pure white with a slightly yellow throat. Really the only difference between the two species is that these flowers are white, slightly larger and frilly around the edges, while *T. asiaticum* has smooth-edged petals. It is sometimes known as "Confederate Star." Introduced by Robert Fortune from Chinese gardens in 1844, it also grows in Taiwan. Height x width 10 ft (3 m). ZONE 7 OR 8.

There is a variegated form: avoid it like the plague. It is horrible. The straight species has such beautiful rich green, glossy leaves there is no reason to pollute them with splashes of muddy white.

Jasminoides = like a jasmine.

Tripterygium spp.

Celastraceae

*T*ripterygium may be nothing special to look at but the may-like scent is blissful. Much as I like these plants, it is hard to find a space for them in a garden. They are a small group of climbing shrubs with cherry-like, deciduous leaves that twine around trees and shrubs to climb to the light. I have seen

Below: *Tripterygium hypoglauca*

them growing on a netting frame but it looked too contrived. I made the mistake of growing mine up through a cherry tree: with the similarity of leaves, I never notice it until the brilliant red seed cases appear in fall. Perhaps the ideal would be to grow one over an old tree stump where it could drape down in flowing fashion. That way the heads of the little, greenish white flowers would be handy enough for you to enjoy the lovely fragrance. In fall they turn into winged, hop-like seeds in a stunning blood red. Sometimes the fall color can be good, too.

If you decide you have a space for *Tripterygium* they are easy enough to grow, being cold-hardy, wind-hardy and able to cope with any soil at all. The stems do need something thin, like wire or twigs, to twine around. They will grow in dense shade but flower much better in full sun. Equally happy in wet or drought-prone regions, and hot or cold zones.

There are three species in cultivation and they are all quite similar. **T. regelii** is the most common. **T. hypoglauca** and **T. wilfordii** are just as scented. They all hail from China, Japan and Korea. Height 6–30 ft (2–10 m). ZONE 5.

Tri = three; *pteron* = wing.

Viburnum

Caprifoliaceae

Viburnums have become garden standbys, to such an extent that we all know at least three types, although they can be tricky to recognize because they vary so much. Some are evergreen, while most are deciduous and hardy. The leaves vary from soft, maple-like, palmate versions to glossy, smooth or even rough corrugated types. Even the flowers are not consistent. Some have a simple cluster of starry flowers, but we are probably more familiar with either the pom-pom heads or the hydrangea-like flat, lace-cap versions where the larger sterile flowers surround the smaller true flowers. Quite a few have the advantage of being scented, and even deliciously so. Others are grown for their attractive berries as well as for their flowers, scent and foliage, so you can see that it is hard to make firm statements about the genus.

Viburnums are content in any soil, including very acidic or alkaline conditions. Some, like *Viburnum opulus* and *V. sargenti*, will grow in swampy places. In fact, if you have a very wet, boggy area, these are two of the best choices for such a site. Most prefer full sun but will cope with a little shade. They tend to look sparse and do not flower as well if they get too much shade.

Most are easy to transplant and even quite large specimens of the deciduous types can be moved in the cooler months. For the most part, they are cold-hardy and have become standbys because they are so easy to grow and have so many fine qualities.

Viburnums are an excellent choice for a shrubbery or mixed border, and some are suited to narrow areas around the house. The added bonus of fragrance is always attractive when planting near paths and windows.

Viburnum = from the Greek *vieo* = to tie, referring to their flexible shoots.

Viburnum x bodnantense 'Dawn'
(*V. farreri* x *V. grandiflorum*)

A very upright bush with shiny, chocolate-colored stems and neat, corrugated leaves. In early spring the bare stems have tight, pendulous clusters of bright pink flowers. They are not only showy but deliciously scented and surprisingly tough, when you think that it is usually very early spring when they emerge. Height 6–10 ft (2–3 m) x width 5 ft (1.5 m). ZONE 7.

Bodnantense = named after the Bodnant garden in North Wales.

Viburnum x burkwoodii (*V. carlesii* x *V. utile*)

A tall, sometimes ungainly shrub, as it is often semi-evergreen and looks untidy during the winter months. In spring the rounded, white, pom-pom heads are nicely scented, like vanilla ice-cream. It is probably a better shrub for colder regions, where it grows slowly and loses its leaves in winter. The leaves are shiny dark green above and furry beneath. Height 6–10 ft (2–3 m) x width 5 ft (1.5 m). ZONE 4.

Some of the named hybrids have a much tidier shape and bigger flowers. Examples are **'Anne Russell'** and **'Fulbrook'**, both with pink and white flowers and a pleasant scent. To be strictly correct these two are *V.* x *burkwoodii* crossed back onto *V. carlesii*, so they are three-quarters *V. carlesii*.

Burkwoodii = named after the plant breeder Albert Burkwood.

Viburnum x carlcephalum (*V. carlesii* x *V. macrocephalum*)
FRAGRANT VIBURNUM

A neat, rounded, hardy bush, ideal for urban gardens, its pink buds open to creamy-white, scented flowers in spring before the leaves emerge. The smell is a combination of primroses and newly mown hay. The starry, five-petaled flowers are packed very closely together to form one dense head. Like so many viburnums, it makes an attractive cut-flower for a small vase, where the scent can fill the room.

The rough, bristly leaves appear in pairs just as the flowers are fading; they eventually become rough, tough, wind-hardy and sun-tolerant. Height x width 6–10 ft (2–3 m). ZONE 6.

Carlcephalum = a combination of *carlesii* (see below) and *macrocephalum*.

Viburnum carlesii
KOREAN SPICE VIBURNUM

Dense, rounded bushes have slightly furry, gray leaves that give the impression they are permanent whereas in fact the bush is deciduous, often with attractive, red fall colors. In spring the rounded heads of pink buds open to white with a strong scent that you will notice all around the garden. In the wild these tough plants grow in rocky gorges on mountainsides, so drought doesn't deter them. *V. carlesii* originates in Korea. Height x width 6 ft (2 m). ZONE 5.

Carlesii = after W.R. Carles, a late 19th-century British vice-consul in Seoul, Korea.

Viburnum 'Eskimo' (*V.* x *carlcephalum* x *V. utile*)

This plant has the perfect name to help us visualize its rounded pom-pom heads. They are the purest white of any flower, with a pleasant perfume to top them off. Shiny, dark blackish green leaves help to highlight the purity of the flower color.

It is semi-evergreen, more so in mild climates. *V. eskimo* only grows into a very small shrub and is therefore ideal for any garden large or small. Height 3 ft (1 m) x width 4 ft (1.2 m). ZONE 6.

Viburnum *farreri*, syn *V. fragrans*

A cold-hardy, upright shrub with handsome corrugated leaves that open in a bronze color in the spring. Rounded heads of sweetly scented flowers open during the winter months. The buds are pink, opening to almost white flowers. This bush would be valu-

Above and left:
Viburnum x
carlcephalum

able even if it only flowered in summer, but is priceless with its winter blossoms. This plant is from China. Height 6–10 ft (2–3 m) x width 3–5 ft (1–1.5 m). ZONES 6 TO 8.

Farreri = named after Reginald Farrer (1880–1920), a British plant collector.

Wisteria

Fabaceae

Wisteria…friend or foe? I have never been quite sure. I know the flowers are stupendous and there is nothing quite like them outside the tropics. Elongated chains of blossom hang like flowery curtains. Perhaps they are at their best along the side of the house, hanging down from the verandah, or simply across a house wall with a mass of vertical flowers. Somehow you have to contrive to grow the plant horizontally. This does two things: it slows the growth and induces the plant to flower. The same is true of all plants: if you take a vertical branch and tie it down, close to horizontal, it will change from a growth stem to a flowering stem. This is because you are changing the hormone balance within that branch. Gardeners do this with apple trees to make them flower and fruit, but it works with all woody plants.

In the case of wisterias, they are extremely vigorous, and if given a free run up a tall tree they will simply race up to the top and their best flowers will be out of sight. Far better to let nature slow the plant down by training it to grow horizontally. Of course, you can always resort to pruning, and in this case it

may seem complicated but it's not. Wisteria put out long, long stems, sometimes 15 ft (5 m) long, looking for new trees to climb, and if you let all these grow you would have a monster on your hands. So in early summer, cut all these stems off at five buds from where they started. The plant then has another rush of energy and the two end buds grow into long stems. In late summer, or during winter, you cut off these two long stems as well, leaving just three buds at the base, and these will have fattened up to be next spring's flowers. It is basically the same training and pruning used for grapes and kiwifruit. When you next see a beautiful wisteria decked in long chains of flowers, and those beautiful, gnarly, twirling branches like a vine in a fairy story, you will realize that it doesn't just happen like that, some diligent gardener has put much time and effort into this "natural" display. Somehow when they are at their best it suggests an idyllic picture, a little cottage with wisteria on one wall and roses on another.

Another possibility is to train your wisteria as a standard. Allow only one leader and tie it to a cane. When it has reached the desired height, cut the top off and allow the bush to send a cascade of weeping stems out like an open umbrella. Keep the best of these stems as permanent and, hey presto, you have a free-standing wisteria bush.

Wisterias like plenty of sun, although the roots can be in shade. The soil must be free-draining but otherwise any type will suffice. They are easy to plant out but you are unlikely to shift them again once the vines are entwined. Winter cold holds no threat, as they are deciduous and hardy. Moderate winds are fine, but it is best not to choose a windy site.

Wisterias are one of the many plants linking North America

Right: *Viburnum carlesii* 'Aurora'

with China and Japan. Actually the North American versions were introduced to Europe first but were overshadowed by the showier Asian species.

Wisteria = named by Thomas Nuttall in memory of Caspar Wistar, an 18th-century physician and professor of anatomy from Pennsylvania. Some spell the plant wistaria and some wisteria. To be correct it should have an "e". Even Nuttall was not consistent, using both spellings, because apparently the family name was Wüster and some members changed to Wistar while others opted for Wister. Under the rules of plant naming the first used name is correct, even if wrongly spelled.

Wisteria floribunda
JAPANESE WISTERIA
The Japanese wisteria was first introduced by Philipp von Siebold, an eye specialist who made Japan his home for many years. The long chains of violet-blue flowers have a pleasant soapy fragrance.

The stems climb clockwise around wires and supports. There is a form called **W. f. macrobotrys** and a cultivar of that called **'Multijuga'**, both with exceptionally long flower chains, longer than your arm. The flowers open progressively from the "top" or base of the flower chain to the tip, thus extending the flowering season. There are numerous named varieties with white, blue or mauve flowers. Height 30 ft (10 m). ZONE 4.

Floribunda = bearing an abundance of flowers.

Wisteria frutescens
AMERICAN WISTERIA
You hardly ever see this plant in cultivation, more's the pity. It winds around supports in a counterclockwise direction. The good forms have rich lavender-purple flowers and are fragrant. I saw my first example of this North American species in North Carolina 30 years into my plant career. I was left wondering why it had taken

Above: *Wisteria floribunda* 'Snow Showers'

Previous pages: *Wisteria* 'Lavender Lace'

me so long to find it. The flowers are a lovely rich blue and the chains, although shorter than the Asian versions, are still stunning. It has the advantage of producing flowers on the new growth in spring and so you can prune it any way you fancy before spring without affecting the flowering display. It is also less vigorous than its Asian cousins. There is a white form, too. Height 15–30 ft (5–10 m). ZONE 5.

Frutescens = shrubby or shrub-like.

Wisteria sinensis
CHINESE WISTERIA
This wisteria climbs counterclockwise. Its flowers are fragrant and a super-rich blue color, with the advantage that they open all at once, creating a more dramatic display. There are white, purple and blue forms, and doubles, too. Height 100 ft (30 m). ZONE 5.

Sinensis = from China.

Zenobia pulverulenta

threat and it will take a breezy site. Typically it forms an open, upright, thin-stemmed bush with small 1 in (2.5 cm) long leaves. It is a deciduous shrub but can be semi-evergreen in warm climates (zone 9 and above).

In late spring the bush is decked with cute white bells, not unlike the related *Pieris*, but with the added bonus of a delicious scent.

Some forms have beautiful blue foliage on a small, compact bush with the white bell flowers held above the leaves. Perhaps an effort should be made to select outstanding clones of this fine native American shrub. Height 6 ft (2 m) x width 5 ft (1.5 m). ZONE 5.

Zenobia = named after Zenobia, the queen of Palmyra (now Syria); *pulverulenta* = powdered, referring to the glaucous blue leaves.

Zenobia

Zenobia pulverulenta
Ericaceae

This plant has two claims to fame, or three if you include its famous name, after the warrior queen. Primarily it is grown for the spicy, exotic, almost cinnamon-scented flowers and the fall colors, an exciting mix of orange, red and purple.

The plant is related to ericas and, like the related rhododendrons, it likes well-drained, acidic soils. The moist forests from North Carolina to Florida are its home and it is quite happy in sun or shade cast by deciduous trees. Winter cold poses no

Ready-reference table

Species or cultivar	page reference	hardiness zones	evergreen ●* / deciduous ○	native to North America	height x width
Abelia chinensis	12	8	○●		5-6 x 5-6 ft (1.5-2 x 1.5-2 m)
Abelia x *grandiflora*	12	5	○●		6 x 6 ft (2 x 2 m)
'Frances Mason'	12	5	○●		6 x 6 ft (2 x 2 m)
'Edward Goucher'	12	5	○●		6 x 6 ft (2 x 2 m)
Abelia schumannii	12	7	○●		6 x 6 ft (2 x 2 m)
Abelia triflora	13	6	○●		6 x 6 ft (2 x 2 m)
Abelia uniflora	13	7	○●		6 x 6 ft (2 x 2 m)
Abeliophyllum distichum	13	4	○		2-3 x 3 ft (0.6-1 x 1 m)
Acacia baileyana	15	8	●		15 x 15 ft (5 x 5 m)
Acacia dealbata	15	8	●		20-30 x 30 ft (6-9 x 6 m)
Acacia longifolia	15	8	●		15 x 15 ft (5 x 5 m)
Acacia melanoxylon	15	8	●		50-80 x 30 ft (15-25 x 10 m)
Acacia pravissima	15	8	●		20 x 15 ft (6 x 4.5 m)
'Golden Carpet'	16	8	●		3-6 x 6-10 ft (1-2 x 2-3 m)
Acacia verticillata	16	8	●		10-12 x 6 ft (3-4 x 2 m)
'Rewa'	16	8	●		6 x 6 ft (2 x 2 m)
Acradenia frankliniae	16	8	●		10-15 x 3-6 ft (3-5 x 1-2 m)
Agonis flexuosa	16	9	●		15-25 x 10 ft (5-8 x 3 m)
Agonis juniperina	17	8/9	●		15-25 x 10 ft (5-8 x 3 m)
'Florist Star'	17	8/9	●		15-25 x 10 ft (5-8 x 3 m)
Akebia quinata	17	5	○●		10-30 ft (3-10 m) climber
Akebia trifoliata	18	5	○●		10-30 ft (3-10 m) climber
Aloysia triphylla	18	8	○●		6 x 6 ft (2 x 2 m)
Amelanchier arborea	19	4-9	○	*	20 x 15 ft (6 x 5 m)
Amelanchier asiatica	19	5-9	○		6-10 x 5 ft (2-3 x 1.5 m)
Amelanchier canadensis	19	3-9	○	*	10 x 6 ft (3 x 2 m)
Amelanchier laevis	20	5-9	○	*	10-12 x 6-10 ft (3-4 x 2-3 m)
Amelanchier lamarckii	20	5-9	○	*	10-12 x 6-10 ft (3-4 x 2-3 m)
Amorpha canescens	20	2	○	*	1-3 x 3 ft (0.3-1 x 1 m)
Amorpha fruticosa	21	5	○	*	6 x 6 f t (2 m)
Argyrocytisus battandieri	21	8/9	●		6-12 x 6-12 ft (2-4 x 2-4 m)
Artemisia absinthium	22	4	●		3-4 x 3-4 ft (1 x 1 m)
Artemisia arborescens	23	5	●		3-5 x 3-5 ft (1-1.5 x 1-1.5m)
Artemisia 'Powis Castle'	23	5	●		3 x 5 ft (1 x 1.5 m)
Azara integrifolia	23	8	●		15-20 x 6 ft (5-6 x 2 m)
Azara lanceolata	23	8	●		15 x 6 ft (5 x 2 m)
Azara microphylla	23	8	●		15-20 ft (5-6 m) x 6 ft (2 m)
Azara petiolaris	24	8	●		15 x 6 ft (5 x 2 m)
Azara serrata	24	8	●		15 x 6 ft (5 x 2 m)
Backhousia anista	25	9	●		10-15 x 10 ft (3-5 x 3 m)
Backhousia citriodora	24	9	●		6-10 x 3-5 ft (2-3 x 1-1.5 m)
Boronia heterophylla	25	9	●		3-6 x 2 ft (1-2 x 60 cm)
Boronia megastigma	25	9	●		2-3 x 1-2 ft (0.6-1 x 30-60 cm)
'Heaven Scent'	25	9	●		2-3 x 1-2 ft (0.6-1 x 30-60 cm)
'Lutea'	25	9	●		2-3 x 1-2 ft (0.6 m-1x 30-60 cm)
Brugmansia					
'California Peach'	27	9	●		15 x 15 ft (5 x 5 m)
'Grand Marnier'	27	9	●		15 x 15 ft (5 x 5 m)
'Noel's Blush'	27	9	●		15 x 15 ft (5 x 5 m)
Brugmansia chlorantha	27	9	●		6 x 6 ft (2 x 2 m)
Brugmansia sanguinea	27	9	●		6-10 x 3-6 ft (2-3 x 1-2 m)
Brugmansia suaveolens	27	9	●		10-15 x 10-15 ft (3-5x 3-5 m)
Brunfelsia calycina	28	9	●		3 x 3 ft (1 x 1 m)
Brunfelsia latifolia	28	9	●		3-10 x 3-5 ft (1-3 x 1-1.5 m)
Buddleja alternifolia	28	6	○		6-10 x 6-10 ft (1-3 x 2-3 m)
Buddleja asiatica	29	8/9	●		6-10 x 6 ft (2-3 x 2 m)
Buddleja davidii	29	6	○		6-10 x 6-10 ft (2-3 x 2-3 m)
Buddleja madagascariensis	29	9/10	●		6-10 x 6 ft (2-3 x 2 m)
Callistemon citrinus	31	8/9	●		10 x 10 ft (3 x 3 m)
Callistemon 'Little John'	31	8/9	●		3-6 x 3-5 ft (1-2 x 1-1.5 m)
Callistemon salignus	31	8	●		15 x 15 ft (5 x 5 m)
Callistemon viminalis	32	9	●		15 x 15 ft (5 x 5 m)
Calocedrus decurrens	32	5	●	*	60-80 x 30-40 ft (18-25 x 10-12 m)
'Aureovariegata'	32	5	●		40 x 20 ft (12 x 6 m)
'Berrima Gold'	32	5	●		40 x 20 ft (12 x 6 m)
'Columnaris'	32	5	●		60-80 x 30-40 ft (18 x 25 x 10-12 m)
'Fastigiata'	32	5	●		60-80 x 30-40 ft (18-25 x 10-12 m)
'Intricata'	32	5	●		3-6 x 3 ft (1-2 x 1 m)
Calocedrus macrolepis	32	8/9	●		100 x 25 ft (30 x 8 m)
Calocedrus formosana	32	9	●		80 x 30 ft (18 x 10 m)
Calycanthus floridus	33	5	○	*	6 x 6 ft (2 x 2 m)
Calycanthus occidentalis	33	6/7	○	*	6 x 6 ft (2 x 2 m)
Camellia japonica	34	8	●		6-12 x 3-6 ft (2-4 x 1-2 m)
'Kramer's Gold'	35	8	●		6-12 x 3-6 ft (2-4 x 1-2 m)
'Kramer's Supreme'	35	8	●		6-12 x 3-6 ft (2-4 x 1-2 m)
'Scented Gem'	35	8	●		6-12 x 3-6 ft (2-4 x 1-2 m)
'Scented Sun'	35	8	●		6-12 x 3-6 ft (2-4 x 1-2 m)
'Scentsation'	35	8	●		6-12 x 3-6 ft (2-4 x 1-2 m)
'Superscent'	35	8	●		6-12 x 3-6 ft (2-4 x 1-2 m)
Camellia lutchuensis	35	8	●		6-10 x 3-6 ft (2-3 x 1-2 m)
Camellia oleifera	35	6	●		20 x 10 ft (6 x 3 m)
Camellia sasanqua	35	8/9	●		6-10 x 6 ft (2-3 x 2 m)
'Hiryu'	36	8/9	●		6-10 x 6 ft (2-3 x 2 m)
'Mini-no-yuki'	36	8/9	●		6-10 x 6 ft (2-3 x 2 m)
'Plantation Pink'	36	8/9	●		6-10 x 6 ft (2-3 x 2 m)
Camellia tsaii	36	8/9	●		6-10 x 3-6 ft (2-3 x 1-2 m)
Camellia yunnanensis	36	8	●		6 x 3 ft (2 x 1 m)
Carpenteria californica	37	8	●	*	6-10 x 6 ft (2-3 x 2 m)
Caryopteris x *clandonensis*	38	6	○		3 x 3 ft (1 x 1 m)
'Arthur Simmonds'	38	6	○		2 x 2 ft (60 x 60 cm)
'Blue Mist'	38	6	○		3 x 3 ft (1 x 1 m)
'Ferndown'	38	6	○		3 x 3 ft (1 x 1 m)
'Heavenly Blue'	38	6	○		3 x 3 ft (1x 1 m)
Caryopteris incana	38	6	○		5 x 5 ft (1.5 x 1.5 m)
Caryopteris mongolica	38	6	○		3 x 3 ft (1 x 1 m)
Catalpa bignonioides	40	5-9	○	*	25-50 x 25-50 ft (8-15 x 8-15 m)
Catalpa ovata	40	5-9	○		30 x 30 ft (10 x 10 m)
Catalpa speciosa	40	4-9	○	*	50-70 x 50-70 ft (15-20 x 15-20 m)
Ceanothus arboreus	40	8	●	*	12 x 10 ft (4 x 3 m)
'Trewithen Blue'	40	8	●		12 x 10 ft (4 x 3 m)
Ceanothus 'Burkwoodii'	41	7	●		6 x 6 ft (2 x 2 m)
Ceanothus 'Concha'	41	8	●		6 x 6 ft (2 x 2 m)
Ceanothus 'Dark Star'	41	8	●		6 x 6 ft (2 x 2 m)
Ceanothus impressus	41	7/8	●	*	6-10 x 6-10 ft (2-3 x 2-3 m)
'Puget Blue'	41	7/8	●		6-10 x 6-10 ft (2-3 x 2-3 m)
Ceanothus papillosus	41	8	●	*	12 x 12 ft (4 x 4 m)

* Some plants usually regarded as deciduous will stay semi-evergreen or evergreen in mild climates (generally zone 9 and above). Often the lower or older leaves will fall off, leaving a crown of foliage at the tips of the stems. Where a plant exhibits this habit, both the evergreen and deciduous symbols have been inserted.

Species or cultivar	page reference	hardiness zones	evergreen deciduous ○	native to North America	height x width
Ceanothus papillosus					
var *roweanus*	42	8	•	*	3-5 x 5-10 ft (1-1.5 x 1.5-3 m)
Cephalotaxus fortunei	42	6	•		6-20 x 6-20 ft (2-6 x 2-5 m)
'Prostrate Spreader'	42	6	•		3-6 x 6-10 ft (1-2 x 2-3 m)
Cephalotaxus harringtonia	42	6	•		6-10 x 6-10 ft (2-3 x 2-3 m)
'Fastigiata'	42	6	•		6-10 x 1.5 - 3 ft (2-3 x 0.5-1 m)
'Prostrata'	42	6	•		2-5 x 2-5 ft (0.6-1.5 x 0.6-1.5 m)
Cercidiphyllum japonicum	42	4-9	○		50 x 50 ft (15 x 15 m)
'Pendulum'	43	4-9	○		20 x 25 ft (6 x 8 m)
Cercidiphyllum japonicum					
var *sinense*	43	4-9	○		50 x 50 ft (15 x 15 m)
Cercidiphyllum magnificum	43	6	○		30 x 25 ft (10 x 8 m)
Cestrum aurantiacum	44	9	•		6-10 x 6-10 ft (2-3 x 2-3 m)
Cestrum 'Newellii'	44	9/10	•		6-10 x 6-10 ft (2-3 x 2-3 m)
Cestrum 'Hugh Redgrove'	43	9	•		6-10 x 6-10 ft (2-3 x 2-3 m)
Cestrum nocturnum	44	8/9	•		3-6 x 3-6 ft (1-2 x 1-2 m)
Cestrum parqui	45	8	•		6-10 x 6-10 ft (2-3 x 2-3 m)
Chimonanthus praecox	45	7	○		6 x 6 ft (2 x 2 m)
'Luteus'	46	7	○		6 x 6 ft (2 x 2 m)
Choisya ternata	46	8	•		3 x 3 ft (1 x 1 m)
'Aztec Pearl'	47	9	•		8 x 8 ft (2.5 x 2.5 m)
'Sundance'	47	8	•		8 x 8 ft (2.5 x 2.5 m)
Cladrastis lutea	47	3	○	*	30-50 x 30 ft (10-15 x 10 m)
'Rosea'	48	3	○		30-50 x 30 ft (10-15 x 10 m)
Cladrastis sinensis	48	6	○		30 x 30 ft (10 x 10 m)
Cladrastis platycarpa	48	7	○		15-30 x 15-30 ft (5-10 x 5-10 m)
Cladrastis wilsonii	48	6	○		15-30 x 15-30 ft (5-10 x 5-10 m)
Clerodendrum bungei	48	7	○		6 x 10 ft (2 x 3 m)
Clerodendrum trichotomum	48	6	○		6-10 x 6-10 ft (2-3 x 2-3 m)
Clerodendrum trichotomum					
var *fargesii*	49	6	○		6-10 x 6-10 ft (2-3 x 2-3 m)
Clerodendrum ugandense	49	9	•		4-6 ft (1.2-2 m) climber
Clethra alnifolia	51	3	○	*	8 x 8 ft (2.5 x 2.5 m)
'Hummingbird'	51	3	○		36 in x 8 ft (0.9 x 2.5 m)
'Rosea'	51	3	○		8 x 8 ft (2.5 x 2.5 m)
Clethra arborea	51	8/9	•		10-15 x 3-6 ft (3-5 x 1-2 m)
Clethra barbinervis	51	6	○		6-10 x 6 ft (2-3 x 2 m)
Clethra delavayi	51	7	○		6 x 6 ft (2 x 2 m)
Clethra fargesii	51	6	○		10 x 10 ft (3 x 3 m)
Clethra monostachya	51	7	○		6 x 6 ft (2 x 2 m)
Colletia hystrix	52	7	•		6 x 6 ft (2 x 2 m)
Colletia paradoxa	52	7	•		6 x 6 ft (2 x 2 m)
Corylopsis himalayana	52	8/9	○		10-15 x 6-10 ft (3-5 x 2-3 m)
Corylopsis pauciflora	53	6	○		5 x 8 ft (1.5 x 2.5 m)
Corylopsis spicata	53	5	○		6 x 10 ft (2 x 3 m)
Corylopsis willmottiae	53	6	○		12 x 12 ft (4 x 4 m)
Crataegus laevigata	54	5	○		25 x 25 ft (8 x 8 m)
'Paul's Scarlet'	54	5	○		25 x 25 ft (8 x 8 m)
'Plena'	54	5	○		25 x 25 ft (8 x 8 m)
Craetaegus monogyna	54	5	○		25 x 25 ft (8 x 8 m)
Cytisus x *beanii*	56	6	○		1-2 x 3 ft (0.3-0.6 x 1 m)
Cytisus x *kewensis*	56	6	○		1-2 x 3 ft (0.3-0.6 x 1 m)
Cytisus multiflorus	56	7	○		10 x 6 ft (3 x 2 m)
Cytisus x *praecox*	56	6	○		6-10 x 6-10 ft (2-3 x 2-3 m)
'Allgold'	56	6	○		6-10 x 6-10 ft (2-3 x 2-3 m)
'Warminster'	56	6	○		6-10 x 6-10 ft (2-3 x 2-3 m)

Species or cultivar	page reference	hardiness zones	evergreen deciduous ○	native to North America	height x width
Cytisus scoparius	56	6	○		6-10 x 6-10 ft (2-3 x 2-3 m)
Daphne bholua	58	8	○ •		10 x 3 ft (3 x 1 m)
'Gurkha'	58	8	○ •		10 x 3 ft (3 x 1 m)
'Jacqueline Postill'	58	8	○ •		10 x 3 ft (3 x 1 m)
Daphne x *burkwoodii*	58	5	○ •		2-3 x 2-3 ft (0.6-1 x 0.6-1 m)
'Carol Mackie'	58	5	○ •		2-3 x 2-3 ft (0.6-1 x 0.6-1 m)
'Somerset'	58	5	○ •		5 x 3 ft (1.5 x 1 m)
'Variegata'	58	5	○ •		2-3 x 2-3 ft (0.6-1 x 0.6-1 m)
Daphne cneorum	58	5-8	•		1 x 2 ft (30 x 60 cm)
'Alba'	58	5-8	•		1 x 2 ft (30 x 60 cm)
'Eximia'	58	5-8	•		1 x 2 ft (30 x 60 cm)
'Major'	58	5-8	•		1 x 2 ft (30 x 60 cm)
'Variegata'	58	5-8	•		1 x 2 ft (30 x 60 cm)
Daphne genkwa	59	6	○		2 x 3 ft (0.6-1 x 0.6-1 m)
Daphne mezereum	59	5-8	○		3 x 3 ft (1 x 1 m)
'Grandiflora'	59	5-8	○		5 x 5 ft (1.5 x 1.5 m)
Daphne odora	60	7	•		2-3 x 2-3 ft (0.6-1 x 0.6-1 m)
'Alba'	60	7	•		2-3 x 2-3 ft (0.6-1 x 0.6-1 m)
'Aureomarginata'	60	7	•		2-3 x 2-3 ft (0.6-1 x 0.6-1 m)
'Leucanthe'	60	7	•		2-3 x 2-3 ft (0.6-1 x 0.6-1 m)
'Variegata'	60	7	•		2-3 x 2-3 ft (0.6-1 x 0.6-1 m
Dipelta floribunda	60	6	○		10 x 6 ft (2 x 3 m)
Dipelta ventricosa	61	6	○		6 x 6 ft (2 x 2 m)
Dipelta yunnanensis	61	7	○		6 x 6 ft (2 x 2 m)
Drimys lanceolata	62	8-9	•		6 x 6 ft (2 x 2 m)
Drimys winteri	62	8-9	•		6-30 x 6-30 ft (2-10 x 2-10 m)
Drimys winteri andina	62	8-9	•		3-4 x 3-4 ft (1-1.2 x 1-1.2 m)
Drimys winteri latifolia	62	8-9	•		30 x 20 ft (10 x 6 m)
Edgeworthia papyrifera	63	6	○		6 x 6 ft (2 x 2 m)
'Grandiflora'	63	6	○		3 x 3 ft (1 x 1 m)
Edgeworthia gardneri	63	8			10-12 x 10-12 ft (3-4 x 3-4 m)
Elaeocarpus dentatus	64	9	•		15 x 15 ft (5 x 5 m)
Elaeocarpus reticulatus	64	8/9	•		15 x 15 ft (5 x 5 m)
Eriostemon myoporoides	64	8/9	•		4 x 5 ft (1.2 x 1.5 m)
Eucryphia cordifolia	66	8	•		20-25 x 6-10 ft (6-8 x 2-3 m)
Eucryphia glutinosa	66	8	○ •		20-30 x 6-10 ft (6-10 x 2-3 m)
Eucryphia x *intermedia*	68	8	•		15-20 x 6-10 ft (5-6 x 2-3 m)
Eucryphia lucida	66	8	•		10-15 x 3-10 ft (3-5 x 1-3 m)
Eucryphia moorei	67	9	•		10-15 x 3-6 ft (3-5 x 1-2 m)
Eucryphia x *nymansensis*	67	8	•		20-30 x 6-10 ft (6-10 x 2-3 m)
'Mount Usher'	67	8	•		20-30 x 6-10 ft (6-10 x 2-3 m)
'Nymansay'	68	8	•		20-30 x 6-10 ft (6-10 x 2-3 m)
Eurya japonica	68	7	•		6-10 x 3-6 ft (2-3 x 1-2 m)
Fothergilla gardenii	69	5	○	*	3 x 3 ft (1 x 1 m)
'Blue Mist'	70	5	○		3 x 3 ft (1 x 1 m)
Fothergilla major	70	5	○	*	5-10 x 6 ft (1.5-3 x 2 m)
'Mount Airy'	70	4	○		5-10 x 6 ft (1.5-3 x 2 m)
Gardenia jasminoides	71	7	•		3-10 x 3-6 ft (1-3 x 1-2 m)
'Florida'	71	7	•		3-10 x 3-6 ft (1-3 x 1-2 m)
'Mystery'	71	7	•		3 x 3-10 ft (1 x 1-3 m)
'Professor Pucci'	71	7	•		3-10 x 3-6 ft (1-3 x 1-2 m)
'Radicans'	71	7	•		2-3 x 3-4 ft (0.6-1 x 1-1.2 m)
Genista lydia	73	6	○		2-3 x 2-3 ft (60-90 x 60-90 cm)
Genista monosperma	72	8/9	○		10 x 6 ft (3 x 2 m)
Genista pilosa	73	6	○		2-3 x 2-3 ft (60-90 x 60-90 cm)
'Lemon Spreader'	73	6	○		12 in x 2-3 ft (30 x 60-90 cm)
'Vancouver Gold'	73	6	○		18 in x 2-3 ft (45 x 60-90 cm)

Species or cultivar	page reference	hardiness zones	evergreen ● deciduous ○	native to North America	height x width
Genista tenera	73	8	○		6 x 5 ft (2 x 1.5 m)
'Golden Shower'	73	8	○		6 x 5 ft (2 x 1.5 m)
'Yellow Imp'	73	8	○		6 x 5 ft (2 x 1.5 m)
Hamamelis x *intermedia*	74	5	○		10-12 x 6-10 ft (3-4 x 2-3 m)
'Arnold Promise'	74	5	○		10-12 x 6-10 x 3-4 x 2-3 m)
'Diane'	74	5	○		10-12 x 6-10 ft (3-4 x 2-3 m)
'Jelena'	74	5	○		10-12 x 6-10 ft (3-4 x 2-3 m)
Hamamelis japonica	74	4	○		10-12 x 10-12 ft (3-4 x 3-4 m)
Hamamelis japonica var *flavpurpurascens*	74	4	○		10-12 x 10-12 ft (3-4 x 3-4 m)
Hamamelis mollis	74	5	○		10-12 x 10-12 ft (3-4 x 3-4 m)
'Brevipetala'	74	5	○		10-12 x 6-10 ft (3-4 x 2-3 m)
'Coombe Wood'	74	5	○		12 x 15 ft (4 x 5 m)
'Pallida'	75	5	○		10-12 x 6-10 ft (3-4 x 2-3 m)
Hamamelis vernalis	75	4	○	*	6 x 6 ft (2 x 2 m)
'Red Imp'	75	4	○		6 x 6 ft (2 x 2 m)
'Sandra'	75	4	○		6 x 6 ft (2 x 2 m)
Hoheria glabrata	75	7	○		20 x 12 ft (6 x 4 m)
Hoheria lyalli	76	7/8	○●		20 x 12 ft (6 x 4 m)
Hoheria populnea	76	8	●		20 x 12 ft (6 x 4 m)
'Alba Variegata'	76	8	●		20 x 12 ft (6 x 4 m)
'Purpurea'	76	8	●		20 x 12 ft (6 x 4 m)
'Variegata'	76	8	●		20 x 12 ft (6 x 4 m)
Hoheria sexstylosa	76	7	●		20 x 12 ft (6 x 4 m)
Hovenia dulcis	76	6	○		50 x 15 ft (15 x 5 m)
Hydrangea aspera var *villosa*	77	6	○		4-12 x 4-12 ft (1.2-4 x 1.2-4 m)
Hydrangea heteromalla	77	6	○		10 x 12 ft (3 x 4 m)
Hydrangea macrophylla	78	6	○		3-8 x 3-8 ft (1-2.5 x 1.2-5 m)
'Nightingale'	78	6	○		3-8 x 3-8 ft (1-2.5 x 1-25 m)
'Opuloides'	78	6	○		4 x 4 ft (1.2 x 1.2 m)
'Rotschwanz'	78	6	○		3-8 x 3-8 ft (1-2.5 x 1-25 m)
'Seafoam'	78	6	○		6 x 6 ft (2 x 2 m)
Hydrangea paniculata	78	3	○		5-10 x 5-10 ft (1.5-3 x 1.5 - 3 m)
'Kyushu'	79	3	○		5 x 5 ft (1.5 x 1.5 m)
'Tardiva'	79	3	○		6 x 6 ft (3 x 3 m)
Hymenosporum flavum	79	9	●		15 x 6 ft (5 x 2 m)
'Golden Nugget'	80	9	●		3 x 4 ft (1 x 1.2 m)
Illicium anistum	80	6	●		3-15 x 5-10 ft (1-5 x 1.5-3 m)
'Pink Stars'	80	6	●		3-15 x 5-10 ft (1-5 x 1.5-3 m)
Illicium floridanum	81	7	●	*	5-6 x 6 ft (1.5-2 x 2 m)
Illicium henryi	81	7	●		5 x 3 ft (1.5 x 1 m)
Illicium majus	81	7	●		6 x 5 ft (2 x 1.5 m)
Illicium mexicanum	81	7	●		6 x 6 ft (2 x 2 m)
Illicium parviflorum	81	8/9	●	*	6-12 x 3-6 ft (2-4 x 1-2 m)
Itea ilicifolia	82	8	●		6-10 x 6-10 ft (2-3 x 2-3 m)
Itea virginica	82	6	○	*	3-5 x 3-5 ft (1-1.5 x 1-1.5 m)
Itea yunnanensis	83	7-9	●		10 x 10 ft (3 x 3 m)
Jasminum azoricum	84	9	●		10 ft (3 m) climber
Jasminum beesianum	84	8	○●		10 ft (3 m) climber
Jasminum humile	84	7/8	○●		10 x 10-12 ft (3 x 3-4 m)
Jasminum mesnyi	84	8	●		6-10 x 6-10 ft (2-3 x 2-3 m)
Jasminum officinale	84	6	○		10-15 x 10-15 ft (3-5 x 3-5 m)
Jasminum polyanthum	84	8/9	●		60 ft (20 m) climber
Jasminum sambac	85	10	●		3 x 6 ft (1 x 12 m)
Kalmia latifolia	85	3-9	●	*	5-6 x 5-6 ft (1.5-2 x 1.5 -2 m)
'Carousel'	86	3-9	●		5-6 x 5-6 ft (1.5-2 x 1.5-2 m)
'Ostbo Red'	86	3-9	●		5-6 x 5-6 ft (1.5-2 x 1.5-2 m)
Kalmia angustifolia	86	7	●	*	3 x 5 ft (1 x 1.5 m)

Species or cultivar	page reference	hardiness zones	evergreen ● deciduous ○	native to North America	height x width
Laburnum x *watereri*	86	5	○		25 x 25 ft (8 x 8 m)
Lavandula angustifolia	87	5	●		3 x 3 ft (1 x 1 m)
'Hidcote'	88	5	●		24 in x 30 in (60 x 75 cm)
Lavandula dentata	88	8	●		4 x 4 ft (1.2 x 1.2 m)
Lavandula dentata var *allardii*	88	8	●		6 x 4 ft (2 x 1.2 m)
Lavandula stoechas	88	8	●		2-3 x 3 ft (60 cm-1 x 1 m)
Ligustrum japonicum	89	7	●		12 x 6 ft (3 x 2 m)
'Rotundifolium'	89	7	●		12 x 6 ft (3 x 2 m)
Ligustrum ovalifolium	89	5	●		10-15 x 6-10 ft (3-5 x 2-3 m)
Lonicera fragrantissima	90	5	○●		6 x 6-10 ft (2 x 1-3 m)
Lonicera x *heckrottii*	91	5	○		10-20 ft (3-6 m)
Lonicera hildebrandiana	91	9	●		60 ft (20 m)
Lonicera japonica	91	5	●		30 ft (10 m)
Lonicera x *purpusii* 'Winter Beauty'	91	6	○		6 x 8 ft (2 x 2.5 m)
Luculia grandifolia	92	9	○●		10 x 6 ft (3 x 2 m)
Luculia gratissima	92	9	○●		6 x 6 ft (2 x 2 m)
Luculia pinceana 'Fragrant Cloud'	92	9	○●		6 x 6 ft (2 x 2 m)
Magnolia denudata	94	5	○		30 x 15 ft (10 x 5 m)
Magnolia grandiflora	94	6	●	*	70 x 70 ft (20 x 20 m)
'Freeman'	94	6	●		30 x 30 ft (10 x 10 m)
'Maryland'	94	6	●		30 x 30 ft (10 x 10 m)
Magnolia x *soulangeana*	94	5-9	○		25 x 15 ft (8 x 5 m)
'Alexandrina'	95	5-9	○		25 x 15 ft (8 x 5 m)
'Lennei'	95	5-9	○		25 x 15 ft (8 x 5 m)
'Rustica Rubra'	95	5-9	○		25 x 15 ft (8 x 5 m)
Magnolia stellata	95	5	○		6 x 6 ft (2 x 2 m)
Magnolia wilsonii	95	7	○		10-12 x 6 ft (3-4 x 2 m)
Mahonia aquifolium	96	6-9	●	*	2-5 x 5 ft (0.6-1.5 x 1.5 m)
Mahonia japonica	96	7	●		6 x 10 ft (2 x 3 m)
Mahonia x *media*	97	8	●		10 x 10 ft (3 x 3 m)
Mandevilla laxa	97	8/9	○●		10-20 ft (3-6 m) climber
Mandevilla splendens	98	9	●		10-20 ft (3-6 m) climber
'Alice du Pont'	98	9/10	●		10-20 ft (3-6 m) climber
Meliosma cuneifolia	98	8/9	○		15 x 10 ft (5 x 3 m)
Meliosma myriantha	99	9	○		15 x 10 ft (5 x 3 m)
Meliosma oldhamii	99	8	○		6-15 x 6-15 ft (2-5 x 2-5 m)
Meliosma veitchiorum	99	8	○		6-15 x 10 ft (2-5 x 3 m)
Michelia alba	99	9	●		30 x 15 ft (10 x 5 m)
Michelia champaca	100	9	●		30 x 15 ft (10 x 5 m)
Michelia doltsopa	100	8/9	●		20-50 x 15-50 ft (6-15 4-15 m)
'Rusty'	100	8/9	●		20-50 x 15-50 ft (6-15 4-15 m)
'Silver Cloud'	100	8/9	●		20-50 x 15-50 ft (6-15 4-15 m)
Michelia figo	101	9	●		10-15 x 10 ft (3-5 x 3 m)
Michelia maudiae	101	8/9	●		10-15 x 10 ft (3-5 x 3 m)
Michelia yunnanensis	102	8	●		6-12 x 6 ft (2-4 x 2 m)
Myrtus communis	102	8	●		10 x 6 ft (3 x 2 m)
'Flore Pleno'	103	8	●		10 x 6 ft (3 x 2 m)
'Microphylla'	103	8	●		10 x 6 ft (3 x 2 m)
'Variegata'	103	8	●		10 x 6 ft (3 x 2 m)
Myrtus luma	103	8	●		15 x 10 ft (5 x 3 m)
'Glanleam Gold'	103	8	●		15 x 10 ft (5 x 3 m)
Oemleria cerasiformis	103	6	○	*	10-12 x 6 ft (3-4 x 2 m)
Osmanthus americanus	104	7	●	*	10 x 6 ft (3 x 2 m)
Osmanthus delavayi	105	7	●		3-6 x 6-10 ft (1-2 x 2-3 m)

Species or cultivar	page reference	hardiness zones	evergreen ● deciduous ○	native to North America	height x width
Osmanthus x fortunei	105	8	●		6 x 6 ft (3 x 3 m)
Osmanthus fragrans	105	7	●		6-15 x 6-10 ft (2-5 x 2-3 m)
Osmanthus fragrans aurantiacus	105	7	●		6-15 x 6-10 ft (2-5 x 2-3 m)
Osmanthus heterophyllus	105	6	●		6-10 x 3 ft (2-3 x 1 m)
'Aureomarginatus'	106	6	●		6-10 x 3 ft (2-3 x 1 m)
'Gulftide'	106	6	●		6-10 x 3 ft (2-3 x 1 m)
'Myrtifolius'	106	6	●		6-10 x 3 ft (2-3 x 1 m)
'Purpureus'	106	6	●		6-10 x 3 ft (2-3 x 1 m)
'Variegatus'	106	6	●		6-10 x 3 ft (2-3 x 1 m)
Oxydendrum arboreum	106	5-9	○	*	10-20 x 6-12 ft (3-6 x 2-4 m)
Paeonia delavayi	107	5	○		5-8 x 5-8 ft (1.5-2.5 x 1.5-2.5 m)
Paeonia lutea	108	5	○		3-6 x 3-6 ft (1-2 x 1-2 m)
Paeonia suffruticosa	108	5	○		3-6 x 3-6 ft (1-2 x 1-2 m)
Perovskia abrotanoides	109	5	○		3 x 3 ft (1 x 1 m)
Perovskia atriplicifolia	109	6	○		5 x 5 ft (1.5 x 1.5 m)
'Blue Spire'	109	6	○		5 x 5 ft (1.5 x 1.5 m)
Philadelphus coronarius	109	5	○		6 x 6 ft (2 x 2 m)
Philadelphus 'Manteau d'Hermine'	110	5	○		2 x 3 ft (0.6 x 1 m)
Philadelphus 'Virginal'	111	5	○		6-10 x 3-6 ft (2-3 x 1-2 m)
Poliothyrsis sinensis	111	7	○		30 x 20 ft (10 x 6 m)
Prostanthera cuneata	112	8	●		3 x 5 ft (1 x 1.5 m)
Prostanthera rotundifolia	112	8/9	●		6 x 6 ft (2 x 2 m)
Ptelea trifoliata	113	2	○	*	12-25 x 12-25 ft (4-8 x 4-8 m)
'Aurea'	113	2	○		12-15 x 12-15 ft (4-5 x 4-5 m)
'Fastigiata'	113	2	○		12-20 x 6-12 ft (4-6 x 2-4 m)
Pterostyrax hispida	113	6	○		15 x 15 ft (5 x 5 m)
Pterostyrax corymbosa	114	6	○		15 x 10 ft (5 x 3 m)
Pyracantha hybrids	114	6/7	●		6-10 x 6-10 ft (2-3 x 2-3 m)
'Navaho'	114	6/7	●		6-10 x 6-10 ft (2-3 x 2-3 m)
'Shawnee'	114	6/7	●		6-10 x 6-10 ft (2-3 x 2-3 m)
'Teton'	114	6/7	●		6-10 x 6-10 ft (2-3 x 2-3 m)
Rhododendron 'Fragrantissimum'	117	9	●		6-10 x 6-10 ft (2-3 x 2-3 m)
'Lalique'	116	6-9	●		6-12 x 6-12 ft (2-4 x 2-4 m)
'Loderi series'	116	6-9	●		6-12 x 6-12 ft (2-4 x 2-4 m)
'Mrs A.T. de la Mare'	116	6-9	●		6-12 x 6-12 ft (2-4 x 2-4 m)
'Van Nes Sensation'	116	6-9	●		6-12 x 6-12 ft (2-4 x 2-4 m)
Rhododendron arborescens	115	4/5	○	*	6 x 6 ft (2 x 2 m)
Rhododendron calendulaceum	115	4/5	○	*	6 x 6 ft (2 x 2 m)
Rhododendron crassum	116	9	●		6-10 x 6-10 ft (2-3 x 2-3 m)
Rhododendron decorum	116	6-9	●		6-12 x 6-12 ft (2-4 x 2-4 m)
Rhododendron edgeworthii	116	9	●		6-10 x 6-10 ft (2-3 x 2-3 m)
Rhododendron formosum	116	9	●		6-10 x 6-10 ft (2-3 x 2-3 m)
Rhododendron fortunei	116	6-9	●		6-12 x 6-12 ft (2-4 x 2-4 m)
Rhododendron griffithianum	116	6-9	●		6-12 x 6-12 ft (2-4 x 2-4 m)
Rhododendron herzogii	117	9/10	●		3-6 x 3-6 ft (1-2 x 1-2 m)
Rhododendron jasminiflorum	117	9/10	●		3-6 x 3-6 ft (1-2 x 1-2 m)
Rhododendron konori	117	9/10	●		3-6 x 3-6 ft (1-2 x 1-2 m)
Rhododendron nuttalli	116	9	●		6-10 x 6-10 ft (2-3 x 2-3 m)
Rhododendron polyandrum	116	9	●		6-10 x 6-10 ft (2-3 x 2-3 m)
Rhododendron prinophyllum	115	4/5	○	*	6 x 6 ft (2 x 2 m)
Rhododendron prunifolium	115	4/5	○	*	6 x 6 ft (2 x 2 m)
Rhododendron superbum	117	9/10	●		3-6 x 3-6 ft (1-2 x 1-2 m)
Rhododendron vaseyi	115	4/5	○	*	6 x 6 ft (2 x 2 m)
Rhododendron viscosum	115	4/5	○	*	6 x 6 ft (2 x 2 m)

Species or cultivar	page reference	hardiness zones	evergreen ● deciduous ○	native to North America	height x width
Rhododendron spp. (azaleas)	117	5/6	○		6-10 x 6-10 ft (2-3 x 2-3 m)
Ribes x gordonianum	119	6	○		6 x 6 ft (2 x 2 m)
Ribes laurifolium	120	8	●		2 x 3 ft (0.6 x 1 m)
Ribes odoratum	119	5	○	*	6 x 6 ft (2 x 2 m)
Ribes sanguineum	119	6	○	*	6 x 6 ft (2 x 2 m)
Ribes speciosum	119	7	○	*	3-6 x 3-6 ft (1-2 x 1-2 m)
Romneya coulteri	120	8	○ ●	*	3-6 x 3-10 ft (1-2 x 1-3 m)
Romneya trichocalyx	120	8	○ ●	*	3-5 x 3-6 ft (1-1.5 x 1-2 m)
'White Cloud'	120	8	○ ●		3-5 x 3-6 ft (1-1.5 x 1-2 m)
Rosa x alba	122	4	○		12 x 12 ft (4 x 4 m)
Rosa banksiae	123	7	○		20-40 x 20-40 ft (6-12 x 6-12 m)
'Lutea'	123	7	○		20-40 x 20-40 ft (6-12 x 6-12 m)
'Lutescens'	123	7	○		20-40 x 20-40 ft (6-12 x 6-12 m)
'Normalis'	123	7	○		20-40 x 20-40 ft (6-12 x 6-12 m)
Rosa bracteata	123	7	○		5-10 x 5-10 ft (1.5-3 x 1.5-3 m)
Rosa x centifolia	123	4	○		3-5 x 5 ft (1-1.5 x 1.5 m)
Rosa damascena	125	4	○		3-6 x 3-6 ft (1-2 x 1-2 m)
Rosa pimpinellifolia	125	3	○		3 x 6 ft (1 x 2 m)
Rosa rugosa	125	2	○		3-6 x 8 ft (1-2 x 2.5 m)
Rosmarinus officinalis	125	8	●		3-6 x 3-5 ft (1-2 x 1-1.5 m)
'Prostratus'	126	8	●		6 in x 3 ft (15 cm x 1 m)
'Tuscan Blue'	126	8	●		3-6 x 3-6 ft (1-2 x 1-2 m)
Ruta graveolens	126	5	●		2 x 2 ft (60 x 60 cm)
Salvia elegans	128	8	○ ●		5 x 7 ft (1.5 x 2 m)
Salvia gesnerifolia	128	8	○ ●		5 x 7 ft (1.5 x 2 m)
Salvia involucrata 'Bethellii'	128	8/9	○ ●		3 x 3 ft (1 x 1 m)
Salvia leucantha	128	8	○ ●		3 x 3 ft (1 x 1 m)
Salvia officinalis	128	5	○ ●		2-3 x 3 ft (0.6-1 x 1 m)
'Icterina'	128	5	○ ●		2-3 x 3 ft (0.6-1 x 1 m)
'Purpurascens'	128	5	○ ●		2-3 x 3 ft (0.6-1 x 1 m)
'Tricolor'	128	5	○ ●		2-3 x 3 ft (0.6-1 x 1 m)
Salvia x sylvestris	128	5	○ ●		2-3 x 3 ft (0.6-1 x 1 m)
Santolina chamaecyparissus	129	7	●		1 x 3 ft (0.3 x 1 m)
'Lemon Fizz'	130	7	●		1 x 3 ft (30 x 30 cm)
'Lime Fizz'	130	7	●		1 x 3 ft (30 x 30 cm)
'Nana'	130	7	●		1 x 1 ft (30 x 30 cm)
Sarcococca confusa	130	5	●		2-3 x 3 ft (0.6-1 x 1 m)
Sarcococca hookeriana var digyna	130	8	●		6 x 3 ft (2 x 1 m)
Sarcococca hookeriana var humilis	130	6	●		18 in x 3 ft (0.45 x 1 m)
Sarcococca ruscifolia	130	8	●		4 x 4 ft (1.2 x 1.2 m)
Schima khasiana	131	8/9	●		30 x 10 ft (10 x 3 m)
Schima superba	131	8/9	●		30 x 10 ft (10 x 3 m)
Schima wallichii	131	8/9	●		30 x 10 ft (10 x 3 m)
Skimmia x confusa	132	7-9	●		3 x 4 ft (1 x 1.2 m)
Skimmia japonica	132	7-8	●		3 x 4 ft (1 x 1.2 m)
Spartium junceum	133	6	○ ●		10 x 6 ft (3 x 2 m)
Staphylea colchica	134	6	○		10 x 6 ft (3 x 2 m)
Staphylea holocarpa 'Rosea'	134	6	○		10 x 6 ft (3 x 2 m)
Staphylea pinnata	134	6	○		10 x 6 ft (3 x 2 m)
Syringa x hyacinthiflora	135	3-8	○		6-12 x 3-10 ft (2-4 x 1-3 m)
Syringa meyeri 'Palibin'	135	4-9	○		3-6 x 3 ft (2-3 x 2 m)
Syringa oblata	135	4-8	○		6-10 x 6 ft (2-3 x 2 m)
Syringa x prestoniae	135	2-8	○		10-12 x 6-10 ft (3-4 x 2-3 m)

Species or cultivar	page reference	hardiness zones	evergreen deciduous	native to North America	height x width
Syringa vulgaris	135	4-8	○		12-20 x 6-12 ft (4-6 x 2-4 m)
Tecoma stans	136	9	○ ●		10-20 x 10-15 ft (3-6 x 3-5 m)
Ternstroemia gymnanthera	137	8	●		3 x 3 ft (1 m)
'Burnished Gold'	137	8	●		3 x 3 ft (1 x 1 m)
'Variegata'	137	8	●		3 x 3 ft (1 x 1 m)
Teucrium chamaedrys	137	5	●		1-2 x 2-3 ft (30-60 x 60-90 cm)
Teucrium fruticans	138	8	●		10 x 10 ft (3 x 3 m)
Tilia x *euchlora*	139	3-8	○		70 x 50 ft (20 x 15 m)
Tilia x *moltkei*	139	4	○		70 x 50 ft (20 x 15 m)
Tilia tomentosa	139	6	○		100 x 70 ft (30 x 20 m)
Trachelospermum asiaticum	140	6	●		6 x 6 ft (2 x 2 m)
Trachelospermum jasminoides	141	7/8	●		10 x 10 ft (3 x 3 m)
Tripterygium spp.	141	5	○		6-30 ft (2-10 m) climbers
Viburnum x *bodnantense*					
'Dawn'	141	7	○		6-10 x 5 ft (2-3 x 1.5 m)
Viburnum x *burkwoodii*	142	4	○ ●		6-10 x 5 ft (2-3 x 1.5 m)
Viburnum x *carlcephalum*	142	6	○		6-10 x 6-10 ft (2-3 x 2-3 m)
Viburnum carlesii	142	5	○		6 x 6 ft (2 x 2 m)
Viburnum 'Eskimo'	142	6	○ ●		3 x 4 ft (1 x 1.2 m)
Viburnum farreri	142	6-8	○		6-10 x 3-5 ft (2-3 x 1-1.5 m)
Wisteria floribunda	146	4	○		30 ft (10 m) climber
Wisteria frutescens	146	5	○	*	15-30 ft (5-10 m) climber
Wisteria sinensis	147	5	○		100 ft (30 m) climber
Zenobia pulverulenta	147	5	○ ●	*	6 x 5 ft (2 x 1.5 m)

Right: *Michelia yunnanensis*

Mail-order sources for trees and shrubs

The importation of live plants and plant materials across state and country borders may require special arrangements, which will be detailed in suppliers' catalogs.

American regulations vary according to the country of origin and type of plant. Every order requires a phytosanitary certificate and may require a CITES (Convention on International Trade in Endangered Species of Wild Fauna and Flora) certificate. For more information contact:

USDA-APHIS-PPQ
Permit Unit
4700 River Road, Unit 136
Riverdale, Maryland 20727-1236
Tel: (301) 734-8645/Fax: (301) 734-5786
Website: www.aphis.udsda.gov

Canadians importing plant material must pay a fee and complete an "application for permit to import." Contact:
Plant Health and Production Division
Canadian Food Inspection Agency
2nd Floor West, Permit Office
59 Camelot Drive
Nepean, Ontario K1A 0Y9
Tel: (613) 225-2342/Fax: (613) 228-6605
Website: www.cfia-agr.ca

Angelgrove Tree Seed Company
P.O. Box 74, Riverhead
Harbour Grace, Newfoundland A0A 3P0
Website: www.tree-seeds.com
Mail order supplier of seeds for hardy trees and shrubs.

ArborVillage
PO Box 227
Holt, Missouri 64048
Tel: (816) 264-3911/Fax: (816) 264-3760
Email: Arborvillage@aol.com
Wide variety of common and unusual trees and shrubs. Catalog available.

Camellia Forest Nursery
125 Carolina Forest Road
Chapel Hill, North Carolina 27516
Tel: (919) 968-0504/Fax: (919) 960-7690
Website: www.camforest.com
Flowering shrubs and trees from China and Japan.

Collins Lilac Hill Nursery
2366 Turk Hill Road
Victor, New York 14564
Tel: (716) 223-1669
More than 200 lilacs from Ted "Doc Lilac" Collins.

Eastern Plant Specialties
P.O. Box 226W
Georgetown, Maine 04548
Tel: (732) 382-2508
Website: www.easternplant.com
Catalog available.

Forestfarm
990 Tetherow Road
Williams, Oregon 97544-9599
Tel: (541) 846-7269/Fax: (541) 846-6963
Website: www.forestfarm.com
E-Mail: forestfarm@rvi.com
Good selection of trees and shrubs. Ships to Canada.

Fraser's Thimble Farms
175 Arbutus Road
Salt Spring Island, British Columbia V8K 1A3
Tel/Fax: (250) 537-5788
Website: www.thimblefarms.com
E-mail: thimble@saltspring.com
Order by fax or e-mail. Ships to U.S.

Great Plant Company
Tel: (415) 362 5430/Fax: (415) 362 5431
Website: www.greatplants.com
E-mail: plants@greatplants.com
Catalog available. Does not ship to Canada.

Greer Gardens
1280 Goodpasture Island Road
Eugene, Oregon 97401-1794
Tel: (541) 686-8266/Toll-free Tel: (800) 548-0111
Fax: (905) 686-0910
Website: www.greergardens.com
Catalog available. Ships to Canada.

Heronswood Nursery, Ltd.
7530 NE 288th Street
Kingston, Washington 98346
Tel: (360) 297-4172/Fax: (360) 297-8321
Website: www.heronswood.com
Excellent catalog.

Hortico Inc.
723 Robson Road, R.R. 1
Waterdown, Ontario L0R 2H1
Tel: (905) 689-6984/Fax: (905) 689-6566
Website: www.hortico.com
Catalog available. Ships to the U.S.

Louisiana Nursery
5853 Highway 182
Opelousas, Louisiana 70570
Tel: (337) 948-3696/Fax: (337) 942-6404
Website: www.louisiananursery.org
Wide selection including over 600 different varieties of magnolias. Full-color catalog. Ships to Canada.

Molbaks's
13625 N.E. 175 Street
Woodinville, Washington 98072
Tel: (425) 483-5000
Wide range of plants and seeds.

Select Plus International Nursery
1510 Pine
Mascouche, Quebec J7L 2M4
Tel: (450) 477-3797
Website: www.spi.8m.com
Informative website. Ships to the U.S.

Wayside Gardens
1 Garden Lane
Hodges, South Carolina 29695
Toll-free: 1 (800) 213-0379
Website: www.waysidegardens.com
Wide selection. Free catalog.

Opposite:
Hydrangea macrophylla 'Nightingale'

Glossary

Acidic Any substance with a low pH. See also pH.

Acuminate Tapering to a point.

Acute Sharp pointed, without tapering.

Adventitious Occurring away from the usual place, e.g. aerial roots on stems.

Alkaline Any substance with a high pH. See also pH.

Alternate With leaves arranged singly on different sides of the stem and at different levels.

Apex The tip of a leaf or organ.

Attenuate Very gradually tapering.

Axil The upper angle between the stem and a leaf.

Bare rooted Trees and shrubs that are lifted from the open ground and sold with their roots wrapped in damp shredded newspaper, sphagnum moss, etc.

Bipinnate A leaf that is doubly pinnate, the primary leaflets being again divided into secondary leaflets, e.g. *Jacaranda*.

Bract A modified leaf or sepal at the base of a flower, often the most colorful part, e.g. *Cornus* and *Bougainvillea*.

Bullate A puckered leaf surface.

Calyx (pl. calyxes) The outer, often decorative, covering of a flower bud, usually consisting of united sepals.

Chlorophyll The green pigment in plants essential for the process of photosynthesis.

Clone An exact replica of an individual plant. Any plant propagated by vegetative means.

Cone The seed-bearing organs of conifers, composed of over-lapping scales on a central axis.

Conifer A plant that bears its seeds in cones.

Container-grown Plants raised entirely in containers, as opposed to open ground or field grown.

Cordate Heart-shaped.

Corymb A more or less flat-topped inflorescence, the outer flowers opening first.

Crenate Having shallow, rounded teeth or scalloped edges.

Crenulate Finely crenate.

Cultivar A botanical term for a variety that has arisen or is maintained in cultivation.

Cuneate Wedge-shaped with a gradual, even taper to the base.

Cyme A type of broad, flat-topped inflorescence in which the central flowers open first.

Dead heading The removal of faded flower heads to prevent the production of seed or to encourage heavier flowering.

Deciduous A plant that sheds all its leaves for part of the year.

Dentate With a serrated or toothed edge.

Denticulate Very finely toothed.

Digitate A leaf shape that resembles the arrangement of the fingers on a hand, e.g. *Aesculus*.

Dioecious Having male and female reproductive organs on separate plants.

Dissected Deeply cut into numerous segments.

Divaricate Spreading widely.

Drip line The circle around the outermost branch tips of a shrub or tree, the limit to which rainwater drips fall from the plant.

Drip tip The tapering, pointed end of a leaf, usually indicating an origin in a wet climate as the drip tip of the leaf helps to shed water.

Endemic Native to a particular restricted area.

Evergreen Retaining foliage throughout the year.

Exotic A plant originating in a foreign country and which is not native or endemic.

Family A group of related genera.

Fastigiate Narrow and upright with branches or stems erect and more or less parallel.

Floret One of many small flowers in a compound head.

Genus (pl. genera) A grouping of closely related species.

Glabrous Without hairs of any kind.

Glaucous A distinct blue or gray tint, especially leaves.

Globose Globe-shaped.

Gymnosperm A plant in which the seeds are not enclosed in an ovary, e.g. conifers and podocarps.

Honeydew The sticky secretion of many sap-sucking insects.

Hybrid The result of cross-fertilization of different parent plants.

Indigenous Native to a particular country or area. See also endemic and exotic.

Indumentum See tomentum.

Inflorescence The flower-bearing part of a plant, irrespective of arrangement.

Internode The length of stem between two nodes.

Invasive Said of a plant that grows quickly and spreads to occupy more than its allotted space, usually to the detriment of surrounding plants.

Juvenile A young or immature plant. Many plants display distinct differences between juvenile and adult foliage and growth habit.

Laciniate Having fine lobes, giving the impression of being cut by hand.

Lanceolate Lance-shaped, long and gradually tapering.

Leader The plant's dominant central shoot or one of several lateral shoots trained to produce a particular growth form.

Leaflet One of the smaller leaf-like parts of a compound leaf.

Leaf scar The mark left after a leaf falls. Very noticeable on some plants, e.g. *Aesculus*.

Legume A plant that produces pea-type seeds attached alternately to both sides of the pod and has root nodules that fix atmospheric nitrogen, e.g. peas, beans and lupins.

Lenticel Breathing hole on a stem or trunk, usually seen as a raised bump.

Lepidote Covered in small scales.

Linear Narrow and short with sides almost parallel.

Monoecious Having male and female reproductive organs in separate flowers on the one plant.

Monotypic A genus containing only one species.

Mucronate With a sharply pointed tip.

Mutant A spontaneous variant differing genetically and often visibly from its parent.

Mycorrhiza A beneficial association between a fungus and plant roots. Some plants, such as *Pinus*, rely on mycorrhizae for proper development.

Native A plant that occurs naturally in the area in which it is growing.

Natural cross A hybrid that occurs between two distinct, but usually related, plant species without human help.

Node A point on a stem on which leaves, buds or branches are borne.

Obovate Egg-shaped, with the broadest end at the top.

Open ground Plants raised in fields and lifted prior to sale, as opposed to container-grown plants.

Opposite Leaves on both sides of the stem at the same node.

Ovate Egg-shaped, with the broadest end at the base.

Palmate Roughly hand-shaped, with three or more lobes radiating fan-like from the petiole.

Panicle A branching cluster of flowers.

Parasite A plant that lives off another plant and which is usually unable to survive without the host plant.

Pathogen An organism, especially a bacterium or fungus, capable of causing disease.

Pedicel The stalk of an individual floret within a compound head.

Peduncle The main stalk of an inflorescence or of a flower borne singly.

Peltate Shield-shaped.

Petiole The stalk of a leaf.

pH The degree of acidity or alkalinity of the soil as measured on a scale from 0 (acidic) to 14 (alkaline), with 7 as the neutral point.

Photosynthesis The process whereby plants use solar energy, through the catalytic action of chlorophyll, to convert water and carbon dioxide into carbohydrates.

Pinnate A leaf form with leaflets arranged on both sides of the stalk, like a feather.

Pubescent Covered, often sparsely, in short hairs.

Raceme A stalk with flowers along its length, the individual blossoms with short stems.

Recurved Bent backward and/or downward.

Reflexed Sharply recurved.

Reticulate A net-like structure or markings.

Rootstock A rooted section of plant used as the base onto which a scion from another plant is grafted.

Russet A rough, brownish marking on leaves, fruits or tubers.

Scandent Having a climbing habit.

Scion A bud or shoot that is grafted onto the stock of another plant.

Sepal The individual segment of a calyx.

Serrate Having a saw-toothed or serrated edge.

Species The basic or minor unit in binomial nomenclature.

Specific name A plant's second name, e.g. *Pinus* **radiata.**

Spike A series of stalkless flowers on a single stem. The lower flowers are the first to open.

Sport A mutation showing distinct variations from the norm, e.g. a different foliage form or flower color.

Stellate Star-like or star-shaped.

Sub-shrub A permanently woody plant with soft pliable stems. Often green barked but woody at the base.

Sucker An adventitious stem arising from the roots of a woody plant, often from the stock rather than the scion of a grafted plant.

Systemic Any substance capable of permeating through the entire plant. Often said of insecticides and fungicides.

Taxonomy The science of plant classification.

Tepal The petal-like structures of a flower that does not have clearly defined sepals and petals, e.g. *Magnolia.*

Terminal bud The bud at the tip of the stem. Usually the first to burst into growth at bud break.

Tomentum The furry coating found on some leaves and stems, e.g. many rhododendrons. Also known as indumentum.

Topiary Trimming shrubs and trees to predetermined shapes for aesthetic appeal rather than growth restriction or function.

Trifoliate A leaf that is divided into three leaflets, e.g. clover.

Triploid A plant with three complete sets of chromosomes.

Truncate Ending or cut off abruptly or at right angles.

Truss A compound terminal cluster of flowers borne on one stalk.

Umbel A group of flower heads growing from a common point on a stem, hence umbellate.

Undulate Having a wavy edge.

Varietal name see Cultivar.

Variety Strictly a subdivision of a species, but often refers to a recognizably different member of a plant species worthy of cultivation.

Whorl A circle of three or more flowers or branches on a stem at the same level.

Bibliography

American Horticultural Society. *A-Z Encyclopedia of Garden Plants*. C. Brickell and J. Zuk (Editors-in-Chief). New York: Dorling Kindersley, 1997.

Bean, W. J. *Trees and Shrubs Hardy in the British Isles*. London: John Murray, 1986.

Benvie, S. *The Encyclopedia of North American Trees*. Toronto: Firefly, 2000.

Bryant, G. (Chief Editor). *Botanica: The illustrated A-Z of over 10,000 garden plants*. Auckland: David Bateman Ltd, 1997.

Callaway, D. *The World of Magnolias*. Portland: Timber Press, 1994.

Chicheley Plowden, C. *A Manual of Plant Names*. Sydney: Allen & Unwin, 1968.

Coates, A. M. *The Quest for Plants*. Studio Vista, 1969.

Harrison, R. E. *Handbook of Trees and Shrubs*. Auckland: Reed, 1981.

Haworth-Booth, M. *Effective Flowering Shrubs*. London: Collins, 1965.

Hillier, H. G. *The Hillier Manual of Trees and Shrubs*. Newton Abbot: David & Charles, 1992.

Johnson, A. T. and Smith, H. A. *Plant Names Simplified*. London: W. H. & L. Collingridge, 1931.

Kim, Tae-Wook. *The Woody Plants of Korea*. Seoul: Kyo-Hak, 1994.

Krussmann, G. *A Manual of Cultivated Broad Leaved Trees and Shrubs*. Portland: Timber Press, 1984.

Krussmann, G. *A Manual of Cultivated Conifers*. Portland: Timber Press, 1984.

Lancaster, R. *Travels in China*. Woodbridge: Antique Collectors Club, 1989.

Lance, R. *Woody Plants of the Blue Ridge*. Self-published, 1994.

Little, E. *National Audubon Society Field Guide to North American Trees*. New York: Alfred Knopf, 1980.

Petrides, G. *Eastern Trees*. Boston: Houghton & Mifflin, 1988.

Petrides, G. *Trees and Shrubs*. Boston: Houghton & Mifflin, 1986.

Pizzetti, I. and Cocker, H. *Flowers: A Guide for your Garden*. New York: Abrams, 1975.

Tripp, K.E. and Raulston, J.C. *The Year in Trees*. Portland: Timber Press, 1995.

van Gelderen, D.M., de Jong P.C., Oterdoom H.J., van Hoey Smith J.R.P. *Maples of the World*. Portland: Timber Press, 1994.

Whittle, T. *The Plant Hunters*. Oxford: Heinemann, 1970.

Index

Page numbers in italics indicate that the plant is illustrated.

Abelia 12
Abelia chinensis 12
Abelia schumannii 12, *13*
Abelia triflora 13
Abelia uniflora 13
Abelia x *grandiflora* 12
  'Edward Goucher' 12, *13*
  'Frances Mason' 12
Abeliophyllum distichum 13, *14*
absinth 22
Acacia 14
Acacia baileyana 14, *15*
Acacia dealbata 15
Acacia longifolia 14, *15*
Acacia melanoxylon 15
Acacia pravissima 15
  'Golden Carpet' 16
Acacia verticillata 16
Acradenia frankliniae 16
Afghan sage 109
Agonis 16
Agonis flexuosa 16, *17*
  'Grace' 17
Agonis juniperina 17
  'Florist Star' 17
Akebia quinata 17
Akebia trifoliata 18
Alleghney serviceberry 20
Aloysia triphylla 18
alpine mint bush 112
Amelanchier 18
Amelanchier arborea 19
Amelanchier asiatica 19
Amelanchier canadensis 19
Amelanchier laevis 20
Amelanchier lamarckii 20
American wisteria 146
amorpha 20
Amorpha canescens 20
Amorpha fruticosa 21
anchor plant 52
angels' trumpets 26
Apocynaceae 97, 139
Arabian jasmine 85
Argyrocytisus battandieri 21
Artemisia 22
  'Powis Castle' 23
Artemisia absinthium 22
Artemisia arborescens 22, *23*
Asian serviceberry 19
Asteraceae 22, 129
Australian frangipani 79
azaleas 117
Azara 23
Azara integrifolia 23
Azara lanceolata 22, *23*
Azara microphylla 23
Azara petiolaris 24
Azara serrata 24

Backhousia anista 25
Backhousia citriodora 24
banana shrub 100
Berberidaceae 95
bigleaf hydrangea 78
Bignoniaceae 39, 136
blackwood 15
bladdernut 133
blue butterfly bush 49
blue glory bower 49
blue spiraea 37
Boronia 25

Boronia heterophylla 25
Boronia megastigma 25
  'Heaven Scent' 25
  'Lutea' 25
bottlebrush 30
boxleaf azara 23
bridalveil broom 72
broom 55, 71
brown boronia 25
Brugmansia 26
  'California Peach' 27
  'Grand Marnier' 27
  'Noel's Blush' 27
Brugmansia x *candida* 27
Brugmansia chlorantha 26, *27*
Brugmansia knightii 27
Brugmansia lutea 27
Brugmansia rosei 27
Brugmansia sanguinea 26, *27*
Brugmansia suaveolens 27
Brunfelsia 28
Brunfelsia calycina 28
  'Eximea' 28
Brunfelsia latifolia 28
buddleja 28
Buddleja alternifolia 29
Buddleja asiatica 29
Buddleja davidii 29, *30*
Buddleja madagascariensis 29
buffalo currant 119
bull bay magnolia 94
burnet rose 125
buttercup winter hazel 53
butterfly bush 28, 29
Buxaceae 130

cabbage rose 123
calico bush 85
California allspice 33
California privet 89
Californian fuchsia 119
Californian lilac 40
Californian tree poppy 120
Callistemon 30
  'Little John' *31*
Callistemon citrinus 30, *31*
Callistemon salignus 31
Callistemon viminalis 32
Calocedrus 32
Calocedrus decurrens 32
  'Aureovariegata' 32
  'Berrima Gold' 32
  'Columnaris' 32
  'Fastigiata' 32
  'Intricata' 32
Calocedrus formosana 32
Calocedrus macrolepis 32
Calycanthaceae 32, 45
Calycanthus 32
Calycanthus floridus 33
  'Athens' 33
Calycanthus occidentalis 33
Camellia 34
Camellia japonica 34
  'Kramer's Gold' 35
  'Kramer's Supreme' 35
  'Kramer's Surprise' *34*
  'Scented Gem' 35
  'Scented Sun' 35
  'Scentsation' 35
  'Superscent' 35
Camellia lutchuensis 35
  'Fairy Bush' *35*
Camellia oleifera 35
Camellia sasanqua 35
  'Hiryu' 36, *37*
  'Mini-no-yuki' 36
  'Moonlight' 36

  'Plantation Pink' 36
Camellia tsaii 36
Camellia yunnanensis 34, 36
cape jasmine 71
Caprifoliaceae 12, 60, 90, 141
Carolina allspice 33
Carpenteria 37
Carpenteria californica 37
  'Ladham's Variety' 37
Caryopteris 37
Caryopteris x *clandonensis* 38
  'Arthur Simmonds' 38
  'Blue Mist' 38
  'Ferndown' 38
  'Heavenly Blue' *38*
Caryopteris incana 38
Caryopteris mongolica 38
Catalina ceanothus 40
Catalpa 39
Catalpa bignonioides 40
  'Aurea' 40
Catalpa ovata 40
Catalpa speciosa 39, 40
Ceanothus 40
  'Burkwoodii' 41
  'Concha' 41
  'Dark Star' *41*
Ceanothus arboreus 40, *41*
  'Trewithen Blue' 40
Ceanothus impressus 41
  'Puget Blue' 41
Ceanothus papillosus 40, 41
Ceanothus papillosus var *roweanus* 42
Celastraceae 141
Cephalotaxaceae 42
Cephalotaxus 42
Cephalotaxus fortunei 42
  'Prostrate Spreader' 42
Cephalotaxus harringtonia 42
  'Fastigiata' *42*
  'Prostrata' 42
Cercidiphyllaceae 43
Cercidiphyllum japonicum *43*
  'Pendulum' 43
Cercidiphyllum japonicum var *sinense* 43
Cercidiphyllum magnificum 43
Cestrum 43
  'Hugh Redgrove' 44
  'Newellii' 44, *45*
Cestrum aurantiacum 43, *44*
Cestrum nocturnum 44, *45*
Cestrum parqui 45
cham-pak 100
Chethraceae 50
chickasaw rose 123
Chilean jasmine 97
Chimonanthus 45
Chimonanthus praecox 45, *46*
  'Luteus' 46
Chinese abelia 12
Chinese anise 80
Chinese catalpa 40
Chinese jasmine 84
Chinese wisteria 147
Chinese witch hazel 74
chocolate vine 17
Choisya ternata 46
  'Aztec Pearl' *47*
  'Sundance' 47
Christmas box 130
Cladrastis 47
Cladrastis lutea 47, *48*
  'Rosea' 48
Cladrastis platycarpa 48
Cladrastis sinensis 48
Cladrastis wilsonii 48
Clerodendrum 48

Clerodendrum bungei 48, *49*
Clerodendrum trichtomum 48, *49*
Clerodendrum trichtomum var *fargesii* 49
Clerodendrum ugandense 49, *50*
Clethra 50
Clethra alnifolia 51
  'Hummingbird' 51
  'Rosea' 51
Clethra arborea 51
Clethra barbinervis 50, 51
Clethra delavayi 51
Clethra fargesii 51
Clethra monostachya 51
clove currant 119
Colletia 52
Colletia hystrix 52
Colletia paradoxa 52
common camellia 34
common gardenia 71
common lilac 135
common myrtle 102
common rue 126
common sage 128
common sweetshrub 33
common white jasmine 84
Confederate jasmine 141
Cootamundra wattle 15
Corylopsis 52
Corylopsis himalayana 52, *53*
Corylopsis pauciflora 53
Corylopsis spicata 53
Corylopsis willmottiae 53
  'Spring Purple' 53
cowtail pine 42
Crataegus 54
Craetaegus monogyna 54
Crataegus laevigata 54
  'Paul's Scarlet' *54*, *55*
  'Plena' 54
Crimean lime 139
crimson bottlebrush 31
crown of thorns 52
Cupressaceae 32
Cytisus 55
Cytisus battandieri 21
Cytisus x *beani* 56, *57*
Cytisus x *kewensis* 56
Cytisus multiflorus 56, *57*
Cytisus x *praecox* 56
  'Allgold' 56
  'Warminster' 56
Cytisus scoparius 56
  'Andreanus' 57

damask rose 125
daphne 57
Daphne 57
Daphne bholua 58
  'Gurkha' 58
  'Jacqueline Postill' 58
Daphne x *burkwoodii* 58
  'Carol Mackie' 58
  'Somerset' 58
  'Variegata' *58*
Daphne cneorum 58
  'Alba' 58
  'Eximia' 58
  'Major' 58
  'Variegata' 58
Daphne genkwa 59
Daphne mezereum 59
  'Grandiflora' 59
Daphne odora 60
  'Alba' 60
  'Aureomarginata' 60
  'Leucanthe' 60
  'Variegata' 60

datura 26
deciduous hybrid azaleas 117
Dipelta 60
Dipelta floribunda 60, *61*
Dipelta ventricosa 61
Dipelta yunnanensis 61
double white banksian rose 123
downy serviceberry 19
Drimys 62
Drimys lanceolata 62
Drimys winteri 62
Drimys winteri andina 62
Drimys winteri latifolia 62
dwarf fothergilla 69
dwarf Korean lilac 135

Edgeworthia 63
Edgeworthia gardneri 63, *64*
Edgeworthia papyrifera 63
  'Grandiflora' 63
Elaeocarpaceae 64
Elaeocarpus 64
Elaeocarpus dentatus 64
Elaeocarpus reticulatus 64
English hawthorn 54
English lavender 87
epaulette tree 113
Ericaceae 85, 106, 114, 117, 147
Eriostemon myoporoides 64, *65*
  'Profusion' 65
Eucryphia 65
Eucryphia cordifolia 66
Eucryphia glutinosa 66
Eucryphia x *intermedia* 68
  'Rostrevor' 68
Eucryphia lucida 66, *67*
  'Pink Cloud' 67
Eucryphia moorei 67
Eucryphia x *nymansensis* 67
  'Mount Usher' 67
  'Nymansay' 68
Eurcyphiaceae 65
European white linden 139
Eurya japonica 68
  'Variegata' 69

Fabaceae 20, 21, 47, 55, 71, 86, 133, 143
false anise 80
false holly 105
false indigo 21
February daphne 59
firethorn 114
Flacourtiaceae 23, 111
florist's hydrangea 78
flowering currant 119
fortune plum yew 42
Fothergilla 69
Fothergilla gardenii 69
  'Blue Mist' 70
Fothergilla major 70
  'Mount Airy' 70
fragrant olive 105
fragrant viburnum 142
French lavender 88
French lilac 135
fringe flower 64
fringed lavender 88
fuschia-flowered gooseberry 119

Gardenia 70
Gardenia 70
Gardenia jasminoides 71
  'Florida' 71
  'Mystery' 71
  'Professor Pucci' 71
  'Radicans' *71*
garland flower 58

Genista 71
Genista lydia 73
Genista monosperma 72
Genista pilosa 73
  'Lemon Spreader' 73
  'Vancouver Gold' 73
Genista tenera 73
  'Golden Shower' 73
  'Yellow Imp' 5, 72, 73
germander 137
giant Burmese honeysuckle 91
glory bower 48
glossy abelia 12
golden chain tree 86
golden wattle 15
goldflame honeysuckle 91
goldspire 23
great double white rose 122
green cestrum 45
Grossulariaceae 119

Hamamelidaceae 52, 69, 73
Hamamelis 73
Hamamelis x intermedia 74
  'Arnold Promise' 74
  'Diane' 74
  'Jelena' 74
Hamamelis japonica 74
Hamamelis japonica var
  flavpurpurascens 74
Hamamelis mollis 74
  'Brevipetala' 74
  'Coombe Wood' 74
  'Pallida' 74, 75
Hamamelis vernalis 75
  'Red Imp' 75
  'Sandra' 75
hardy eucryphia 66
harlequin glory bower 48
hawthorn 54
hedgehog rose 125
Himalayan daphne 58
Hoheria 75
Hoheria glabrata 75
Hoheria lyalli 76
Hoheria populnea 75, 76
  'Alba Variegata' 76
  'Purpurea' 76
  'Variegata' 76
Hoheria sexstylosa 76
holly osmanthus 105
hollyleaf sweetspire 82
honeysuckle 90
hop tree 113
houhere 75
Hovenia dulcis 76
Hydrangea 77
Hydrangea 77
Hydrangea aspera var villosa 77
Hydrangea heteromalla 77
Hydrangea macrophylla 78
  'Nightingale' 78, 155
  'Opuloides' 78
  'Rotschwanz' 9, 78
  'Seafoam' 78
Hydrangea paniculata 78
  'Kyushu' 4, 79
  'Tardiva' 79
Hydrangeaceae 77
Hymenosporum flavum 79
  'Golden Nugget' 79

Illiciaceae 80
Illicium 80
Illicium anistum 80, 81
  'Pink Stars' 80
Illicium floridanum 81
  'Halley's Comet' 81

Illicium henryi 80, 81
Illicium majus 81
Illicium mexicanum 81
Illicium parviflorum 81
incense cedar 32
Indian bean tree 40
Italian yellow jasmine 84
Itea 81
Itea ilicifolia 82
Itea virginica 82
Itea yunnanensis 83
Iteaceae 81

Jacobite rose 122
Japanese clethra 51
Japanese honeysuckle 91
Japanese privet 89
Japanese raisin tree 76
Japanese rose 125
Japanese skimmia 132
Japanese wisteria 146
Japanese witch hazel 74
jasmine 83
Jasminum 83
Jasminum azoricum 84
Jasminum beesianum 84
Jasminum humile 83, 84
  'Revolutum' 84
Jasminum mesnyi 84
Jasminum officinale 84
Jasminum polyanthum 84
Jasminum sambac 85
jessamine 83
juneberry 18
juniper myrtle 17

Kalmia augustifolia 86
  'Rubra' 86
Kalmia latifolia 85
  'Carousel' 86
  'Ostbo Red' 86
katsura tree 43
Korean abelia leaf 13
Korean spice viburnum 142
kwai fa 105

Laburnum 86
Laburnum x watereri 86
  'Vossii' 86
lacebark 75, 76
Lady Bank's rose 123
Lamiaceae 87, 108, 112, 125, 127,
  137
lanceleaf azara 23
Lardizabalaceae 17
large fothergilla 70
Lavandula 87
Lavandula augustifolia 87
  'Hidcote' 88
Lavandula dentata 88
Lavandula dentata var allardii 88
Lavandula stoechas 88
  'Merle' 88
lavender 87
lavender cotton 129
lead plant 20
lemon ironwood 24
lemon-scented verbena 18
lemon-scented jasmine 84
lemon-scented myrtle 24
Ligustrum 89
Ligustrum japonicum 'Rotundifolium'
  89
Ligustrum ovalifolium 89
lilac 134
lilac daphne 59
lily of the valley tree 51
lily tree 94

lime tree 138
linden tree 138
Lippia citriodora 18
Loganiaceae 28
long-leaf waxflower 64
Lonicera 90
Lonicera fragrantissima 90
Lonicera x heckrottii 90, 91
Lonicera hildebrandiana 91
Lonicera japonica 91
Lonicera x purpusii 'Winter Beauty'
  91
Luculia 91
Luculia grandiflora 8, 92
Luculia gratissima 92
  'Early Dawn' 92
Luculia pinceana 'Fragrant Cloud' 92
lydia woodwaxen 73

Macartney rose 123
Magnolia 92
Magnolia 92
  'Caerhay's Belle' 94
  'Claret Cup' 94
  'Manchu Fan' 94
Magnolia denudata 93, 94
  'Forrest's Pink' 94
  'Purple Eye' 94
Magnolia grandiflora 94
  'Freeman' 94
  'Maryland' 94
Magnolia x loebneri 94
Magnolia salicifolia 94
Magnolia sieboldii 94
Magnolia x soulangeana 94
  'Alexandrina' 95
  'Lennei' 95
  'Rustica Rubra' 94, 95
Magnolia stellata 95
Magnolia wilsonii 95
Magnoliaceae 92, 99
Mahonia 95
Mahonia 95
Mahonia aquifolium 96
Mahonia japonica 96
Mahonia x media 97
  'Charity' 96, 97
  'Lionel Fortescue' 97
Malvaceae 75
Mandevilla 97
Mandevilla laxa 7, 97
Mandevilla splendens 98
  'Alice du Pont' 98
matilija poppy 120
may 54
Meliosma 98
Meliosma cuneifolia 98
Meliosma myriantha 98
Meliosma oldhamii 98, 99
Meliosma veitchiorum 98
Mexican bush sage 128
Mexican orange blossom 46
mezereon 59
Michelia 99
Michelia alba 100
Michelia champaca 100
Michelia doltsopa 100
  'Rusty' 100
  'Silver Cloud' 100
Michelia figo 100, 101
Michelia maudiae 101, 102
Michelia yunnanensis 101, 102, 152-3
mimosa 14
Mimosaceae 14
mint bush 112
mock orange 109
mollis azaleas 117
Mount Atlas broom 21

mountain laurel 85
mountain witch alder 70
moutan 108
mugwort 22
Myrtaceae 16, 24, 30, 102
myrtle 102
Myrtus communis 102, 103
  'Flore Pleno' 103
  'Microphylla' 103
  'Variegata' 103
Myrtus luma 103
  'Glanleam Gold' 102, 103

night-scented jessamine 44
northern catalpa 40

Oemleria 103
Oemleria cerasiformis 103
oil seed camellia 35
Oleaceae 13, 83, 89, 104, 134
orange cestrum 43
Oregon grapeholly 96
Osmanthus 104
Osmanthus americanus 104
Osmanthus delavayi 104, 105
Osmanthus x fortunei 104, 105
Osmanthus fragrans 105
Osmanthus fragrans aurantiacus 105
Osmanthus heterophyllus 105
  'Aureomarginatus' 105
  'Gulftide' 106
  'Myrtifolius' 106
  'Purpureus' 106
  'Variegatus' 106
oso berry 103
oval leaf privet 89
oven's wattle 15
Oxydendrum 106
Oxydendrum arboreum 106
Ozark witch hazel 75

Paeonia 107
Paeonia delavayi 107
Paeonia lutea 108
Paeonia suffruticosa 108
Paeoniaceae 107
pak-lan 100
Papaveraceae 120
paper bush 63
peony 107
pepper tree 62
peppermint tree 16
Perovskia 108
Perovskia abrotanoides 109
Perovskia atriplicifolia 109
  'Blue Spire' 5, 109
Philadelphaceae 37, 109
Philadelphus 109
  'Manteau d'Hermine' 110
  'Virginal' 111
Philadelphus coronarius 2-3, 109
  'Aureus' 110
pikake 85
pineapple sage 128
pinkwood 67
Pittosporaceae 79
plum yew 42
poet's jasmine 84
poison bay 81
Poliothyrsis 111
Poliothyrsis sinensis 111
port wine magnolia 100
Portuguese broom 56
Preston lilac 135
prickly Moses 16
primrose jasmine 84
privet 89
Prostanthera 112

Prostanthera cuneata 112
Prostanthera rotundifolia 112
Provence rose 123
Ptelea 113
Ptelea trifoliata 113
  'Aurea' 113
  'Fastigiata' 113
Pterostyrax 113
Pterostyrax corymbosa 114
Pterostyrax hispida 113
purple anise 81
purple sage 128
Pyracantha hybrids 114
  'Navaho' 114
  'Shawnee' 114
  'Teton' 114

ramanas rose 125
red angel's trumpets 27
red boronia 25
red cestrum 44
Rhamnaceae 40, 52, 76
Rhododendron 114
Rhododendron 114
  'White Waves' 117
Rhododendron spp. (azaleas) 117, 118
Rhododendron arborescens 115
Rhododendron calendulaceum 115
Rhododendron crassum 117
Rhododendron decorum 116
Rhododendron edgeworthii 116
Rhododendron formosum 117
Rhododendron fortunei 116
Rhododendron Fortunei series 116
  'Fragrantissimum' 117
  'Lalique' 116
  'Loderi series' 116
  'Mrs A.T. de la Mare' 116
  'Van Nes Sensation' 116
Rhododendron herzogii 117
Rhododendron jasminiflorum 117
Rhododendron konori 117
Rhododendron maddenii 117
Rhododendron Maddenii series 116
Rhododendron polyandrum 117
Rhododendron prinophyllum 115
Rhododendron prunifolium 115
Rhododendron nuttalli 117
Rhododendron superbum 117
Rhododendron vaseyi 115
Rhododendron viscosum 115
ribbonwood 76
Ribes 119
Ribes x gordonianum 119
Ribes laurifolium 120
Ribes odoratum 119
Ribes sanguineum 119
  'King Edward VII' 119
Ribes speciosum 119, 120
Romneya 120
Romneya coulteri 120, 121
Romneya trichocalyx 121
  'White Cloud' 121
Rosa 121
  'Abraham Darby' 122
  'Mary Rose' 122
Rosa x alba 122
Rosa banksiae 123
  'Lutea' 123
  'Lutescens' 123
  'Normalis' 123
Rosa bracteata 123
Rosa x centifolia 123
  'Fantin-Latour' 125
  'La Noblesse' 125
Rosa damascena 125
  'Tringinipetala' 125
Rosa pimpinellifolia 125

Rosa rugosa 125
  'Roseraie de L'Hay' *124*, 125
Rosaceae 18, 54, 103, 114, 121
rose 121
rosemary 125
Rosmarinus 125
Rosmarinus officinalis 125
  'Prostratus' *126*
  'Tuscan Blue' *126*
rosy jasmine 84
rosyleaf sage 128
round-leaved mint bush 112
Rubiaceae 70, 91
Russian sage 109
Ruta 126
Ruta graveolens 126, *127*
  'Jackman's Blue' 126
Rutaceae 16, 25, 46, 64, 113, 126,
  132

Sabiaceae 98
sage 127
sagebrush 22
Salvia 127
Salvia elegans 128
Salvia gesnerifolia *127*, 128
Salvia involucrata 'Bethellii' *1, 8, 128*
Salvia leucantha 128
Salvia officinalis 128
  'Icterina' 128
  'Purpurascens' *128*
  'Tricolor' 128
Salvia x *sylvestris* 128, *129*
Santa Barbara ceanothus 41
Santolina 129
Santolina chamaecyparissus *129*
  'Lemon Fizz' 130
  'Lime Fizz' 130
  'Nana' 130
Sarcococca 130
Sarcococca confusa 130
Sarcococca hookeriana var *digyna* 130
Sarcococco hookeriana var *humilis* 130
Sarcococca ruscifolia *130*
sasanqua camellia 35
saucer magnolia 94
scented boronia 25
Schima 130
Schima khasiana 131
Schima superba *131*
Schima wallichii 131
Scotch broom 56
Scotch rose 125
Scots rose 125
sea tomato 125
shadbush 18, 19
shrubby germaner 138
silky leafwoodwaxen 73
silver broom 21
silver lime 139
silver linden 139
silver wattle 15
singleseed hawthorn 54
Skimmia 132
Skimmia x *confusa* 132
  'Kew Green' 132
Skimmia japonica *132*
  'Fragrans' 132
snowy Mespilus 18
Solanaceae 26, 28
sorrel tree 106
sourwood 106
southern catalpa 40
southern magnolia 94
Spanish broom 133
Spartium 133
Spartium junceum *6, 133*
Staphylea 133

Staphylea colchica *134*
Staphylea holocarpa 'Rosea' 134
Staphyleaceae 133
star anise 80
star jasmine 141
star magnolia 95
stinking ash 113
strawberry shrub 33
Styracaceae 113
summer lilac 29
summersweet 50
sweet box 130
sweet olive 105
sweet pepperbush 50, 51
sweetspire 81
Syringa 134
Syringa x *hyacinthiflora* 135
Syringa meyeri 'Palibin' 135
Syringa oblata 135
Syringa oblata var *dilatata* *134*
Syringa x *prestoniae* 135
Syringa vulgaris 135
  'Souvenir de Louis Späth' *135*

Tasmanian leatherwood 66
Tecoma stans 136
Ternstroemia gymnanthera 137
  'Burnished Gold' *137*
  'Variegata' 137
Teucrium 137
Teucrium chamaedrys 137
Teucrium fruticans *138*
  'Azureum' 138
Theaceae 34, 131, 136
Thymelaeaceae 57, 63
Tilia 138
Tilia x *euchlora* 139
Tilia x *moltkei* 139
Tilia tomentosa *139*
  'Sterling' 139
Tiliaceae 138
Trachelospermum 139
Trachelospermum asiaticum *140*
Trachelospermum jasminoides 141
tree anemone 37
tree germander 138
tree peony 107
tree poppy 120
Tripterygium spp. 141
Tripterygium hypoglauca *141*
Tripterybium wilfordii 141
trumpet bush 136

ulmo 66

Verbenaceae 18, 37, 48
vernal witch hazel 75
Viburnum 141
  'Eskimo' 142
Viburnum x *bodnantense* 'Dawn' 141
Viburnum x *burkwoodii* 142
Viburnum x *carlcephalum* *142*
Viburnum carlesii 142
  'Aurora' *143*
Viburnum farreri 142
vireya rhododendrons 117
Virginia sweetspire 82

wall germander 137
Warminster broom 56
wattle 14
weeping bottlebrush 32
western catalpa 40
white alder 50
white bottlebrush 31
white forsythia 13
white rose of York 122
white Spanish broom 56

whitey wood 16
willow bottlebrush 31
willow myrtle 16
willow-leafed jessamine 45
winter daphne 60
winter hazel 52
winter honeysuckle 90
Winteraceae 62
winter's bark 62
wintersweet 45
Wisteria 143
  'Lavender Lace' *144-145*
Wisteria floribunda 146
  'Snow Showers' *146*
Wisteria frutescens 146
Wisteria sinensis 147
witch alder 69
witch hazel 73
wormwood 22

yellow bells 136
yellow elder 136
yellow tree peony 108
yellowwood 47
yesterday, today and tomorrow 28
Yulan magnolia 94

Zenobia 147
Zenobia pulverulenta *147*

Acknowledgements

I would like to thank everyone who helped in any way with the making of this book. Most especially, I would like to thank Pat Greenfield for the fantastic photographs; Gail Church for help, advice and support; Theresa Greally for running my nursery and garden during my absence at the computer; Michael Hudson, the most knowledgable plantsman I know, for being my botanical dictionary; and Graham Smith for leading me onto this book-writing trail.

I would also like to thank Tracey Borgfeldt, Jennifer Mair, Errol McLeary, Brian O'Flaherty and Paul Bateman for editing and producing the book, and for frequent advice.

Thank you to the people who hosted us during research trips and who helped with photographs, especially Garry Clapperton, Michael and Carola Hudson, Bob and Lady Anne Berry, John and Fiona Wills, David and Noeline Sampson, Mr Min Pyong-gal (Mr Ferris-Miller), Peter Cave, Graham Smith, Andrew Brooker, Greg Rine, Gwyn Masters, Mark and Abbie Jury, Ian McDowell, Ian and Sheryl Swan, Tony Barnes and John Sole, Margaret and Richard Hodges, Margaret Bunn, Les Taylor, Alan Jellyman, Frédéric Tournay and Geoff Bryant.

And my thanks to Joni Mitchell, for the music to write to.

Picture credits

All photographs by Pat Greenfield except for the following:
Geoff Bryant p. 32 *Calocedrus decurrens*; p. 34 *Camellia* 'Kramer's Supreme'; p. 34 *Camellia yunnanensis*; p. 112 *Prostanthera cuneata*; p. 125 *Rosa* x *damascena*; p. 127 *Ruta graveolens*; p. 132 *Skimmia japonica* with berries.
Glyn Church p. 24 *Backhousia citriodora*, tree; p. 105 *Osmanthus fragrans*; p. 132 *Skimmia japonica* in flower; p. 137 *Ternstroemia* species and cultivars.
Alan Jellyman p. 37 *Carpenteria californica*.
Frédéric Tournay p. 61 *Dipelta floribunda*; p. 98 *Meliosma myriantha*; p. 99 *Meliosma oldhamii*; p. 111 *Poliothyrsis sinensis*.